Witches'
Spell-A-Day
Almanac

Holidays & Lore   Spells & Recipes
Rituals & Meditations

Copyright 2009 Llewellyn Worldwide.
Editing: Ed Day; Design: Michael Fallon
Cover Design: Lisa Novak; Background Photo: © PhotoDisc
Monthly Introductions by Ember; Interior Art: © 2005, Terry Miura (illustra-
tions: pp. 9, 29, 49, 71, 91, 113, 133, 153, 173, 193, 213, 233);
© 2005 Eris Klein (holiday and day icons)

You can order Llewellyn books and annuals from *New Worlds*,
Llewellyn's catalog. To request a free copy of the catalog, call toll-free
1-877-NEW WRLD, or visit our website at http://subscriptions.llewellyn.com

ISBN: 978-0-7387-0696-2
Llewellyn is a registered trademark of Llewellyn Worldwide, Ltd.
2143 Wooddale Drive, Dept. 978-0-7387-0696-2
Woodbury, MN 55125

Table of Contents

About the Authors

Elizabeth Barrette has been involved with the Pagan community for more than twenty years. She serves as the managing editor of *PanGaia* and the Dean of Studies at the Grey School of Wizardry. She lives in central Illinois and enjoys gardening for wildlife and stone magic. Visit her LiveJournal "The Wordsmith's Forge" at http://ysabetwordsmith.livejournal.com

Boudica is reviews editor and co-owner of *The Wiccan/Pagan Times* and owner of *The Zodiac Bistro*, both online publications. She is a high priestess with the Mystic Tradition Teaching Coven of Pennsylvania, Ohio, New Jersey, New York, and Maryland and is a guest speaker at many local and East Coast events. A former New Yorker, she now resides with her husband and six cats in Ohio.

Castiel is a Green Witch who embraced Neopaganism in 1993 and has been a member of the Elder Grove of the Coven of the Tangled Pines, Tangled Woods Tradition of Witchcraft, since 2006. She has a master's in Theological Studies from the Vanderbilt Divinity School and is pursuing professional studies in massage therapy and herbalism. She lives in her East Nashville, Tennessee, cottage with her husband and eight non-human children.

Dallas Jennifer Cobb has made a magical life in a waterfront village on the shore of Lake Ontario. She teaches Pilates, works in a library, and writes to finance long hours spent with her daughter. She regularly writes for Llewellyn almanacs and wrote two novels with support from National Novel Writing Month (www.NaNoWriMo.org). Contact her at: jennifer.cobb@live.com

Raven Digitalis is a Neopagan priest of the "disciplined eclectic" shadow magick tradition Opus Aima Obscuræ, and is a radio and club DJ. He is the author of *Goth Craft: The Magickal Side of Dark Culture*. With his Priestess Estha, Raven holds community gatherings, tarot readings, and a variety of ritual services. The two also operate the metaphysical business Twigs and Brews.

Ellen Dugan, a.k.a. "The Garden Witch" is an award-winning author and a psychic-clairvoyant. She has been a practicing Witch for more than twenty-four years. Ellen has written many books, including *Garden Witchery*, *Cottage Witchery*, and *How to Enchant a Man*. www.ellendugan.com

Ember, a freelance writer, poet, and regular contributor to Llewellyn's annuals, wrote the monthly introductions as well as many spells. She lives in Missouri with her husband of thirteen years and their two feline companions.

Lily Gardner has been studying and collecting bits of folklore and myth since childhood. In addition to writing for Llewellyn, she has written several short stories, a murder mystery, and is completing a work on saint folklore. Lily has been practicing witchcraft in Portland, Oregon, for fifteen years.

Abel R. Gomez is a freelance writer who also performs, sings, leads ritual, goes to school, and worships Maa Kali in the San Francisco Bay Area. His magick is aimed at uncovering the beauty of the Earth for use as a tool of transformation and deep healing. An active member of the Reclaiming community of Witches, he also studies Shakta Tantra.

Igraine is a Zen Witch, astrologer, tarotist, writer, teacher, and yogini living in Bucks County, Pennsylvania. She designs curriculum, exercises, and reflections for the MSN online community Tarot for Life, and is the founder of The Morrisville Metaphysical Society. She is working on an original tarot deck, *The Witches Altar* with artist Ted Enik and is co-writing a book with her sister about meditations, spreads, and rituals on the 22 major arcana of the tarot.

James Kambos is a regular contributor to Llewellyn annuals whose spellcrafting spark began when he watched his grandmother create spells based on Greek folk magic. When not writing, he paints in the American primitive style. He calls the beautiful Appalachian hill country of southern Ohio home.

Lupa is a neoshaman living in Portland, Oregon, with her husband and fellow author, Taylor Ellwood, two cats, and a lot of books and art supplies. She is a ritual tool artist and the author of several nonfiction books on Pagan topics. Learn more at www.thegreenwolf.com and http://therioshamanism.com

Estha McNevin is a Neopagan Priestess and is the head of the Opus Aima Obscuræ tradition. Besides public sabbat rituals, Estha hosts personal women's divination rituals each Dark Moon and holds private spiritual consultations and tarot readings for the community. www.myspace.com/twigsandbrews

Gail Wood is a Witch, high priestess, author, and tarot reader. She's been on the Pagan path for nearly thirty years. She can be contacted at www.rowdygoddess.com or by email at darkmoonwitch@earthlink.net

S. Y. Zenith is a lifelong solitary Pagan in Eastern and Western traditions. She has traveled to India, Nepal, Thailand, Malaysia, Singapore, Borneo, and Japan. Now residing permanently in Australia, she experiments with remedies and recipes and teaches the use of sacred objects from India and the Himalayas. She is also a member of the Australian Society of Authors.

A Note on Magic and Spells

The spells in the *Witches' Spell-A-Day Almanac* evoke everyday magic designed to improve our lives and homes. You needn't be an expert on magic to follow these simple rites and spells; as you will see if you use these spells through the year, magic, once mastered, is easy to perform. The only advanced technique required of you is the art of visualization.

Visualization is an act of controlled imagination. If you can call up in your mind a picture of your best friend's face or a flag flapping in the breeze, you can visualize. In magic, visualizations are used to direct and control magical energies. Basically, the spellcaster creates a visual image of the spell's desired goal, whether it be perfect health, a safe house, or a protected pet.

Visualization is the basis of all good spells, and as such it is a tool that should be properly used. Visualization must be real in the mind of the spellcaster so that it allows him or her to raise, concentrate, and send forth energy to accomplish the spell.

Perhaps when visualizing you'll find that you're doing everything right, but you don't feel anything. This is common, for we haven't been trained to acknowledge—let alone utilize—our magical abilities. Keep practicing, however, for your spells can "take" even if you're not the most experienced natural magician.

You will notice also that many spells in this collection have a somewhat "light" tone. They are seemingly fun and frivolous, filled with rhyme and colloquial speech. This is not to diminish the seriousness of the purpose, but rather to create a relaxed atmosphere for the practitioner. Lightness of spirit helps focus energy; rhyme and common language help the spellcaster remember the words and train the mind where it is needed. The intent of this magic is indeed very serious at times; and magic is never to be trifled with.

Even when your spells are effective, magic won't usually sparkle before your very eyes. The test of magic's success is time, not immediate eye-popping results. But you can feel magic's energy for yourself by rubbing your palms together briskly for ten seconds, then holding them a few inches apart. Sense the energy passing through them, the warm tingle

in your palms. This is the power raised and used in magic. It comes from within and is perfectly natural.

Among the features of the *Witches' Spell-A-Day Almanac* are an easy-to-use "book of days" format; new spells specifically tailored for each day of the year (and its particular magical, astrological, and historical energies); and additional tips and lore for various days throughout the year—including color correspondences based on planetary influences, obscure and forgotten holidays and festivals, and an incense-of-the-day to help you waft magical energies from the ether into your space.

In creating this product, we were inspired by the ancient almanac traditions and the layout of the classic nineteenth-century almanac *Chamber's Book of Days*, which is subtitled *A Miscellany of Popular Antiquities in Connection with the Calendar.* As you will see, our fifteen authors this year made history a theme of their spells, and we hope that by knowing something of the magic of past years we may make our current year all the better.

Enjoy your days, and have a magical year!

2010
Year of Spells

January is the first month of the Gregorian calendar, named for the Roman god Janus, god of doorways. Janus is often depicted with two faces, one looking forward and the other back, signifying the ending of one year and the beginning of another. January's Full Moon is called the Wolf Moon. Its astrological sign, Capricorn, the Goat (December 21–January 20), is a cardinal-earth sign ruled by Saturn. Though the ground is cold and bare, a sense of newness can be felt. Traditions around the world include personal resolutions to make a fresh start. This is a time to assess the past year, make future plans, and organize the home. Twelfth Night celebrations, which originated with the concluding Roman Saturnalia festivities, are held during January. In some cultures, a cake is baked with charms, such as a coin for prosperity or a ring for marriage, inside to predict the future for those who find them. In the Norse tradition, the Yule log was extinguished and the ashes saved to kindle next year's fire. This brought good fortune and ensured the transition of one year to the next. Making toasts is a popular way to ring in the New Year. Wassail has been a drink of good wishes since the 1400s. It's an ale-based drink with honey and spices, served in small bowls. Toast with the words *Waes hael*, which is old English for "be well."

January 1
Friday

New Year's Day – Kwanzaa ends

 3rd ♋

☽ → ♌ 9:41 pm

Color of the day: Coral
Incense of the day: Yarrow

A New Year's Knot Spell

Time. It has no beginning; it has no ending. At New Year's, we stand at the threshold and once again face another wheel of the year. For this spell, you'll need a piece of red yarn about three feet long. Red represents the life force and the yarn symbolizes the endless cord of time. Think of one wish you want to come into your life this year. Begin tying four knots in the yarn, working from left to right and spaced about equally. When done, open your front door while holding the yarn in your hands. Feel each knot while thinking of your wish, and say: "I hope. I wish. I believe. I receive." Tie the ends of the yarn together to represent the Wheel of the Year. Keep the yarn on your altar, and reflect on your wish occasionally.

James Kambos

Notes:

Holiday lore: New Year's Day calls for safeguards, augurs, charms, and proclamations. All over the world on this day, people kiss strangers, shoot guns into the air, toll bells, and exchange gifts. Preferred gifts are herring, bread, and fuel for the fire.

January 2
Saturday

 3rd ♌

Color of the day: Gray
Incense of the day: Magnolia

A Ritual to Isis

Isis is the supreme goddess of the Egyptian tradition, patron of motherhood, and mistress of magic. In ancient Egypt, this day was celebrated as the Advent of Isis. Worshippers would gather to celebrate Isis' return from Phoenicia with the Ark of Osiris. Celebrate and honor this sacred festival of Isis by creating a small altar in her honor. To do so, gather a white candle, an image of Isis, and any pearl or moonstone jewelry you fancy. Burn lotus, jasmine, or myrrh incense. When the altar space is prepared to your liking, take a moment to breathe and be present in the space. Invite Isis to join your space and spend some time in meditation and prayer with her. Ask her to bless the jewelry you brought.

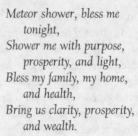

Wear the jewelry in her honor and to connect to her power.

Abel Gomez

Notes:

January 3
Sunday

3rd ♌

☽ → ♍ 9:52 pm

Color of the day: Orange
Incense of the day: Hyacinth

Shower Yourself with Purpose

While Earth enjoys the Quadrantids meteor shower, cast a spell for purpose and renewed energy for the return to school and work after the holidays. At its peak, the Quadrantids meteor shower will bless us with up to forty meteors per hour. Meteors, also called shooting stars, are visible from Earth as space debris becomes heated by friction, becoming bright and seeming to streak across the sky. So go outside after 10 pm, and look for meteors radiating from the constellation Bootes. With each streak of light feel the excitement.

*Meteor shower, bless me
tonight,
Shower me with purpose,
prosperity, and light,
Bless my family, my home,
and health,
Bring us clarity, prosperity,
and wealth.*

Envision your life being brightened with purpose and magical blessing. See your work, school, and endeavors glowing with renewed purpose. Know you are newly energized.

Dallas Jennifer Cobb

Notes:

January 4
Monday

3rd ♍

Color of the day: White
Incense of the day: Lily

Placating a Negative Moon

According to vedic astrology, if the Moon is not placed positively in a person's birth chart, it is called Chandra Dosha. The Moon's mantra, a mystical Sanskrit chant, "Om Som Somaye Namah Om," can be recited 108 times daily in order to appease

the Moon's negative influences. To enhance the effect, Hindu wise men and vedic astrologers have long recommended donating white clothes, white sugar, and tumbled moonstones to charity. The Moon, the presiding deity for the element water, rules over the tides of the ocean as well as emotions. It also represents the Mother aspect of divinity which is the energy that creates and preserves. The Moon also governs peace of mind, comfort, wisdom, general well-being, and fortune. Long-term chanting of the mantra results in illumination, sense of purpose, and intuition.

S. Y. Zenith

Notes:

January 5
Tuesday

3rd ♏

☽ → ♎ 11:58 pm

Color of the day: Red
Incense of the day: Bayberry

Banish Negative Emotions

Today, the Moon is waning and the Sun is in Capricorn. One of Capricorn's rulerships is work. Because the Moon—your internal

landscape—is waning, contemplate negative emotions attached with your job, career, or occupation. If you have more than one of these, contemplate all negative aspects associated with the various forms of work. Write these negative aspects—as many as you can think up—with black ink on a piece of parchment paper. Step outside, ignite the paper, and say something like:

> Sacred flame of
> transformation, banish these
> stresses, woes, and fears.
> Take from me these
> trepidations for now
> and all my years.

Finish by sprinkling a good amount of banishing herbs (such as nettles, black pepper, and valerian root) on the ashes. Stomp once on the pile with a "so mote it be!" Also, be sure to do everything you can to lessen your stresses on the job and make your work life the best it can be.

Raven Digitalis

Notes:

January 6
Wednesday

3rd ♎

Color of the day: White
Incense of the day: Lilac

Make No Misspeak

It's the first Wednesday of the new year, so let's work on our communication skills. Traditionally, Wednesdays are linked to Mercury, the fleet-footed god of communication. Since we are in a waning Moon, let's banish verbal misunderstandings and all types of communication problems. I suggest using an orange candle for the planet Mercury, and to bring some energy and enthusiasm to the spell. Light the candle and repeat the spell verse three times.

> Clever Mercury is the Roman fleet-footed god,
>
> Bring clear communication, as into my life you trod.
>
> In this waning Moon, let's banish troubles far away,
>
> Misunderstandings are gone, only harmony will stay.
>
> By all the power of three times three,
>
> As I will it, then so shall it be!

Ellen Dugan

Notes:

Holiday lore: Twelfth Night and the night following it are when wassailing used to take place. The word "wassail" comes from the Anglo-Saxon words *waes hael*, meaning "to be whole or healthy." People drank to each other's health from a large bowl filled with drink such as "lamb's wool," which was made of hot ale or cider, nutmeg, and sugar with roasted crab apples. In some parts of Britain, trees and bees are still wassailed to ensure a healthy crop. Having drunk to the tree's health, people fire shotguns into the branches. Different regions sing different wassail songs to the tree. Here's one from Worcestershire:

> Here's to thee, old apple tree,
> Whence thou mayest bud,
> Whence thou mayest blow,
> Whence thou mayest bear
>   apples enow.

January 7
Thursday

3rd ♎
4th Quarter 5:40 am

Color of the day: Crimson
Incense of the day: Myrrh

Straighten Up Spell

It's been exactly a week since we sincerely declared our resolutions for this New Year with the best of intentions! If you find yourself tilting sideways, feeling off center, and sensing your foundation is beginning to crumble, it's no wonder! Thirty years ago today the Leaning Tower of Pisa was shut down to the public due to a faulty structure. Use this as an inspiration to realign your intentions, pledging your commitment anew with greater determination to straighten up your act. Write down your New Year's vow clearly stated on a slip of paper. Place it on your altar dressed with a red cloth for rootedness, stability, and passion. Prop an image of the Tower from your tarot deck or printed from your computer to use as a focal point. Sit before this provocative card and picture yourself scaling to the very spire, standing strong as you hold both arms skyward. Now state your resolution for this year as if proclaiming it to the world. Then, in your mind's eye, cast a bolt of lightning earthbound like the great god Zeus himself and declare, "it is so!" Find your foundation re-established and resolute!

Igraine

Notes:

January 8
Friday

4th ♎
☽ → ♏ 5:00 am

Color of the day: Purple
Incense of the day: Alder

Midwives Day

In the mountains of Greek Macedonia, this day was set aside for honoring village midwives with gifts of practical tools such as towels and soap, but also wine and food. This event was also celebrated with a festive meal and a parade. Find a way to show appreciation for someone who has helped you "deliver," whether a midwife, doctor, nurse, or a friend. This does not need to be related specifically to childbirth. If you are expecting a child, working on any kind of creative project (which is another way of "giving birth"), or going through an adoption of a child or pet, use this spell to help facilitate the process. Light a green or white candle and speak these words:

Midwives all, hear my plea,

Assist my efforts faithfully.

May what I bring to fruit be well,

To grow in love, I cast this spell.

Ember

Notes:

you perform this simple spell, think clearly and carefully on what you want to begin. You'll need three white cords. (White is the color of virginity, purity, and newness.) To draw this energy to your own being, measure one cord to the length of your body, the second to the circumference of your torso, and the third to the length of the previous two combined. Draw the energy of your ventures into the cords as you stew in the crisp awakening energy of the day. Tie the ends together to create a circle, then stand within it until it is fully charged. Allow this essence to vibrate through you as you seal the energy into the rope. When done, wrap and store the cords in an undisturbed place. Untie the knots when you are feeling overanxious or hopeless in your pursuits and recharge on this energy.

Estha McNevin

Notes:

January 9
Saturday

4th ♏

Color of the day: Brown
Incense of the day: Sage

Knotwork for Transitions
Performing cord magic near the solar new year helps us hold on to the energy of the wheel's shift and this transformative power. As

January 10
Sunday

 4th ♏

☽ → ♐ 1:10 pm

Color of the day: Amber
Incense of the day: Juniper

Save the Eagles Day

Today is Save the Eagles Day. Eagles eat rabbits, fish, snakes, birds, and many other animals. Some eagle species are endangered due to habitat loss, poaching, and pesticides. Eagles appear widely in mythology and heraldry. The bald eagle, America's national bird, is shown on many American documents and emblems. A black eagle spreads its wings on Germany's coat of arms. In Rome, the eagle represented the god Jupiter and symbolized the senate. The Turks and the Byzantine Empire used a two-headed eagle as their emblem. To honor the renowned bird, work to protect eagles and their habitat. Donate to a wildlife sanctuary or ask officials to strengthen environmental protections. As you do, say this charm to attract the Spirit of Eagle:

> Strong wings and clear sight
> Guide us in our flight.
> You watch over all
> From your high blue hall.
> We will guard your home,
> Treetop and wave-foam.

Elizabeth Barrette

Notes:

January 11
Monday

4th ♐

Color of the day: Ivory
Incense of the day: Clary sage

Commuter Protection

January and February can be stormy months that bring all sorts of bad weather. Our children travel back and forth to school, our spouses travel back and forth to their places of business. This protection spell is to watch over your family while they travel to and from home.

> Bad weather will come
> as it may
> Goddess watch us
> night and day
> Protect us wherever
> we may roam
> Bring my loved ones
> safely home.

Boudica

Notes:

January 12
Tuesday

4th ♐
☽ → ♑ 11:54 pm

Color of the day: Black
Incense of the day: Geranium

Compitalia

Today is the Roman celebration of Compitalia that honors the protective household spirits called the Lares, who were considered to be the children of Mercury and the Naiad Lara. They were often depicted in art as a pair of dancing youths. According to tradition, Roman homes had a shrine dedicated to the Lares and on this special day, they were celebrated and given offerings of wine, bread, milk, and honey. Here is a modern charm that celebrates the old gods or spirits of the household. I suggest leaving an offering to these household spirits. Light a white candle in their honor and repeat the charm.

> I call upon the Lares,
>   guardians of the hearth
>   and home,
> To honor your day, as
>   celebrated in ancient
>   Rome.
> I ask for protection and joy,
>   with the aid of the Lares,
> Bless this magical home and
>   family, with love to spare.

Ellen Dugan

Notes:

January 13
Wednesday

4th ♑

Color of the day: Brown
Incense of the day: Bay laurel

Russian New Year

With the excitement of the holidays behind us and the coldest, grayest parts of winter still to come, it's easy to sink into the doldrums and let resolutions slide. But today, the old Russian New Year, is a great day to push the reset button and get back on track! Dig through your junk drawer or craft cabinet and find a shiny button and a piece of string about 18 to 20 inches long. Run the string through the button and hold an end in each hand. Focus your energy on your desire to get things started and see things through. Repeat the following charm:

> Every second a fresh start
> Every moment new
> One touch of a button
> Gives the power to redo!

Wear the button on the string around your neck. When you feel yourself losing your momentum, grab the button, give it a push, and let yourself start over again!

Castiel

Notes:

candle next to your tarot board. Find your Seeker card (often the Fool) and place it in the center of the circle. When you feel centered, start shuffling cards, holding the first aspect firmly in your mind. Draw the card when you feel it's right. Continue through each aspect. Blessings.

Lily Gardner

Notes:

January 14
Thursday

 4th ♑

Color of the day: Green
Incense of the day: Clove

Dark of the Moon Divination

Now that the holidays are well and truly over, sink into the restful, contemplative energies of winter. Tonight, cast this special tarot divination to use as guide for the rest of the year. Make a large paper circle. Divide the circle in pie-shaped wedges, one wedge for every aspect in your life: love, family, money, self-discovery, health, friends, etc. Draw a symbol to represent each of these aspects along the perimeter of the circle and color in each wedge. Place your tarot board in a quiet room. Light the room with candlelight, using a black

January 15
Friday

4th ♑
New Moon 2:11 am
☽ → ♒ 12:17 pm

Color of the day: Rose
Incense of the day: Vanilla

A Candlelight Divination

Tonight the New Moon of January forms a frosty crescent on an ebony sky spangled with starlight. The shadows of the night lie deep, and snow crunches underfoot. Tonight is a perfect time to tap into the power of the New Moon and scry into a candle flame to foretell your

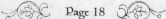

future. When the New Moon rides high, light a silver candle and concentrate on one question you'd like answered. Gaze intently at the flame and feel the energy of the New Moon surrounding you, drawing the answer to you. As you scry, speak this charm:

> Lady Luna, as you increase
> in light,
> Bring my answer into sight.

Let the visions you see in the flame come and go freely. Close the ritual by snuffing out the flame and moving the candle to a window where the moonlight can shine on it. You may repeat this ritual every night until you see your answer in the candlelight. When the question is answered, ask another on a different night. As the Moon increases in size, your visions may become stronger. During this process you can expect to have some prophetic dreams.

James Kambos

Notes:

January 16
Saturday

1st ♒︎

Color of the day: Blue
Incense of the day: Patchouli

Feast Day of Concordia

This is a good time for resolving conflicts in your home, work, school, or circle of friends—let go of old grudges and confront issues in a respectful, constructive manner. Before you talk to anyone with whom you have a quarrel, whether in person, by phone, or e-mail, take a shower or bath (or wash your hands well). As you do, call on Concordia, Roman goddess of harmony and agreement, to help smooth the conversation:

> Goddess, sweet Concordia
> dear,
> I ask your guidance in my
> time of need.
> I invite your peaceful
> presence here,
> To guide and bless the words
> I speak.
>
> May I listen well to what
> (person's name) says,
> May my response be patient
> and kind,
> May I respect (person's name)
> and myself today,
> So that balance and agreement
> we both shall find.

Lupa

Notes:

Buy your pet a treat or a new toy in celebration for all that they do in your life. A feast of pork can be enjoyed among the animal owners.

Estha McNevin

Notes:

January 17
Sunday

1st ≈

Color of the day: Gold
Incense of the day: Frankincense

Animal Blessings and Protection

Today's Western animal-blessing traditions originated from Italy and are associated with St. Anthony of Abad, patron saint of the animal kingdom. These ceremonies are performed in England, Austria, Switzerland, Spain, and Mexico. Blessings of the feast day occurs on the Sunday closest to January 17, which was the date of St. Anthony's physical death but observed as his birth date in heaven. Give thanks and show gratitude to household pets and farm animals with an improvised ceremony at home or with other animal lovers by having them blessed by a priest or priestess sprinkling holy water. Cats can wear homemade capes, dogs can wear sunglasses and leather collars. When animals are sanctified, they receive the additional protection of St. Anthony.

January 18
Monday

Martin Luther King, Jr. Day

1st ≈
☽ → ♓ 1:17 am

Color of the day: Silver
Incense of the day: Hyssop

A Spell for Activism

As we all know, Dr. King devoted his life to championing the oppressed. Through his efforts and leadership, African-Americans realized a better life. But think of how many people on this planet still suffer from oppression through bigotry. Think of how animals suffer at the hands of humans. Don't get depressed! Make a vow to dedicate however many hours you feel you can commit this year to a cause that moves you. Write your vow on a sheet of paper, fold it three times,

and place it beneath a blue candle. Next to the candle, place an image of Martin Luther King. Sit before the candle and center. When you're ready, light the candle. Ask the Spirit to embolden you to act for what you believe in. Stay with that prayer until you feel it. Leave the candle burning until it's nearly spent, then burn your vow in its flame. Bury the remains of the candle in your garden or in a pot.

Lily Gardner

Notes:

paper. As you think of your wish, the shape of the star should be filled in with one of these colors—gold, yellow, or orange. Place your power hand over this star after it is colored and speak your Words of Power. Place the star on your altar between orange or gold candles and let them burn down. Hide your star and let no one else touch it.

James Kambos

Notes:

January 19
Tuesday

1st ♓
☉ → ♒ 11:28 pm

Color of the day: White
Incense of the day: Ylang-ylang

A Four-Pointed Star Spell
Four-pointed stars are used in hex sign magic and are very powerful. These stars are symbols of prosperity, fertility, abundance, and the Wheel of the Year. To attract abundance and good luck, simply draw the shape of a four-pointed star on white

January 20
Wednesday

1st ♓
☽ → ♈ 1:36 pm

Color of the day: Topaz
Incense of the day: Lavender

Breadbasket Festival
A celebration of abundance in Portugal, this day marks the miraculous relief from a plague. Little girls dress in white and carry huge baskets of bread and flowers on their heads. In honor of this day, celebrate abundance in your life by giving gifts of bread and flowers to others—or use this spell to ask for what you

need. Start by obtaining a loaf of bread and some flowers. Place them on your altar or a table with a white cloth, and say the following blessing:

Loaf and flowers, lend your gifts,
Let them grow from seed.
Send relief for what I crave,
Satisfy my need.

Cut the bread and share it with others; keep the flowers in your home for decoration.

Ember

Notes:

January 21
Thursday

1st ♈

Color of the day: Purple
Incense of the day: Nutmeg

Synthetic Technomagic

Synthetic materials work best for holding and manipulating synthetic energy, just as natural materials work best for natural energy. Plastic comes in many useful shapes and colors. Among the most convenient items are dice. Ordinary six-sided dice work fine, but like most magical tools, fancier ones may hold

more energy or otherwise deliver better results. Fantasy role-playing games use dice with four, six, eight, ten, twelve, and twenty sides. They include opaque, translucent, marbled, metallic, and many other styles that work especially well with synthetic energy. You can use a single die, like a rheostat, to control the intensity of a technomagic spell. Cast the spell— for instance, a simple protection spell for your computer—into the die. You might leave it at "3" most of the time, and turn it up to "5" or "6" if the computer starts to waver. More faces give finer control.

Elizabeth Barrette

Notes:

Holiday lore: Feast Day of Saint Agnes of Rome. Since the fourth century, the primitive church held Saint Agnes in high honor above all the other virgin martyrs of Rome. Church fathers and Christian poets sang her praises, and they extolled her virginity and heroism under torture. The feast day for Saint Agnes was assigned to January 21. Early records gave the same date for her feast, and the Catholic Church continues to keep her memory sacred.

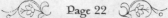

January 22
Friday

1st ♈

☽ → ♉ 11:39 pm

Color of the day: Pink
Incense of the day: Thyme

Privacy Spell

Today is the anniversary of the Roe v. Wade Supreme Court decision protecting a woman's right to choose in privacy. If you have an issue you wish to hide from prying eyes, write out that issue on a piece of paper. Fold the paper with the writing on the inside, chanting, "Until it's ready to unfold, keep my secret well untold." Tuck the paper into a small bag or box and keep on your altar until it's ready. Do not speak of either the spell or your issue. When you're ready for others to know your secret, open the bag or box and unfold the paper, chanting, "What was once concealed can now be revealed." Burn the paper to ashes, chanting, "The work is done and the magic has begun. As I will it, so mote it be!" Sweep up the ashes and bury the ashes with thanksgiving.

Gail Wood

Notes:

January 23
Saturday

1st ♉

2nd Quarter 5:53 am

Color of the day: Black
Incense of the day: Pine

Overcoming Obstacles

Today is a great day for facing seemingly insurmountable obstacles—on this day in 1855, the first bridge spanning the mighty Mississippi River opened. Decide on a goal that you would like to achieve in the next one, two, or even five years. Sit down with a piece of paper and write a basic list of things you would need to do to achieve that goal, such as find a program of study, save money, etc. Read over your list, then sit comfortably and close your eyes. Envision that you are standing on the bank of a large river, looking at the bank on the other side. Now imagine that a bridge begins to form on your side of the bank, and span to the other side. See this happening in as much detail as possible, and when the bridge is completed, see yourself walking across. Open your eyes, and post your list somewhere you will see it every day. Now go get started!

Castiel

Notes:

January 24
Sunday

2nd ♉

Color of the day: Orange
Incense of the day: Almond

Share a Prosperous Life

Today, the Aymara Indians of Bolivia celebrate Ekeko, god of prosperity. Symbols of local prosperity—coffee, sugar, flour, and beans—are seen everywhere. A generous deity, Ekeko holds a prominent place in most households, even here in North America where we love our morning coffee and pastry. Today, consciously invoke Ekeko and summon prosperity to your life. As you sip your coffee, savor the simple pleasures of rich taste, stimulating caffeine, and generous warmth in your life. Bite a pastry and let the sweetness on your tongue remind you of the sweetness of life. In this moment you are rich indeed, fully aware of the abundance that is yours every day. Now, whenever you encounter the tantalizing scent of coffee or sweet pastries, return to your awareness of prosperity. Inhale and fill yourself with prosperity. Invite a friend for a cup of coffee, and share your wealth.

Dallas Jennifer Cobb

Notes:

January 25
Monday

2nd ♉

☽ → ♊ 6:11 am

Color of the day: Gray
Incense of the day: Neroli

The Burns Supper

Every January 25, folks in Scotland (and elsewhere) celebrate the life and creativity of poet Robert Burns, who died in 1796. An active Freemason for many years, Burns was also an honorary member of several lodges across Scotland. "Burns suppers" started shortly after his death, held initially on his death-day, July 21, then moved to January 25. While a full Burns supper is an elaborate group affair, with much good food and readings of Burns' poetry, you can take the opportunity today to celebrate the creativity of poets throughout history as well as Burns himself. Make today a day of poetry. If you've been planning to write rituals for any reason, especially those that involve reciting verse, use today to research the poetry of others or create your own. Contact the muse Calliope and other beings who watch over the rhymes and rhythms of poetry.

Lupa

Notes:

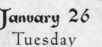

January 26
Tuesday

2nd ♊

Color of the day: Maroon
Incense of the day: Cinnamon

Fun at Work Day

Today is Fun at Work Day. Whether you like or hate your workplace, you can cast a little spell to bring fun into your day. You will need small pictures of you and of a fun place, whether or not you have ever been there. The night before, cut out the picture of you and paste it on the other picture; as you do this think about fun things you enjoy. On the back, write, "Today, give me a smile once in a while. In the midst of every task, find a laugh to help me last!" Charge the picture with happiness by smudging it with lavender incense, and place it on your altar underneath three cloves and a quartz crystal. Take the picture to your job and tuck it somewhere around you. Be aware, and things are more fun.

Gail Wood

Notes:

January 27
Wednesday

2nd ♊
☽ → ♋ 9:01 am

Color of the day: Brown
Incense of the day: Honeysuckle

Nevermore Nepenthe

On this day in 1845, Edgar Allen Poe's timeless poem, "The Raven" was first published. As a bird totem a raven suggests second sight, mystery, forgotten knowledge, and, in some cases, ill omen. In this haunting Plutonian poem of death and beauty, our narrator pores over old books of "forgotten lore" pondering the loss of his lover Lenore in hopes of divining some mysterious elixir or soothing balm to mend his broken heart and uplift his shattered soul. The raven suddenly appears, casting his dark shadow as he perches atop the bust of Pallas as if to prophesy the wisdom of the goddess, revealing the magic to mend and heal. "Nevermore!" he cries. Be free of memories that bind you to the past. Take the beak from out your heart and find respite with this Nevermore Nepenthe, a potion to forget one's sorrows.

Ingredients
1 dram of spring water
1 T. of vodka

1 chip of lapis lazuli (to charge
    the elixir)
6 drops of basil for melancholia
6 drops of marjoram for happiness
6 drops of passionflower for peace

Burn pine incense to heal bereave-
ment or wear nightshade tucked into
a medicine bag to dispel the memory
of a lost love.

Igraine

Notes:

tool. Gather magazines, clip art, pho-
tos, symbols, and other images that
represent your desire, a glue stick,
scissors, and some paper. Once all
the collage is completed to your liking, take it to your magic space and
breathe a blessing onto it. Bless and
charge your collage and leave it on
your altar until your desire manifests.

> *I charge and bless this*
>   *magical art*
> *May it be the beginning*
>   *and the start*
> *Of (your desire) coming*
>   *my way*
> *Drawing closer with each day.*

Abel R. Gomez

Notes:

January 28
Thursday

 2nd ♋

Color of the day: White
Incense of the day: Apricot

Collage Wish Spell

Collage spells are some of the
most fun and creative forms of
spellcasting. They allow you to draw
from myriad sources and materials
to help focus and manifest magical
desires. The first step is figuring out
what you desire. If you are unsure,
take a moment to breathe and listen to your heart. If you need extra
assistance, consult your divination

January 29
Friday

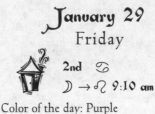 2nd ♋
)→♌ 9:10 am

Color of the day: Purple
Incense of the day: Orchid

Bleak Stew

For our ancestors, the bleak days
of winter brought with them a
scarcity in food and nourishment,
particularly the luxury of meat and

fresh produce. Hardy preserves and root stews remain a beloved and comforting winter staple. The following vegetarian stew offers readers a taste of the savory desperation for winter survival.

4 cups vegetable stock
1 large potato
1 large yam
3 large carrots
1 large turnip
16 ounces pumpkin (1 can)
1 large onion
1 pinch clove
Bay, thyme, parsley, pepper, salt, and
    garlic to taste.

In a soup pot, combine vegetable stock with diced potatoes, yams, carrots, and turnips. Boil on medium for 30 minutes. Add canned pumpkin and return to a boil. As the flavors blend together, say:

> In my pot I marry the earth,
> I beg of the gods a loving
>   rebirth.

Season to taste and serve. Slice and brown the onion in a separate pan and serve as garnish.

Estha McNevin

Notes:

January 30
Saturday

2nd ♌
Full Moon 1:18 am

Color of the day: Indigo
Incense of the day: Ivy

The Full Moon Energy Experience
It's the Full Moon! On this most glorious of evenings, venture outside to an area of land heavily guarded by trees and shrubbery. For this solitary ritual, seat yourself in a location where the Moon is visible (if possible). Bring a small, white tealight candle and a brewed pot of jasmine green tea with a cup. When comfortable, stare at the Moon (or gaze in the direction in which She sits in the sky) and take nine very deep, slow breaths in through the nose and out through the mouth. Envision silver, soft white, and violet energy circulating from the Moon to your body. Fill yourself with Her lunar radiance, aligning your own energy to that of the exalted Lady of the Night Sky. Light the tealight candle and hold it up to the Moon. Say something like:

> This illumination reflects the
> glory and beauty of the Great
> Mother. As She is pure, I thus
> purify my body and mind.

Pour yourself a cup of tea and hold it to the Moon. Say:

This tea of jasmine and green represents the cleansing, joy, and abundance of Lady Luna. As I take it into my body, I also take of her infinite essence.

Set the cup behind the candle, allowing their energies to intermingle for a few moments. Drink the tea, finish the pot, and blow out the candle. Be sure to pour a cup of tea on the ground as an offering to the spirits and the Moon.

Raven Digitalis

Notes:

January 31
Sunday

 3rd ♌

☽ → ♍ 8:23 am

Color of the day: Yellow
Incense of the day: Heliotrope

Fit and Trim

You become especially aware of your health during the winter months. You may seem to be susceptible to colds and flu, and your clothes seem to be tighter. You can get into bad eating habits and continue them without realizing what you are doing to your body. You feel sluggish, bloated, and tired. This is the time to take a look at how much exercise you are getting, how many junk or rich foods you are eating, and how to try to get yourself back into a program of exercise and healthy diet. Take trips to the mall and walk a good brisk pace when the weather is bad outside. Join a local Y or see if the local school offers a healthy family program. Look at your diet and start substituting wholesome foods for those quickie box meals, as well as dropping some of the mindless munching items. Eat right and stay fit.

Boudica

Notes:

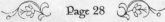

February is the second month of the Gregorian calendar. Its astrological sign is Aquarius, the Water-bearer (January 20–February 18), a fixed-air sign ruled by Uranus. The name February comes from the Latin term *februum*, which means "purification," referring to a Roman purification ritual called Februa that was held on the fifteenth. We also celebrate an important Celtic quarter-day, Imbolc, usually on February 1 or 2. The Wheel of the Year has turned toward the first stirrings of renewal, and Imbolc is a time to honor the spark of new life by paying homage to Brigid, the Celtic goddess of creativity (the spark of inspiration), the hearth and forge (spark of fire for the home), and childbirth and healing (spark of life). Honor her with candle flames and decorative lights. The church later named her St. Brigid and Christians celebrate Candlemas on this day. This is a time to shake off the winter blues and look ahead. Groundhog Day has its origins in the Imbolc celebration, as this is a good time to practice divination. And don't forget the romance of St. Valentine's Day—a time to indulge in sweets and flowers while celebrating the warmth of love. The Finnish call this month *helmikuu*, "the month of the pearl," to describe the beads of ice that form on tree branches when snow melts. The Full Moon of February is called the Snow Moon.

February 1
Monday

3rd ♏︎

Color of the day: Gray

Incense of the day: Narcissus

Plant Your Wishes

It is the midpoint of winter turning into spring—a time to plan for the year and make wishes for the future. There once was a custom to tie ribbons on branches for the wishes of the year. To plant your wishes, you will need a fallen tree branch and some ribbon in colors that symbolize your wishes. Create sacred space by lighting candles in white, red, and black for the goddess Brigid and burn cinnamon incense in her honor. Breathe in deeply the peace of the slumbering Earth at the moment before waking. Now tie each ribbon onto the tree branch, stating your wish three times. When you are done, chant, "Ribbons of colors oh so bright, bring my wishes to the light," three times. Plant your wishing tree on your altar until the Spring Equinox when you will plant it outdoors. At the first harvest, Lammas, on August 1, burn the branch in thanksgiving for what you have harvested from your wishes.

Gail Wood

Notes:

February 2
Tuesday

Imbolc – Groundhog Day

3rd ♏︎

)) → ♎︎ 8:42 am

Color of the day: Black

Incense of the day: Bayberry

Spell for New Beginnings

Today is Imbolc, a day sacred to Brigid, Celtic goddess of the hearth flame. Let's work some fire magic! If you have a fireplace in your home or an outdoor fire pit, build the fire, and cast the spell while gazing into the flames. If you need to remain inside, a cluster of white or red candles in various shapes and sizes arranged on a large charger plate will work out beautifully. Wait until dark if you are outside, or turn off all the lights if you are inside. Then light a wooden match and see how much light that one little flame actually creates. Now light the fire or your arrangement of candles and take a few moments to ground and center yourself. Once your fire is burning nicely or the candles have all been lit and are merrily flickering away, begin the spell.

I banish darkness, on this Imbolc night,

In its place I create both warmth and light.

May the goddess Brigid hear
my heartfelt call,

Bless my home and all who
live here, one and all.

Now I close this verse,
bringing harm to none,

By fire's bright magic, this
spell is done.

                    Ellen Dugan

Notes:

Holiday lore: On Imbolc, a
bundle of corn from the harvest
is dressed in ribbons and becomes
the Corn Bride. On February 2, the
Corn Bride is placed on the hearth
or hung on the door to bring
prosperity, fertility, and protection
to the home.

February 3
Wednesday

 3rd ♎

Color of the day: Yellow
Incense of the day: Bay laurel

The Bean Throwing Rite

In China, February 3 is known as
Risshun or Setsubun. Similar to
New Year's Eve, the festival has long
been renowned as a most auspicious
time for driving away evil, bad luck,
and harmful energies. One of the
most common Risshun practices is
called *mamemaki*, which can translate
as "bean throwing." As part of the
exorcism of evil, tradition holds that
members of the household should
throw roasted soybeans out of the
doors and windows of the home.
To take this element of practice into
our own purification rite, do the
same: buy a good amount of roasted
soybeans, place them in a bowl, and
carry them through the house. As
you throw handfuls of them out of
the open doors and windows, say:
Apo pantos kako daimonos! This is a
Greek phrase that roughly translates
as "Away, all evil spirits!" For added
effect, you can wear the mask of a
devil or demon when performing
this. After the ritual, you can also
eat the number of soybeans that cor-
respond to the number of years you
have lived, with one extra to ensure

additional good luck. Both are traditional practices for the holiday.

Raven Digitalis

Notes:

oil must be more than the essential oils. Mix thoroughly and let stand in a dark cupboard for two weeks before decanting into small dark-colored bottles with droppers. This oil may also be given to people who are in need.

S. Y. Zenith

Notes:

February 4
Thursday

 3rd ♎︎
☽ → ♏︎ 11:56 pm

Color of the day: Green
Incense of the day: Mulberry

Oil to Attract Jupiter's Blessing
Jupiter, the planet of expansion, prosperity, and abundance, rules over Thursday. Blend a container of oil that helps to draw Jupiter's blessings. This oil can be worn on the skin, rubbed on candles and petition parchments, poured into prosperity baths with other ingredients, and utilized for spells requiring improved finances and an abundance of good luck. Wash and sterilize one small jar. Pour some cold-pressed carrier oil such as almond or jojoba into the jar. Add a few drops of peppermint, spearmint, and cinnamon essential oils, as well as the oil of cinquefoil and High John the Conqueror to the carrier oil. The volume of the carrier

February 5
Friday

 3rd ♏︎
4th Quarter 6:48 pm

Color of the day: White
Incense of the day: Thyme

Mayoresses' Festival
In parts of northern Spain, women have adopted this day as a celebration of a St. Agatha, a virgin who was tortured and killed in the third century for refusing the attention of a man. Two women are selected to be mayoresses for a day to parade around dressed in lavish black and red adornments. Men do the chores while the women celebrate. Today is a great day to honor women. Ladies, dress up for a night on the town or

gather at someone's home for some quality girl-talk. Gentlemen, give the women in your life an unexpected gift. To increase your bond with the women in your life, use this spell:

> Companions, family, and
>   friends,
> Let our bond be without end;
> Keep our ties of friendship
>   true,
> Honor me as I honor you.

Light pink and red candles and spend time with the women you cher‑ish—and ladies, don't forget to do something nice for yourself!

Ember

Notes:

February 6
Saturday

 4th ♏
☽ → ♐ 7:04 pm

Color of the day: Black
Incense of the day: Patchouli

To Draw Spring Growth
On a large sheet of green parch‑ment, write the qualities of your ideal spring activities in dove's blood ink. As the ink soaks into the

paper, feel the fresh and fertile Venus listening to your prayers and detail your desires and fantasies for her to draw in and manifest. As you con‑vey your thoughts and passions, try to evoke a feeling of having already achieved them. Before you are done, visualize the new experiences hap‑pening to you and focus on these feelings of manifestation and fate as you sign the parchment and seal it to the future with your own right-handed thumb print. In a burning bowl, draw the force of Mars and set the parchment alight; as you do so chant seven times:

> By the power of Mars as he
> beds his bride; by love and
> lust and the Venus tide; with
> this so has my hopelessness
> died.

Estha McNevin

Notes:

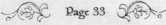

February 7
Sunday

 4th ♐

Color of the day: Orange

Incense of the day: Eucalyptus

Playing for Peace Spell

Today the Super Bowl XLIV will be played at Dolphin Stadium in Miami, Florida. Organized sporting events bring together large numbers of people and accumulate some very powerful energy. Too often we see this energy turn mean or ugly, so let's cast a spell for peaceful play, energetically directing the accumulated energy for positive purpose. State your intent: to magically influence the masses attending (and watching the event on television) for the good of all. Not just for big events like the Super Bowl, this spell can be quietly cast from the bleachers at your kids' games, or from the sidelines before you run out onto the field in your own sport.

> We play the game not to win or lose,
>
> Between bad and good it's time to choose,
>
> Let the Goddess' peace reign across the field,
>
> And to her spirit make evil yield.

Dallas Jennifer Cobb

Notes:

February 8
Monday

 4th ♐

Color of the day: Lavender

Incense of the day: Rosemary

Glamour Bombing

Engage your spontaneous and playful side today by throwing a glamour bomb. This term refers to random acts of weirdness and senseless acts of beauty. These actions refer to myriad things that are aimed at helping people reconnect to their inner Fey and sense of wonder. Think about what you can do today to inspire and catch someone off guard. Perhaps write "believe" in chalk when no one is looking or leave an anonymous note that reads, "you are beautiful" in a book at your public library. Draw a happy face on a sticky note and post it in a random place. Find something that you feel called to do and bring it out into the world. The sky's the limit! May your divine and magical soul help someone else remember the beauty and mystery of the world this day.

Abel R. Gomez

Notes:

Holiday lore: Today is the Buddhist Needle Memorial. On this day, as part of the principle of endless compassion espoused by the Buddhist faith for all sentient and nonsentient beings, all the sewing needles that have been retired during the year are honored. That is, needles are brought to the shrine and pushed into a slab of tofu that rests on the second tier of a three-tiered altar. Priests sing sutras to comfort the needles and heal their injured spirits.

February 9
Tuesday

 4th ♐
☽ → ♑ 5:43 am

Color of the day: Red
Incense of the day: Ginger

A Spell to Let Go
With the darkness of the Moon, cast a spell to let go of what worries you or arouses fear. Write your worry or fear upon a small piece of paper. Now fold the paper in half, removing the list from your sight. Say:

> Out of sight
> Dark of night
> There is no light
> For you to grow.

Tear the paper into tiny pieces, consciously dissembling your fear or worry as you do. Now flush the bits down the toilet or take them outside and let them fly away with the wind. As they leave your hand, invoke:

> This small worry, I let it go.
> This small fear, I will not
>   sow.
> Be gone worry, be gone fear,
> Be gone sadness, and peace
>   be here.

Take a deep breath, and know peace is yours.

Dallas Jennifer Cobb

Notes:

February 10
Wednesday

 4th ♑

Color of the day: Brown
Incense of the day: Marjoram

how Am I Doing?

Take time to look at your life, job, and family to see what you want to achieve for this year. Pull out your favorite divination tool and a notebook and spend a little time taking inventory of what you want, what you need, and where you want to go. Pull out the checkbook and examine your financials. How well have you done at your job and how well is your company doing? Should you be looking for another job? This is the time of year employers will hire. Brush up your résumé and see if a better position for you is in the cards. Maybe you need to look at a better relationship with your family. While the home front may be fine, how are your parents or in-laws? Do they need special attention? Use your magical skill set to get a good idea of what the year ahead has to offer.

Boudica

Notes:

February 11
Thursday

4th ♑

☽ → ♒ 6:24 pm

Color of the day: Turquoise
Incense of the day: Jasmine

Kick the Cold Tea

Frost may still etch a filigree pattern on the windowpane and the snow still rides the howling wind, but deep within Mother Earth, the Goddess begins to stir. To relieve the late winter blues, pamper yourself tonight with this spell. Run a hot bath and use a floral-scented bubble bath. After the bath, apply your favorite moisturizing lotion to your body. Slip into a comfy robe or pajamas. Grab a book you've been dying to read and brew some tea or hot chocolate. Settle in and cocoon for the evening. Snuggle under a soft blanket. As you stir your hot drink, envision the Goddess stirring to life outside, beneath the earth. And the Earth itself is resting beneath a blanket of snow, just as you're relaxing beneath your warm blanket. You are now One with the Goddess and the earth. Rejuvenate. Heal. Now your spirit is renewed, like the earth is renewing itself for the next cycle of growth.

James Kambos

Notes:

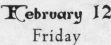

February 12
Friday

4th ≈

Color of the day: Rose
Incense of the day: Rose

Darwin Day

This is Darwin Day, honoring the scientist Charles Darwin. He presented the theory of evolution, in which natural selection causes minor variations in plants and animals to create new species better suited to their environments. This idea shaped much of modern biology and botany. Some revelatory religions base their worldview on descriptions in ancient liturgy, which can lead to apparent conflicts between science and religion. Pagan religions generally do not do this; instead, they base their worldview on what the world itself reveals through its creatures and processes. Thus science and Paganism do not conflict, as new discoveries simply illuminate new aspects of the world we already revere. Choose a plant or animal you admire. Study it closely and consider how its features suit it for its particular role in nature. Meditate on the ever-changing perfection of life and how elegantly the Divine has shaped the processes of nature.

Elizabeth Barrette

Notes:

Holiday lore: Lincoln is called the Great Emancipator and is thought of as one of our greatest presidents. Know this, however: Lincoln was an almost unknown figure until the age of forty, when he first entered the Illinois state legislature. His later assassination threw the country into widespread mourning, inspiring Walt Whitman to write:

> Coffin that passes
>   through lanes and street,
>   through day and night
>   with the great cloud
>   darkening the land . . .
> I mourned, and yet shall
>   mourn with ever-
>   returning spring.

February 13
Saturday

 4th ≈

New Moon 9:51 pm

Color of the day: Blue
Incense of the day: Magnolia

herbs for health

The New Moon is a perfect time to start something new and empower it for success. To create a healthy new lifestyle, gather these herbs: chicory for removing obstacles, ginger for power, and thyme to attract good health. Also get a small blue bag, a piece of paper, a blue candle, sandalwood incense, and glitter. Light the candle and call in the Spirit. On a piece of paper, draw a picture of the healthy new you and put it in the bag; put in the herbs in this order: chicory, thyme, and ginger. Then add glitter just for the fun of it. Shake the bag and breathe in your desire. Smudge with incense and carry it close to your body until the Full Moon, talking to it every day. At the Full Moon, bury the bag in the ground, thanking your magic and the spirits that empower it.

Gail Wood

Notes:

February 14
Sunday

Valentine's Day
Chinese New Year (tiger)

1st ≈

☽ → ♓ 7:23 am

Color of the day: Gold
Incense of the day: Juniper

Inner Strength Spell

The Chinese New Year celebration traditionally lasts fifteen days, much longer than the public holiday. Homes are decorated with vases of pretty blossoms, plates of oranges and tangerines, as well as a candy tray containing eight varieties of candied fruit and sweets. Auspicious words in Chinese calligraphy on red paper are pasted on doors and walls. Each year is governed by one of the twelve animals signs of the Chinese zodiac. This is the year of the tiger. Both New Year's Eve and New Year's Day are celebrated as family affairs, a time for reunion and thanksgiving. Some hold a ceremony in honor of the gods of heaven and Earth, the gods of the household, and ancestors. Altars have platters of fruit, flowers, food, and Chinese wine placed before them. (White wine can be substituted.) Small red packets of money are given to children and unmarried young adults. A banquet dinner consisting of special dishes with auspicious names is eaten together. For regaining or achieving inner strength in dealing with difficult problems, meditate on the strength, courage, and sharp sight of the tiger. Place some oranges, sweets, fruit, flowers, and wine on the altar with an image of a tiger and connect with the animal's energies.

S. Y. Zenith

Notes:

for luck and peaceful sleep, catnip for visions and prosperity, thyme for prophecy, and oregano for the courage to follow your dreams. Before you sew the bag closed, add a few drops of bergamot oil for success. Slipstitch the top shut and tuck inside your pillowcase. When you get into bed at night, repeat this charm:

> Give me sight
> In the night
> That I may fight
> For what is right
> At the dawn of morning light.

Castiel

Notes:

February 15
Monday

Presidents' Day (observed)

 1st ♓

Color of the day: Silver
Incense of the day: Hyssop

President-Sized Dreams

Today is Presidents' Day, a great day to think about leadership in general. Great leaders have dreams, even visions, that they fight to make come true. To inspire your own great dreams, try making this dream pillow. Get a swath of purple fabric, preferably cotton, about 8 × 4 inches. Fold it in half, sew it closed on two sides, and turn it so the seams are on the inside. Fill the bag with lavender

February 16
Tuesday

Mardi Gras (Fat Tuesday)

 1st ♓
☽ → ♈ 7:30 pm

Color of the day: Scarlet
Incense of the day: Cedar

The Magic Talisman of Denari

Aside from love, attracting material abundance might be the most frequently requested spell.

Talismans are potent magic we can wear on our bodies. This energetic connection between the spell and the physical body creates a magnetic link to the desired outcome. The power of attraction cannot be denied when we adorn ourselves with symbols of what we want to manifest! The Magic Talisman of Denari is your own creation. Will it be your words written on parchment wrapped in a dollar bill and worn at your belt? You might consider drawing a penta‑gram—a symbol of manifestation—and folding it around a silver dollar. Use your rich imagination to conjure your personal talisman and then wear it in faith of the law of attraction.

> This is my talisman close to
>   my skin,
> Charged by my chalice, my
>   sword, and paton.
> I conjure by fire the wealth
>   I desire.
>
> Pointing my wand to the
>   north, I conspire
> With gods! Hear my request!
> Make my abundance
>   manifest!

Igraine

Notes:

February 17
Wednesday
Ash Wednesday

1st ♈

Color of the day: Topaz
Incense of the day: Lilac

Hope Incense

Combine equal parts frankincense, myrrh, dragon's blood, benzoin, copal, and camphor. Add 6 drops of rosemary oil, 6 drops of cassia bark oil, and 6 drops of ylang ylang oil. This fumitory is meant for inspira‑tional healing sessions, meditations, and ritual work. It draws on the sap and vital essence of the forest life and carries many properties of protec‑tion, empowerment, and endurance. Though best burned on charcoal rounds, this blend can be finely pow‑dered before adding the oils and then rolled onto honeyed sticks. Once hung upside down and left to cure for thirty days, these sweet sticks make a wonderful offering for hope and prosperity within the home. Blend thoroughly to evenly distribute oils and store any unused portion in an airtight glass jar.

Estha McNevin

Notes:

February 18
Thursday

1st ♈

☉ → ♓ 1:36 pm

Color of the day: White
Incense of the day: Clover

Fertility Spell

Persian priestesses cast fertility spells to honor their goddess, Spandarmat, on this day. Whether you desire a baby, a garden, or an artistic project, begin by making a fertility doll to manifest your desire. Assemble your materials using the rule of three. Three fertility stones might be coral, agate, and chrysoprase and three plants might be cucumber seeds, motherwort, and mustard seeds. You will need green cloth, sewing tools, rice grains (to stuff into the doll), and ornamentation materials. Before you begin, light a green candle and ask Spandarmat to empower your spell. I leave it to you to decide the shape of your doll; she doesn't need to take a human form. Sew her together, leaving an opening (vagina) through which you can fill her with your crystals, herbs, and rice. Then sew her shut. Leave an offering of nuts and dates at the base of a tree for Spandarmat with your thanks.

Lily Gardner

Notes:

February 19
Friday

1st ♈

☽ → ♉ 5:55 am

Color of the day: Purple
Incense of the day: Vanilla

Talking to the Animals

Take the day to communicate with animals. If you have pets, simply being with them in the house is a good starting point. Wear brown clothing and light a brown candle (for animal magic) and practice simply being with your animal(s). Even if the pet is a speechless fish, all animals communicate with one another telepathically and energetically. This subtle communication is something that professional animal psychics take years to hone, but this ability can certainly be tapped briefly for the sake of experimentation. Take the brown candle to an area of nature that has a variety of wildlife. Light the candle, secure it in a holder, and listen for the voices of nature to make themselves apparent. Spend some time just "hearing them out." After a while, try to discern what they could possibly be communicating—is it instinctual? What other cues, such as their walk or flight pattern, hint at their communication? Do you observe animals communicating with one another? Can you discern what they are "saying?" The intuitive find-ings may surprise you.

Raven Digitalis

Notes:

February 20
Saturday

1st ♉

Color of the day: Gray
Incense of the day: Rue

Complete Home Cleansing

Well it's Saturday—a per-fect time to banish and to cleanse. Let's tap into the energies of the waxing Moon and turn up the volume on your personal wards at your home. Begin by physically cleaning the house. Dust, vacuum, mop, take out the trash, and remove clutter. Then light a new white candle of any size or shape. Set up a work area in the heart of your home and repeat the protection charm three times.

> As this New Moon-white
>   candle glows,
>
> All around me, protection
>   does grow.
>
> I banish all negativity and ill
>   intent,
>
> This spell will hold even after
>   the candle is spent.
>
> By Saturn's day and the
>   element of fire,
>
> This spell is now sealed by
>   my will and desire.

Move the candle to a safe place and let it burn until it goes out on its own.

Ellen Dugan

Notes:

February 21
Sunday

 1st ♉

☽ → ♊ 1:47 pm

2nd Quarter 7:42 pm

Color of the day: Amber
Incense of the day: Hyacinth

Festival of Feralia

In ancient Rome, the festival of Feralia was celebrated on this day to honor the dead. Take the time today to remember your beloved dead. Look through old photo albums. Watch old home movies. Visit the cemetery where they are buried. Bring them flowers and honor their mark in the world and in your life. Speak their names and send them messages and prayers. Set out a plate and leave offerings to them. Give gratitude for your ancestors of blood and of spirit that guide your path. Send prayers to the earth that holds their bodies just as it will receive yours. Remember that you, too, will become an ancestor soon. What is remembered, lives.

> Beloved ones beyond the veil,
>
> I honor your life, I honor your love.
>
> Accept these offerings as tokens of gratitude and love.

> Thank you for your protection and guidance.
>
> You are gone, but not forgotten.
>
> Blessed be.

> Abel R. Gomez

Notes:

February 22
Monday

 2nd ♊

Color of the day: White
Incense of the day: Neroli

Caristia (Roman)

The word *Caristia* comes from *cara*, meaning "dear." This day was a life-affirming celebration in ancient Rome, a day to spend time with family. Arguments and differences were set aside and Concordia, goddess of peace, ruled the day. Symbols include a cornucopia and olive branch and the day was celebrated with a banquet. Today, find a way to honor your family and spend time with them. Prepare a meal together or go out. Visit people who are dear to you. Use the following charm to increase family harmony. Charge a clear quartz cluster by visualizing a peaceful and harmonious environment and keep it in your kitchen or other room where people often gather.

> Harmony and peace
> be found,
>
> May this family be bound
>
> By love and honor and
> respect—
>
> Help us never to forget.

Ember

Notes:

Holiday lore: We all know the lore about our first president—cherry tree, silver dollar, wooden teeth—but the truth behind this most legendary of American figures is sometimes more entertaining than the folklore. For instance, did you know that once when young George went for a dip in the Rappahannock River, two Fredericksburg women stole his clothes? This story was recorded in the Spotsylvania County records. Picture then the young man scampering home flustered and naked, and the icon on the dollar bill becomes just a bit more real.

February 23
Tuesday

2nd ♊
☽ → ♋ 6:29 pm

Color of the day: Gray
Incense of the day: Geranium

House Protection Spell

The festival of Terminalia honors Terminus, the Roman god of boundaries. Using the energies of Terminus and some ingredients from the old customs honoring him, cast this spell. Begin with a fire. Light tealights in every window of your home. Then build a fire outdoors if possible or light a white candle in your cauldron if not. If you use a candle, burn it in the center of your home. As you perform these tasks, feel the element of fire working as a powerful force for protection. Make an offering of honey and white wine to Terminus by sprinkling drops of each into the fire. Pray to him to protect your home from all evil and negativity. Then take a small dish of sea salt and sprinkle it around the boundary of your property. For some traditions, this is good neighbor day. Can you think of some way to be a better neighbor?

Lily Gardner

Notes:

February 24
Wednesday

2nd ♋

Color of the day: Yellow
Incense of the day: Lavender

Turning the Wheel

In late February, winter winds down and spring approaches. Although the first signs of life appear, such as sprouts of crocus and snowdrop, the weather can still turn nasty. Few things are as frustrating as a bright sunny day followed by a blizzard. When cold weather keeps you inside when you'd rather be outdoors daydreaming about spring flowers, work a little magic to help turn the wheel of the year. If you have a fireplace or a wood stove, build a fire in it. Otherwise a small fire of twigs in a metal cauldron will suffice. Gather some friends and sing:

> Though the winds of
>   winter blow
>
> Wrapping all in ice
>   and snow
>
> Fires burn and seasons turn
>   and
>
> We can see the springtime,
>   oh!

Elizabeth Barrette

Notes:

February 25
Thursday

 2nd ♋

☽ → ♌ 8:08 pm

Color of the day: Crimson
Incense of the day: Carnation

Pay the Bills Spell

Holiday bills and heating bills at this time of year can stack financials against you. Sometimes all you can do is just make ends meet. My favorite money spell involves putting the bills in your cauldron. Then take a blank check, make it out to yourself, but don't put any money in the amount box—just dollar signs. Do not limit the amount that you will need. Sign it with the name of your god and goddess. Put that in your cauldron as well, and place it on your altar with a yellow candle. Use a small votive candle in a fireproof container. Add bills when they come in, remove them as you pay them. Ask deity to enable you to make ends meet for the hard financial crunch months. It is also a great idea to review your income and expenditures regularly to keep your budget balanced.

Boudica

Notes:

February 26
Friday

2nd ♌

Color of the day: Pink
Incense of the day: Yarrow

Bear Blessing

While spring is still a few weeks away, some species of bear are beginning to stir in their dens. Mother bears, having given birth to cubs during the long winter, have been feeding them and caring for them even during hibernation. The totem Bear watches over all of her children who sleep. Not all of them may make it through the winter, especially if they are found by hunters or didn't get enough food in the fall to build up a sufficient layer of fat to live on during hibernation. Since all species of bear are threatened by extinction, you may wish to bless the bears during this crucial period of their yearly cycle.

> Bruin, Bera
> Grandfather, Grandmother
> You of long claws and teeth
> You of the thick, shaggy coat
> Fish-eater, berry-picker, lover
>   of honey
> Brave bear, bold mother,
>   young cub
> May you return safely into
>   the waking world.

Lupa

Notes:

goes out, don't make your decision at this time. Like the Hermit, you'll find your way.

James Kambos

Notes:

February 27
Saturday

 2nd ♌
☽ → ♍ 7:52 pm

Color of the day: Black
Incense of the day: Sandalwood

Inner-Wisdom Spell

Sometimes when we must make a decision, we need to turn inward and rely on our inner wisdom. That can be hard to do when we're surrounded with so many distractions. This spell will help you focus on your need. Remove the Hermit card from your tarot deck, place it before you, and light a yellow candle. Study the card. The Hermit is alone. He carries a lantern and he's looking carefully before he takes a step. But he can make his own decisions, for he is the Wise One. Thinking of your question, simply say, "Light my way." Meditate and pay attention to the candle flame. If the flame burns steadily during the ritual, follow your first instinct. If the flame sparks or

February 28
Sunday

Purim

2nd ♍
Full Moon 11:38 am

Color of the day: Gold
Incense of the day: Marigold

Sacrifice for Your Health

We hold a flaming candle of devotion and willing surrender as our Sun has moved into Pisces and the Moon shines full in Virgo. Virgo is the most feminine and receptive form of Earth. It is a powerful time in our yearly cycle to examine personal service and sacrifice. We recall the vestal virgins of ancient Rome who tended the hearth fires at the Temple of Vesta and kept them forever burning. We can use this time to consider what fire needs feeding in our own inner dwelling. Our physical bodies request our attention.

Health, self-discipline, and practical application of skills are the principles we must manifest, embodying purity, duty, and order. Here we linger at the Temple of Vesta to make an offering at her altar. Think on what that offering might be from you. What is your willing sacrifice? What will you devote yourself to that requires self-care and inner healing? What service can you provide that honors the Earth?

Igraine

Notes:

March is the third month of the Gregorian calendar, and it was the first month of the Roman calendar. Its astrological sign is Pisces, the fish (February 18–March 20), a mutable-water sign ruled by Neptune. Named in honor of Mars, the Roman god of war, March can be a tumultuous month with blustery winds, storms, and snow, yet it carries on its breath the promise of spring. It feels as though the seasons are waging a battle for control. In some places, cold temperatures still reign, but inevitably the days are growing longer. This is the month of the Vernal Equinox; day and night are equal in length. March is a good time for reflection (wells and springs can be good places to visit) and seeking balance when weather can be unstable. A feeling of renewal can be sensed in nature as birds begin nesting and the brave crocus peeks out through the snow. Spring bulbs such as tulips and daffodils begin to emerge in our gardens and brighten the landscape. This is a good month for blessing seeds and preparing for the gardening season. The Full Moon of March is often called the Worm Moon or Sap Moon.

March 1
Monday

3rd ♏
☽ → ♎ 7:31 pm

Color of the day: Silver
Incense of the day: Narcissus

Plant the Seeds of Love

Here is a little love spell for the one looking for love. It is a love spell for you. You need to love yourself first before you can ever learn to love someone else.

> Plant a seed and watch
>   it grow
> and as you plant so you
>   shall sow.
> Plant a thought and give
>   it care
> and it will take you
>   everywhere.
> Plant some love inside
>   your heart
> and love to all you
>   will impart.

Plant love in your own life first. Remember, if you feed it and nurture it, the love will steadily grow. You will be amazed at how people around you will notice and will be affected. And it will attract just the right kind of person you want and need in your life.

Boudica

Notes:

Holiday lore: On March 1, Roman matrons held a festival known as Matronalia in honor of Juno Lucina, an aspect of the goddess Juno associated with light and childbirth. Some records indicated that her name was derived from a grove on the Esquiline Hill where a temple was dedicated to her in 375 BCE. Whenever a baby entered the world in Roman times, it was believed that the infant was "brought to light." Women who worshipped Juno Lucina untied knots and unbraided their hair to release any entanglements that might block safe delivery.

March 2
Tuesday

3rd ♎

Color of the day: Gray
Incense of the day: Basil

Evoke Childlike Wonder

Today is birthday of Theodore Geissel (1904–1991). We know him as Dr. Seuss, the author of *Green Eggs and Ham* and other childhood favorites. To evoke the delightful lightness of a life fully and humorously lived in magic and joy, as well as work up your magical confidence, put on your funniest garments and recite with full merriment:

> I am a magical spellcaster
> All this magic I can master.
> Herbs and incense and
>   the candle
> All this lore I can handle.
>
> Fire, water, earth, and air
> Twirl in spells that I dare
> To speak, and to know
> My magical energy glows!
>
> In a cone the energy goes
> To my goal's purpose
>   it flows.
> As I will it so mote it be
> Come back to me three
>   times three!

Go about your day with a smile of joy and feel the lilting power of a life magically led. Blessed be.

Gail Wood

Notes:

March 3
Wednesday

 3rd ♎
$\mathbb{D} \to \mathbb{M}$ 9:11 pm

Color of the day: Topaz
Incense of the day: Marjoram

Leave a Legacy

If you left this Earth tomorrow, how would you be remembered? What legacy have you created for those you care about? If you've never thought about it, today is a great day to start a legacy that can touch lives long after you are gone. If you want your loved ones to be financially secure, you could open a savings account today—add a little magic by putting the account number in an envelope with some cinnamon and mint, for prosperity, and keep it under your altar. If you want to know more than money, you could start a journal and leave the benefit of your wisdom to future generations. You could also benefit future generations by starting to recycle, or donating to a foundation that plants trees. Whatever you decide to do, send your thoughts today forward a couple of years, and see what you can get started.

Castiel

Notes:

March 4
Thursday

3rd ♏

Color of the day: White
Incense of the day: Apricot

Emotional housekeeping

Emotions are the seat of sensitivity within our spiritual bodies. Emotions are a spiritual guide, and becoming aware of them and their influence is vital to any living spiritual path. For this spell, light a blue candle and anoint your neck with lavender, jasmine, or rose oil. Put yourself in a meditative state of mind and think about the role emotions play in your life—to what extent are you in control of your emotions, and to what extent do you feel they control you? Next, take some herbs associated with the element water and sprinkle them at the base of the candle. Cup your hands around the flame and say something like:

> As this candle burns, I
> attune my soul to emotional
> awareness. I vow, from this
> day forth, to truly monitor
> and become aware of my
> emotions as I experience
> them. I recognize my
> emotional body as a profound
> spiritual vehicle that deserves
> the utmost care and
> compassion. So mote it be.

Going forth, stay true to your vow and reinforce it when necessary.

Raven Digitalis

Notes:

March 5
Friday

3rd ♏

Color of the day: Coral
Incense of the day: Mint

Love Spell

The weekend is here, winter is finally letting go of its frozen hold over you, and your thoughts move to finding the perfect companion to spend your life with. Spruce up your happy clothes, use those great-smelling soaps and shampoos, and get out and socialize. Nothing says you're hot like looking great and smelling like springtime itself. Get some new shoes, dust off those party clothes, and get out on the dance floor. Make it a point to visit events that are held locally and check out the local Pagan singles scene. Give a local "singles spot" a try for one evening and see if it's really as good as they say. You will never find that perfect mate sitting in front of the

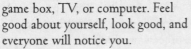

game box, TV, or computer. Feel good about yourself, look good, and everyone will notice you.

Boudica

Notes:

stone, malachite is said to break into pieces to warn you of danger. If worn against the skin, it promotes sleep and general well-being, cures depression, and attracts love. And if that's not enough, malachite is one of the most beautiful gems in the world.

Lily Gardner

Notes:

March 6
Saturday

 3rd ♏
☽ → ♐ 2:36 am

Color of the day: Indigo
Incense of the day: Patchouli

Malachite for Protection

It was once thought that nothing positive could be achieved on March 6, a day considered "perilous." Perhaps you are the cautious sort who likes to be extra careful just in case, or maybe you have your own unlucky days. Try wearing a small piece of malachite either as a piece of jewelry or in a bag around your neck for luck. Malachite is one of the earliest gems to be discovered and used. A malachite decoration estimated to be more than ten thousand years old was unearthed in Iraq. Because of its high copper content, malachite has a magnetic quality. Known as a traveler's

March 7
Sunday

 3rd ♐
4th Quarter 10:42 am

Color of the day: Yellow
Incense of the day: Juniper

Sun Mantra Ritual

According to vedic astrological gem remedies, ruby is governed by the Sun, a planetary deity representing the male or father principle. The Sun's color is blood red. Its nature is bile-dominated, and it presides over the east direction. The Sun is responsible for our immunity and physical makeup. It is also said to govern the brain, nerves, liver, lungs, heart, and bones. For gaining self-confidence, vitality, resistance, ambition, understanding of parapsychic phenomena, intellect, prosperity, success in worldly affairs, and strength, the Sun's gems are worn after sanctification and repetition of the Sun's mantra:

Om Hring Hamsah Suryaye Namah Om.

For horoscopes where the Sun is not well posited, it is advisable to perform "Mantra Yoga" by reciting the Sun's mantra 108 times daily for a period of thirty days. Incense and tealight candles can be lit during mantra recital. Begin by clearing all mundane thoughts and breathing in a relaxed manner.

S. Y. Zenith

Notes:

Holiday lore: Although the month of June is named for Juno, principal goddess of the Roman pantheon, major festivals dedicated to her are scattered throughout the year. For instance, today marks Junoalia, a festival in honor of Juno celebrated in solemnity by matrons. Two images of Juno made of cypress were borne in a procession of twenty-seven girls dressed in long robes, singing

a hymn to the goddess composed by the poet Livius. Along the way, the procession would dance in the great field of Rome before proceeding ahead to the temple of Juno.

March 8
Monday

 4th ♐
☽ → ♑ 12:13 pm

Color of the day: White
Incense of the day: Lily

March Hare Energy to Spare Spell

Out of soft sculpting putty, create a small hare. As you sculpt, envision the boundless energy of spring flowing all around you. Let the excitement and rebirth of life, as it peeks through the veil of winter, invigorate you as you give your March hare shape and detail. On a scrap of parchment, list the things you want to have more energy to accomplish. Dry your hare on the paper and try to envision yourself completing those tasks with ease and nimble skill. Communicate with your hare often and carry her around when you find yourself feeling sluggish. Enjoy talking openly to your creation and develop an entire life story of wild adventures for

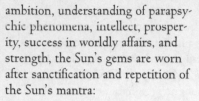

your hare. Opening our lives to the enlivening essence of this amazing creature can help fuel us in those last lingering days of winter. The hare reminds us that life is meant to be playful and inspiring.

Estha McNevin

Notes:

Holiday lore: While most holidays across the world celebrate the lives and achievement of men, March 8 is one day wholly dedicated to the achievement and work of women. Originally inspired by a pair of mid-nineteenth-century ladies' garment workers' strikes, today the holiday is little known in its country of origin; though this day's legacy is clear in March's designation by the U.S. Congress as Women's History Month. Throughout the month, women's groups in many American towns hold celebrations and events, concerts, exhibitions, and rituals that recall heroic and gifted women of every stripe.

March 9
Tuesday

4th ♑

Color of the day: Black
Incense of the day: Cedar

Sweep Away Winter Spell

We've made it through another winter. There may still be wintry blasts, but spring whispers to us from just over the horizon. During the winter, negative energy can collect in our homes, but today we're going to sweep away winter. Open both your front and back doors. Grab your faithful broom and symbolically begin sweeping out all that trapped negative power. Start at the back door and work your way toward the front door. At the front door, sprinkle a few grains of salt along your threshold and sweep out to your front porch. As you sweep toward the street, visualize a blue-white light coming from your broom's bristles. This psychic house-cleaning ritual dates back to early German magic.

James Kambos

Notes:

March 10
Wednesday

 4ℏ ♑
Color of the day: Brown
Incense of the day: Lavender

Giving Thanks

When we begin to acknowledge the blessings that are present all around us, our life becomes more blessed. Take some time today to give thanks and honor the gods for the blessings they have bestowed to you. One technique I learned from my first Witchcamp was the use of a prayer mala. Our teacher taught us to acknowledge something for which we are grateful on each of the 108 rudraksha beads. It's a simple practice that can bring amazing results to the way we see and interact with the world. If you do not have a mala or set of prayer beads, make one or do this exercise in your Book of Shadows or magical journal. Number 108 spots and fill them in as you are moved. Really take your time with this. Ritualize if you wish and create the list inside sacred space. May your day be blessed.

Abel R. Gomez

Notes:

March 11
Thursday

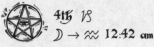 4ℏ ♑
☽ → ♒ 12:42 am

Color of the day: Crimson
Incense of the day: Jasmine

Trusting Your Intuition

We all sometimes get "psychic hits" that warn us away from something or urge us to make a choice we otherwise wouldn't, but it can be hard to listen to those feelings when it seems as if the world is looking at us with raised eyebrows. Today, try this spell to get back in touch with your intuition. Make a little pouch by tying a quartz crystal or moonstone, some star anise, and some mugwort in a piece of purple or black fabric. Carry it in your purse or pocket, or hang it from a string around your neck. When you have a moment of self-doubt, hold the pouch, close your eyes, and say to yourself:

Voices within, verily
Tell me what shall really be

In the quiet of the moment, your intuition should be able to work through. All you have to do then is follow your own lead!

Castiel

Notes:

streets. As you walk, breathe deeply. Let your eyes delight in your surroundings as your feet lead you to a sense of peace. This spell takes a mere fifteen minutes. At the end you will be magically uplifted with increased oxygenation and a slightly elevated heart rate. The endorphins released by exercise will leave you feeling good and able to appreciate the profound magic of health and well-being.

Dallas Jennifer Cobb

Notes:

March 12
Friday

 4th ♒

Color of the day: Purple
Incense of the day: Cypress

A Walking Spell

Walking is wonderful exercise that provides gentle muscle toning and builds cardio function. Buddhist monks incorporate walking in some meditation, using the rhythm of their footfalls as a tool for being present in the moment. Walking is also an amazing form of transportation. It's cheap, fossil-fuel free, and can be done anywhere. No special equipment is needed, but a well-fitting pair of shoes is recommended. Today cast a walking spell. Get outdoors in the sunshine, indoors in a mall, or brave the snowy

March 13
Saturday

 4th ♒
☽ → ♓ 1:44 pm

Color of the day: Black
Incense of the day: Pine

Daily Exercise

Magic is a force that flows through the world, pooling in certain places and objects. People have varying levels of affinity for it. Whatever your current level, you can increase it with regular exercise.

The practice of witchcraft is not just about big spells and seasonal rituals. It relies at heart on the exercise of basic skills. A few minutes of meditation and energy manipulation every day will make for better progress than an hour-long ritual once a month. Each day, hold one of your magical tools and concentrate on sensing its stored power. Add energy to its reservoir if you have some to spare. Here is a daily blessing to say during your magical exercise:

> Power is the tinder,
> Magic is the spark.
> Spinning from the center,
> Spanning light and dark.
> Circle is the cauldron,
> Sacred to Her name.
> Witchcraft is the fire,
> And I am the flame.

> Elizabeth Barrette

Notes:

March 14
Sunday

Daylight Saving Time begins 2 am

 4th ♓

Color of the day: Yellow
Incense of the day: Almond

Nature Spell

> To know and to love:
> the same thing.

We can deepen our spiritual practice by learning more about nature. Whether it's tree, wildflower, bird, or rock identification, take time now to learn more about a particular aspect of nature. Start a notebook and decide how much time each month you're willing to spend on this project. For tree identification, sketch or take photographs of a tree you've chosen. Write its botanical name and its folk name if you can find it. What are its magical properties? Is it native to your area? Does it like dry or humid conditions, sun or shade? You may want to press leaves and include them in your notebook next to the tree you've identified. Try to spend some time with the tree and see if you can feel the spirit of the tree. At the end of the year, review your experiences. Do you feel this study has deepened your love of nature?

> Lily Gardner

Notes:

March 15
Monday

4th ♓
New Moon 5:01 pm

Color of the day: Gray
Incense of the day: Rosemary

New Moon Fertility Spell

On March 15, the annual Shinto fertility festival Tagata Honen-Sai is celebrated. Carrying a giant wooden phallus through the streets, worshippers bless local farmers and farms with fertility. With the New Moon, turn your focus to fertility: nourishment, growth, and rebirth. What is started now grows with the waxing Moon, becoming gloriously full, abundant, and bright. What has lain dormant during the Moon's darkness can now be resurrected and enjoy rebirth. Whatever your focus, be it a thought, feeling, belief, action, activity, or idea, it will grow. You are the cultivator of your life. What will you plant? What needs a fertile blessing? What do you want to grow? A new habit, a relationship, or a work project that requires completion can benefit from the swelling energy of the New Moon and a fertility blessing. As you clearly envision what you want to plant and grow, say:

> Within me I plant a
> tiny seed,
> Of what I want, I love, and
> believe,

> With light comes growth
> swelling long,
> I grow this seed big, bold,
> and strong.

See the project, friendship, or habit growing and evolving. See its fruition and completion. Feel the charge of accomplishment, and know yourself fertile in your endeavors. As the vision becomes detailed and finite, say:

> With the Moon this shall
> succeed.

In the days ahead as the Moon swells, affirm each day the growth and flowering of your intention. See the results.

Dallas Jennifer Cobb

Notes:

Holiday lore: Why is March 15 so notorious? On this date in 226 BCE, an earthquake brought the Colossus of Rhodes—one of the Seven Wonders of the Ancient World—to its knees. But a more famous event likely accounts for the notoriety of the "Ides of March." Julius Caesar's rule, somewhere along the way, became tyrannical. In February of 44 BCE, Caesar had himself named

Dictator Perpetuus—Dictator for Life. Brutus assassinated him on March 15. Caesar's murder was foretold by soothsayers and even by his wife, Calpurnia, who had a nightmare in which Caesar was being butchered like an animal. Caesar chose to ignore these portents and the rest, of course, is history.

March 16
Tuesday

 1st ♓
☽ → ♈ 2:32 am

Color of the day: Maroon
Incense of the day: Ylang-ylang

Three Bowls of Wine Ritual

We all know by now that a glass of red wine is an elixir of good health. Long revered by Witches as the divine nectar of the gods, celebrate this day, the first day of Bacchanalia, with a glass or two to honor the Roman god Bacchus. It's been said three bowls of wine define our limits. The first glass promotes "health," the second "love," and the third, precious "sleep." But move on to the next and you are traversing into dangerous territory as this fourth glass promotes "violence," the fifth is said to create "uproar," the sixth "drunken revelry," the seventh a "black eye," and it just keeps getting

worse! So make a toast in the spirit of responsible revelry, lifting your chalice as you say:

> Hail Bacchus on this eve
> Of feasting, rite, and revelry.
> May my health be dually
>   blessed
> And love unbound sweet
>   words confessed.
> Then honor me one last
>   request,
> And wisely lay me down to
>   rest!

                    Igraine

Notes:

March 17
Wednesday
St. Patrick's Day

 1st ♈

Color of the day: White
Incense of the day: Lilac

Enchanting Green Attire Day

Happy St. Patrick's Day! Let's employ a little color magic and turn the traditional "Wearing of the green" into your own Pagan celebration of the return of the Green Man. The waxing Moon is the perfect time to work for blessings and abundance. Enchant your item of emerald-colored clothing for good luck, magic, and prosperity. Can't you feel the Green Man returning? Spring is on the way!

> *Green is the color of the God,*
> *new life, and the spring,*
>
> *His magic surrounds me*
> *now, in an enchanting ring.*
>
> *The Green Man blesses me,*
> *with good luck and success*
> *so true,*
>
> *May I be graced with his love*
> *in all that I say and do.*
>
> *For the good of all with*
> *harm to none,*
>
> *By color and rhyme this spell*
> *is done!*

Ellen Dugan

Notes:

Holiday lore: Much folklore surrounds St. Patrick's Day. Though originally a Catholic holy day, St. Patrick's Day has evolved into more of a secular holiday today. One traditional icon of the day is the shamrock. This stems from an

Irish tale that tells how Patrick used the three-leafed shamrock to explain the Trinity of Christian dogma. His followers adopted the custom of wearing a shamrock on his feast day; though why we wear green on this day is less clear. St. Patrick's Day came to America in 1737, the date of the first public celebration of the holiday in Boston.

March 18
Thursday

1st ♈

☽ → ♉ 12:29 pm

Color of the day: Purple
Incense of the day: Myrrh

Celtic Tree Month of Alder

Today marks the first day of the Celtic tree month of *Fearn*, the alder tree. A fast-growing species, alders are often used to repopulate scorched or barren lands because of their hardiness and their ability to transport airborne nitrogen into the soil, enriching it. Their fallen leaves make for excellent compost. Take time today to look at areas of your life that have been damaged that could benefit from some fast yet thorough healing. While there may still be long-term work, the tree totem alder can aid in some temporary

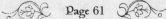

quick fixes while you sort out the more difficult aspects of your situation. Ask alder for help:

> Red alder, black alder,
>   white alder, and green,
> Help me to heal my wounds,
>   make them clean.
> Though the road to true health
>   may be long and dark,
> With you as my guide I'll
>   bravely embark!

Lupa

Notes:

all the small stuff you would like to banish from your life. When you are through, extinguish the candle with a snuffer—don't blow it out. Wrap the candle in the black cloth and tie it securely. Place it in the dish of salt to purify it. Keep it there and be free of worrying about the small things in life. At the next Full Moon when you are free of the stress, dismantle the bundle and dispose of it by either burying it or burning it all.

Gail Wood

Notes:

March 19
Friday

1st ♉

Color of the day: Pink
Incense of the day: Violet

Don't Sweat It Spell

Today is the day that the swallows traditionally return to the San Juan Capistrano mission in California. The swallow teaches us to not let the small stuff get to us. To not sweat the small stuff, gather a small scrap of black fabric, a small black candle, string, and a dish of salt. Light the black candle and tell it

March 20
Saturday

Ostara – Spring Equinox –
International Astrology Day

1st ♉
☉ → ♈ 1:32 pm
☽ → ♊ 8:28 pm

Color of the day: Gray
Incense of the day: Sage

Laying Eggs

Bless and pray over one dozen eggs. Fill them with the energy of your dreams and desires. When they are fully charged, hard boil and

decorate them to express the things you most want to manifest in your life. Gather cozy pillows and blankets to create a nest for your eggs that will evenly distribute their weight and prevent them from getting squished. As you begin this meditation, position yourself over your nest as a devoted mother would and do not break from meditation until you feel your eggs radiating warmth and life beneath you. Draw energy out of your own heart and place a little spark of it inside of each egg. While you tend to your nest, envision each of your desires coming to fruition and focus clearly on the details of their fruition. When each of them is fully realized in your mind's eye, gather your eggs and store in the icebox; eat one egg a day until they are gone.

Estha McNevin

Notes:

March 21
Sunday

1st ♊

Color of the day: Amber
Incense of the day: Marigold

Iranian New Year

Spring-cleaning and feasting mark this day for Muslims and non-Muslims alike. Traditional foods include herb and spinach omelets and snacks made with nuts, seeds, and dried fruit. A table is decorated with candles, incense, fruit, garlic, pastries, coins, and a mirror for every person in the family—and a live goldfish in a bowl of water. This represents the world floating in space and time. Everyone sits perfectly still at the stroke of midnight, as the Earth rolls into a new year. Create your own version of this celebration by cleaning house and performing a cleansing ritual, followed by a feast. Mix a few pinches of dried rosemary and sage in water and use a spray bottle to mist the air.

> Water and herbs, cleanse
>   this space,
> Bring peace and good will to
>   this place.
> As we feast, please bless us,
>   too,
> Our hopes and dreams we
>   now renew.

Ember

Notes:

You will be surprised at the amount of negativity you will remove and how good your home feels.

Boudica

Notes:

March 22
Monday

1st ♊

Color of the day: Lavender
Incense of the day: Clary sage

There's No Place Like Home Spell

Your home should be a haven for yourself. It should be a zone of comfort and you should feel protected and loved. This is the time of year to work on cleaning up your home, clearing out negative energy and reinforcing your protective spellworks. Chalk pentacles on the doors and windows for protection; clean everything up with lavender and rose (if you are allergic, make proper substitutions) and either smudge or use a mixture of salt, lavender buds, and bay leaf ground up fine on the rugs and furniture to ground out negativity. Sweep that all up in a twenty-four-hour period. Spray a lavender oil/water mix and burn some cedar incense to release calm. Wash up window coverings and bedding, and wash down the kitchen and bath.

Holiday lore: Cybele was the Great Mother of the gods in Ida, and she was taken to Rome from Phrygia in 204 BCE. She was also considered the Great Mother of all Asia Minor. Her festivals were known as *ludi*, or "games," and were solemnized with various mysterious rites. Along with Hecate and Demeter of Eleusis, Cybele was one of the leading deities of Rome when mystery cults were at their prime. Hila'aria, or "Hilaria," originally seemed to have been a name given to any day or season of rejoicing that was either private or public. Such days were devoted to general rejoicing and people were not allowed to show signs of grief or sorrow. The Hilaria actually falls on March 25 and is the last day of a festival of Cybele that commences today. However, the Hilaria was not mentioned in the Roman calendar or in Ovid's *Fasti*.

March 23
Tuesday

1st ♊

☽ → ♋ 2:16 am

2nd Quarter 7:00 am

Color of the day: Red
Incense of the day: Bayberry

Festival of Minerva

On this day, ancient Romans celebrated the Festival of Minerva. To honor her, musicians and poets paraded to her shrines and performed their greatest works. Minerva rules wisdom, poetry, warcraft, medicine, and commerce. Born from the head of her father, this virgin goddess bows to neither god nor man. Even now, she appears in statues and seals of universities. Celebrate her festival by going to a civic event, practicing martial arts, performing poetry, or learning a self-sufficient skill. Decorate with images of owls, shields, and spears. Her colors are white and Tyrian purple. Invoke her with these words:

> Minerva of the quick wit
> And steel-strong spine,
> I call on you!
> The flash of your eyes
> Is the sun on a sword's blade
> Teach me to cut to the heart
> Of all things
> And to listen for wisdom
> In the silence of an owl's flight.

> Elizabeth Barrette

March 24
Wednesday

2nd ♋

Color of the day: Brown
Incense of the day: Bay laurel

Day of Blood

This day was a day of mourning for the Roman god Attis, who castrated himself out of guilt after he betrayed his lover, Cybele. He bled to death, and was then resurrected. This represents the life cycle of cutting down and rising again, as mourners held a vigil over an empty tomb, symbolizing the god's resurrection. This universal cycle is celebrated in many different ways in various religious traditions during the springtime of the year. To symbolize the blood of life and the cycle of renewal, decorate your altar (or other sacred space) with red and white flowers and candles. Fill a goblet with red wine or red fruit juice and chant the following:

> As all things, wax and wane,
> Life does, too, again and
> again.

Celebrate the cycle of life as you drink and save a little liquid to pour outside on the ground as an offering to the Earth.

Ember

Notes:

shortening, eggs, and milk and form it into dough. Break dough into small pieces and roll each between palms until it is 1 inch in length. Flatten slightly and roll in sesame seeds. Place them on cookie sheets about 3 inches apart. Bake at 375 degrees F for 12 to 15 minutes or until cookies are browned.

S. Y. Zenith

Notes:

March 25
Thursday

 2nd ♋

☽ → ♌ 5:39 am

Color of the day: Green
Incense of the day: Nutmeg

Cookies to Smooth Relationships

Spring is the season of new life, Lady Day biscuits called "Queen's Biscuits" can be made and shared with family and friends to smooth relations for the year. This recipe makes about six dozen cookies. Ingredients include 4 cups sifted flour, 1 cup sugar, 1 tablespoon baking powder, ¼ teaspoon salt, 1 cup shortening, 2 slightly beaten eggs, ½ cup milk, and ¼ pound sesame seeds. Grease two cookie sheets lightly. In a bowl, sift together flour, sugar, baking powder, and salt. Cut mixture with a pastry blender or two knives until pieces resemble size of small peas. Add

March 26
Friday

 2nd ♌

Color of the day: Coral
Incense of the day: Thyme

Blooming Creativity

Though the possibility of some late wintry weather is not out of the question, in most parts of the world life is bursting out everywhere in shades of light green and rich, earthy brown. Perhaps the creative force inherent at this time of year inspired the poet Robert Frost, whose birthday is today. Take some time today and see if you can't tap into some of that creativity, and try to incorporate something from the natural world around you. Write a poem about new leaves, make a sculpture out of cold spring mud, arrange a bouquet of daffodils. Consider making your nature creation an offering to the creative life force within all things—leave it under a tree or in an icy, rushing brook, or set it on your altar to remind you of the beauty and power life can hold.

Castiel

Notes:

March 27
Saturday

2nd ♌
☽ → ♍ 6:57 am

Color of the day: Blue
Incense of the day: Magnolia

A Spell for Safe Travel

To craft a spell bag attuned to safety in travel, draw the rune Raido on a fabric drawstring bag made of orange fabric. On the opposite side, draw the astrological symbol for Mercury. Fill the bag with any amount of moss (Spanish moss, Icelandic moss, oak moss, general tree moss, etc.) and seaweed (kelp or another variety), as well as a large tiger's eye stone for clear sight. Draw a giant eye on either side of an orange sheet of construction paper, fold it three times, and stick it inside the bag. Close the bag and knot it tightly shut. Hold it to your third eye (Ajna) chakra and say something like:

> Spirits of Mercury and spirits of air; spirits of travel and spirits of care, with this bag I do intend; to keep me safe until the end. In all my travels and all my jaunts, know that it's your protection I want. Keep me aware and keep me secure; these prayers of safety I humbly ask of you.

Repeat this prayer eight times and carry the bag with you on any trip by car, bus, plane, boat, or bicycle.

Raven Digitalis

Notes

:

March 28
Sunday
Palm Sunday

 2nd ♍

Color of the day: Orange
Incense of the day: Eucalyptus

Pansy Love Magic

One of the first flowers I plant each spring is pansies. Their cheery colors bring a touch of spring to flowerbeds, pots, and window boxes. These old-fashioned flowers have been used in love magic since the Victorian era, and can be easily used to enhance a love spell. To create some pansy love magic of your own, try this. First, write your name and your lover's name on a small piece of paper; place the paper in the bottom of a six-inch flowerpot. Fill with potting soil. Plant your pot with pansies in the color associated with your wish. Here are some examples. For better communication, plant yellow or orange pansies. For understanding, use pink or maroon pansies. To promote peace and understanding, plant blue and violet pansies. Use white for faithfulness. Water your pansies regularly and watch your love grow.

James Kambos

Notes:

March 29
Monday

2nd ♍
☽ → ♎ 7:21 am
Full Moon 10:25 pm

Color of the day: Gray
Incense of the day: Hyssop

Yemaya Bath Ritual

Yemaya is the supreme mother goddess of the Yoruba traditions and presides over all waters. Call upon her deep powers of love and healing this night in a bath ritual. You'll need seven blue candles, a lunar stone (preferably moonstone), seven white rose petals, seven pinches of sea salt, and seven drops of lavender, peppermint, or passionflower essential oil. Begin by lighting the candles around the tub and drawing a bath. Take a few deep breaths and meditate on what needs to be healed. Allow yourself to call out to Yemaya with your heart as you add the essential oils and salt to your bath. Breathe once more and when you are ready immerse yourself in her waters. Feel her soft caress against your skin as she heals your deepest wounds. Take your time and allow the process to unfold. When you are ready, step out of the bath and leave the rose petals as an offering to Yemaya.

Yemaya. Mother, goddess of the Sea,

Be in this place, come forth unto me,

Lady of the oceans, the lakes, and the rivers,

Beautiful Queen, ebb and flow bringer,

Heal my mind, my body my soul.

For with your sweet love, I become whole.

Ashe, Great Mother

Abel R. Gomez

Notes:

March 30
Tuesday
Passover begins

 3rd ♎

Color of the day: White
Incense of the day: Geranium

A Spell to Protect Your health

This is a perfect day to begin a new healthier lifestyle, to start losing weight, and become more physically fit. Since it is a waning Moon phase we can use this for "decreasing"

your weight. We will use the energies of Tuesday, a Mars day, to stir up some courage and enthusiasm. You can begin by making a vow to walk at least thirty minutes a day. You just need some walking shoes, the outdoors, and your own personal will to make a positive change. Try enchanting your walking shoes for success.

Today I begin a healthier way of life,

May the god Mars make me strong and strengthen my stride.

Tuesday's magic is for vigor, bravery and derring-do,

I will lose weight as I exercise in these enchanted shoes.

Congratulations on becoming a healthier Witch!

Ellen Dugan

Notes:

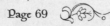

March 31
Wednesday

3rd ♎︎
☽ → ♏︎ 8:41 am

Color of the day: Yellow
Incense of the day: Honeysuckle

Baby Blessing

It is the first blush of spring. The pussy willows press forth their furry heads expectantly and epimedium push their delicate fairy petals up from the dark, black dirt. Winter's edge begins to fade as wondrous new life emerges. The belly of the Goddess is swollen with the God's seed as the ripening rhythm of spring calls forth her babe. Across the land the fairies gather in preparation, collecting blessings and well wishes for these new arrivals. A child is born! Cast your wish for the little prince or princess with this simple baby blessing. To ensure the baby's wisdom and joy plant an iris bulb in a clay pot. With a silver marker, write your wish around the outside of the pot, wrapping your words in a spiral around the bulb to energize your blessing. Gift the new parents with this offering tucked in a box with sprigs of arborvitae considered to be the "Tree of Life."

Igraine

Notes:

April is the fourth month of the Gregorian calendar and the first month of the astrological calendar. Its astrological sign is Aries, the Ram (March 20–April 20), a cardinal-fire sign ruled by Mars. The Roman war god Mars equates with the Greek Ares, or Aries, the first sign of the zodiac. The Latin word *aperire* means "to open" and is thought to be one possible origin of the name. April brings the blooming time, a dazzling display of fragrant flowers and budding trees. Spring makes her presence fully known in April. Redbud, dogwood, crab apple, forsythia, lilac, and many other plants create a splendid color palette in neighborhoods, parks, and forests. Trees are bursting with fresh, tender green leaves—yet unexpected cool weather can threaten new growth. We are reminded of this by April Fools' Day on the first—a day to honor the Trickster. As Anglo-Saxons found April sacred to Eostre or Ostara, the goddess of spring, they referred to it as Oster-monath or Eostur-monath. This is the origin of the modern Easter. April is a month of beauty and new life—symbolized by popular fertility symbols such as eggs and rabbits. And don't forget Earth Day on April 22. Do something special in honor of Mother Earth—plant a tree or find ways to go green and make every day Earth Day. April's Full Moon is called the Pink Moon.

April 1
Thursday
April Fools' Day

 3rd ♏

Color of the day: Green
Incense of the day: Mulberry

Creative Trickery

Rabbit, a trickster in the myths of cultures in North America and Africa (as well as modern myths such as *Watership Down* by Richard Adams), is particularly appropriate for this day. While Rabbit (as with any trickster) should be approached with care, he tends to be gentle in his lessons. Rabbit and his children are renowned for their fertility. While fertility is often taken literally, as procreation of various species, it can also mean more general growth. As spring is the beginning of the growing season in the Northern Hemisphere, it's a great time for putting projects and endeavors into motion. When things go wrong, ask the trickster for tips on creative solutions:

> *Rabbit, Rabbit, as you run*
>
> *Stop a moment by my fire*
>
> *To teach, to show, and to inspire*
>
> *Some fertile growth (and a lot of fun!)*

Lupa

Notes:

April 2
Friday
Good Friday
Orthodox Good Friday

 3rd ♏
☽ → ♐ 12:53 pm

Color of the day: Purple
Incense of the day: Orchid

The Fountain of Youth

Ponce de Leon arrived on the shores of what is now known as Florida on this day in search of the Fountain of Youth. Since that adventurous day in the early 1500s, we have continued to explore the possibility of eternal youth and lasting beauty, hoping to discover some magical elixir or mysterious formula. The secret is revealed through the power of the meditative mind and the expression of youthful optimism. Sit or lie quietly, closing your eyes. Focus on a gentle breath and allow yourself to drift slowly back in time. Take yourself to a special place in your flowering youth where you felt completely content. Explore this terrain, observing your feelings. Remember your daydreams. Experience all of the wonder that surrounds you. Embody this sensation of innocence and joy. When you are ready to return, open your eyes and affirm aloud:

> *I am forever young in mind, body, and soul!*

When finished, smile.

Igraine

Notes:

put the cloth on a table and be seated before it. Put the bowl of water on top of the cloth and the lighted candle on the table directly opposite you on the other side of the bowl. Turn out the lights, soften your vision, and ask the Spirit for revelation. Stare into the bowl and allow things to emerge from the watery wisdom. Without judgment, remember these things. When you are finished, extinguish the candle and thank the Spirit. Pour the water outdoors or into a houseplant.

Gail Wood

Notes:

April 3
Saturday

3rd ♐

Color of the day: Brown
Incense of the day: Sage

heed What You have

On this day in 1944, the U.S. Supreme Court handed down the landmark decision giving African Americans the right to vote. The day reminds us that our basic rights should never be taken for granted. To bring the things you take for granted into your awareness, you will need a clear bowl of water, a dark cloth, and a white candle. In a darkened room,

April 4
Sunday
Easter
Orthodox Easter

3rd ♐
☽ → ♑ 9:07 pm

Color of the day: Amber
Incense of the day: Eucalyptus

The Egg Wish Spell

You may have something you really would like to have or do in your life. While this is not a time to start a new project, it may be time

to incubate and hatch an old desire. Make a pinhole at the top of a raw egg. On the bottom, make a small hole that is wide enough to insert a rolled up piece of paper. Blow the egg out, rinse, and let dry. Carefully paint with watercolors or magic marker a symbol on the egg to represent a planetary influence or deity. Write your wish on a piece of paper, roll it up real tight and place inside the egg. Place this egg on your altar to remind you of your desire and make sure you work toward this goal. When the wish is fulfilled, smash the egg and burn the paper before burying it all in a secret place.

Boudica

Notes:

Offerings of candles, flowers, incense, and food—especially pastries—are left at the graves. This is a good day to connect with and contact the spirits of your ancestors. If you can visit a loved one's grave, honor their memory with a small decoration and a bit of their favorite sweet treat. At dinner, set a place for them at the table; let them be the guest of honor. Celebrate their life by telling fun and happy stories about them. If you wish to contact them at this time, use a magic mirror, a pendulum, or meditation. You may notice their presence in subtle ways—a scent, a touch, or a flicker of light. Or they may contact you during a dream.

James Kambos

Notes:

April 5
Monday

3rd ♑

Color of the day: Lavender
Incense of the day: Hyssop

Remember Your Ancestors Spell
On this day in Taiwan, family graves are visited and deceased loved ones are remembered. The graves are cleaned and decorated.

April 6
Tuesday

Passover ends

 3rd ♑
4th Quarter 5:37 am

Color of the day: Red
Incense of the day: Ginger

Break Fast from Technology

Far too often, we forget the role that technology plays in our lives. Personally, I strongly suggest taking a break (a "fast") from technology for a number of days. (This is described in my book *Shadow Magic Compendium*.) For the space provided here, I suggest this blessing after any fast from technology, or at any time you feel overwhelmed to express gratitude to the neo-gods of technology. Get a bag of fifty tealight candles and a little bottle of peppermint or spearmint essential oil (non-synthetic). At precisely 8 pm, anoint one of the tealights with the oil and fire up the wick. Place this next to the first item of electronic technology you see in the house—perhaps on top of the television, on the computer tower, next to a light fixture, on the car, or on the washing machine. When placing the candle, say something like:

> I honor you, gods of technology and electricity. Please always serve me positively, as I shall do the same for you.

Continue this process with every piece of technological equipment you see in the house. Check the candles constantly to make sure the flames are safe, secure, and contained.

Raven Digitalis

Notes:

April 7
Wednesday

 4th ♑
☽ → ♒ 8:51 am

Color of the day: White
Incense of the day: Bay laurel

Clear the Path to Enlightenment

Wednesday's are named after the Norse god Woden (or Odin). This god traveled the Earth in disguise as a one-eyed man with a long beard and a gray hat. He was always seeking wisdom. Woden/Odin is a god of mystery and magic, and of course the runes. Today, with a little help from Woden/Odin, let's remove any obstacles in your path toward enlightenment. Light a white candle and visualize the safe and easy removal of any obstacles that are in

your path. Now repeat the charm
three times:

> Today is sacred to the old
> Norse god Woden,
>
> Knowledge I seek, hear me as
> the charm is spoken.
>
> Safely remove from my path
> all troubles and strife,
>
> May I attain wisdom and
> guidance throughout my life.
>
> For the good of all with
> harm to none,
>
> In Woden's name this spell
> is done!

Ellen Dugan

Notes:

April 8
Thursday

4th ≈

Color of the day: Turquoise
Incense of the day: Balsam

Prosperity Talisman Ritual

After acquiring a prosperity talisman, choose a time of day when
you will not be disturbed. Clean an
area in a quiet room and sit down.

Play some relaxing music. Place the
talisman in the middle of where you
are seated and surround it in four
quarters with candles. A gold candle
represents east, red for south, blue
for west, and green for north. Light
the candles. Cleanse, consecrate,
and empower the talisman by first
connecting with the energies of the
east, then south, west, and north.
Contemplate on what you wish to
receive and write your petition on a
piece of parchment paper, then recite
its contents out loud. Pass the talisman and parchment around the candles like the cycles of seasons. Keep
the parchment on the altar. As you
put on the talisman, envision being
blessed with abundance in prosperity,
love, and unity.

S. Y. Zenith

Notes:

April 9
Friday

 4th ♒

☽ → ♓ 9:48 pm

Color of the day: Pink
Incense of the day: Mint

Love Spell

Cast your love spells on Friday, the day sacred to Venus. Your spells will be especially potent in April, the month dedicated to her. You can cast many kinds of love spells: self-love and acceptance, personal beauty, attracting love, promoting love, deepening a relationship to one of commitment, or adding spark to an existing relationship. To attract a special person into your life, write his or her name on a piece of parchment paper and plant it beneath a teacup rose. These lovely plants are sacred to Venus and can be grown indoors or out. Place the rose in your window, preferably in the direction of your loved one's house. Cup the plant in your hands every day and say:

> As your roots deepen
> And your leaves drink the
>   light,
> (Name of loved one)'s love
>   awakens.
> And as you blossom, so
> (Name of loved one)'s love
>   will bloom.

Lily Gardner

Notes:

April 10
Saturday

4th ♓

Color of the day: Gray
Incense of the day: Ivy

Stretching Time Spell

In spring, the days grow longer as the Sun returns from the south. But it's not summer yet—and there's a lot to do. Sometimes you need more time than a day holds. For this spell, you need some honey, a gold-colored metal image of the Sun, wax, and a clean empty jar with a lid. In the morning light, hold up the metal sun and say:

> Sun in the sky
> Sun in my hand
> Be now as one
> By my command!

Place the metal sun into the empty jar. Pour the honey over the metal sun until the jar fills, saying:

> May the hours of the day
> Be bright and sunny
> And may the river of time
> Flow slow as honey.

Cap the jar tightly and seal it with wax. When you need more daylight, hold the jar and imagine the hours stretching out like a strand of honey.

Elizabeth Barrette

Notes:

April 11
Sunday

4th ♓

Color of the day: Orange
Incense of the day: Hyacinth

Fire Spell

Life isn't always exciting. It's easy to get lost in the daily grind of work, school, errands, and the constant demands of life. Call upon the energy of fire today to break free from the routine and engage your true passion. Go to your ritual space and gather as many candles as you need to create a complete circle around you. Be sure there is enough space to prevent any sort of accident. Breathe and invite the spirits of fire to surround you. In your mind's eye, visualize the flames burning away all that no longer serves and giving form to your deepest yearning, the desire

to live and breathe as a human in the world. When ready, bid farewell and give gratitude to the fire.

> Powers of fire, of passion, and delight,
>
> Burn away all sorrow, take away all plight.
>
> Conjure forth my desire and yearning to be,
>
> Fire is my freedom, so mote it be!

Abel R. Gomez

Notes:

April 12
Monday

4th ♓
☽ → ♈ 9:31 am

Color of the day: Silver
Incense of the day: Neroli

A Penny for Your Protection

In 1877, a mask was worn by the catcher at a Harvard baseball game. This is believed to be the first time a catcher's mask was used. To weave a spell of protection, gather a penny, some thin white string or embroidery floss, a birthday candle, and a red marker. Take a centering breath, tapping into your strength and power as well as the power of Mother Earth, then draw a pentacle on the candle with the marker. Concentrate on bringing the power of the elements to your aid by saying,

> By air, fire, water, earth, and spirit, give me strength and protection.

Light the candle and begin wrapping the string around the penny, chanting:

> Light and wisdom will surround me, as all evil moves around me.

When you are done, tie a knot and say:

> As I will it, so mote it be, protection come to me three times three.

Carry the penny close to your body.

Gail Wood

Notes:

H istorical note: On April 12, 1961, Yuri Gagarin piloted the first manned spaceship to leave the pull of our planet's gravity. This achievement is given much less attention than it deserves. Part of that is politics, since Gagarin was a cosmonaut for the Soviet Union. Part of it, too, is time; today, space pilots live and work for months aboard space stations, so a simple space flight seems routine. Still, Yuri Gagarin's 108-minute flight in space represented a triumph of science and engineering, and it also broke a psychological barrier. It was literally a flight into the unknown. "Am I happy to be setting off on a cosmic flight?" said Yuri Gagarin in an interview before the launch. "Of course. In all ages and epochs people have experienced the greatest happiness in embarking upon new voyages of discovery . . . I say 'until we meet again' to you, dear friends, as we always say to each other when setting off on a long journey."

April 13
Tuesday

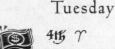 4th ♈

Color of the day: Black
Incense of the day: Cedar

Sprouting Wealth

I n a large bowl place ¼ cup dry mung beans. Rinse them thoroughly and let stand in 4 cups cool

water overnight. As you rinse them chant:

> Awaken life; embolden seed;
> bring me wealth with this
> deed.

The following morning, draw wealth and luck symbols on a large wide-mouthed mason jar with permanent marker. Rinse the beans and place them inside. Secure a cheesecloth over the opening with a strong rubber band and replace the ring only. Rinse the beans every day, repeating the chant. Tilt the jar over a large bowl to drain excess water after rinsing and place on a sunny kitchen table. Sprouts can be grown year-round and jars can be specially decorated to cultivate different intentions. They make a nutritious addition to sandwiches and salads and keep a constant life cycle rejuvenating in the home, which helps immensely in attracting luck and wealth. Enjoy!

Estha McNevin

Notes:

April 14
Wednesday

4th ♈

🌙 New Moon 8:29 am

☽ → ♉ 6:55 pm

Color of the day: Yellow
Incense of the day: Lavender

A Gardener's New Moon Spell

A New Moon in spring is the time for amazing new beginnings. It is a time for drawing, attracting, and seeding. Diana, goddess of the waxing and New Moon, will work with you as you plant seeds for summer's abundance—literally and symbolically. In the mundane world, soak your seeds tonight for planting tomorrow in tiny peat pots. These seeds will produce this summer's harvest. In the magical realm, state your clear intention of what you want to seed, sprout, grow, blossom, and come to fruit in the season ahead. Focused, detailed, and filled with belief, state your intention as though it exists now. Whether you have a greenhouse where you can start real plants, or if you plant seeds in the spiritual realm, know that what you sew now will grow with the Moon, the months and the seasonal cycle:

> As I sew my seeds tonight,
>
> Diana guide my magic rite.

Planting goodness, planting peace,

Diana goddess be with me.

Tiny seeds will always grow,

I know the power of this I sew.

That it will grow to flower and feed,

Let goodness grow from what I seed.

Dallas Jennifer Cobb

Notes:

a day to do something for Tellus Mater to let her know just how important she is to you. Take some time, regardless of the weather, to go outside and open yourself wide to her energy. Research "green" changes you can easily make in your life and then put them into practice. Volunteer to pick up trash or remove harmful invasive species. Donate money to an eco-friendly nonprofit group. Write a letter to an elected official or other decision-maker in support of an environmentally friendly law or practice, and work some magic to give the letter extra "oomph" before sending it.

Lupa

Notes:

April 15
Thursday

 1st ♉

Color of the day: Purple
Incense of the day: Clove

Give Thanks to the Earth Mother

Today is the festival of Tellus Mater, the Earth Mother. While many Pagans follow nature-based religions, we sometimes forget to give back to the Mother who gives us our very lives through food, water, shelter, and even the molecules that make up our bodies. Make today

April 16
Friday

 1st ♉

Color of the day: White
Incense of the day: Alder

A Rah Ra Ritual

Today is the Holiday of Ra. Ra was considered the king of the Egyptian gods, the patron of the

Pharaoh and all-father of creation. As the Sun god, he was said to ride a chariot across the sky every day. So today, when the Sun rises directly overhead, go outside and tip your face up to its light and thank Ra for his illuminating presence in your life.

> May the presence of Ra shine
> down upon me,
>
> Bring sunshine into my life
> and warmth, gently.
>
> The gold solar disc is your
> symbol and sign,
>
> May I be blessed and
> protected for all time.

Ellen Dugan

Notes:

April 17
Saturday

 1st ♉
)) → ♊ 2:08 am

Color of the day: Blue
Incense of the day: Rue

Inner Wisdom Spell

Sophia, goddess of wisdom, the divine feminine, and mother of creation, knows all that was and all that ever will be. Characterized by

the dove, her spirit is infinite and pure. Chant a tribute to Sophia to align yourself with her divine influences. Know that within you is the accumulated wisdom of your life, your parents, and teachers, and the collective wisdom of our evolution. With quiet introspection, cultivate your timeless wisdom: the whispers in your head, the feeling in your gut, and the tingling vibration on your scalp are all communications of intuition and instinct, the ancient tools of wisdom. They speak the truth of generations of learning, and survival. Today, hear the voice of your intuition and instinct. Affirm your own divine wisdom.

> Each particle of information
> Contributes to my knowing
>
> Each experience and
> revelation within me wisdom
> growing.
>
> What I know, within me
> grows, grounded in the divine
>
> As I act, speak, and think,
> Sophia's wisdom is mine.

Dallas Jennifer Cobb

Notes:

April 18
Sunday

 1st ♊

Color of the day: Gold
Incense of the day: Frankincense

A Cherry Blossom Love Spell

At this time of year in Japan, flower festivals honor many fruit trees—but especially cherry trees. For many years, all parts of the cherry tree have been used in love spells. The blossoms, bark, leaves, and the fruit itself are known to attract love, fertility, and friendship. This spell calls for cherry blossoms, which should be abundant now. Begin this spell by gathering a handful of cherry blossoms that have fallen to the ground. Light a pink candle and scatter the blossoms on a piece of white fabric or a pretty handkerchief. Tie the corners of the fabric with a pink or red ribbon. While not thinking of anyone specific, tie the ribbon in a knot as you say:

Love is sweet, love is fine,
love is mine.

Hide your bundle in a secret place.

James Kambos

Notes:

April 19
Monday

1st ♊
☽ → ♋ 7:39 am

Color of the day: Gray
Incense of the day: Rosemary

Pickled Garlic for Magical Use

A pickled and refrigerated jar of garlic comes in very handy when in a rush to prepare a ritual that requires it. Used in protection spells, garlic bulbs can be mashed and rubbed on candles, pentagrams, and other magical accoutrements. After touching an object filled with negative energies, use a mashed garlic bulb to rub your hands before washing with soap. Extra jars can be made for giving to friends or selling at fairs, Pagan gatherings, and school fetes. It is simple and fast to make. This recipe makes 4 quarts. The ingredients include 4 quart jars full of peeled garlic bulbs, enough cold water to top off the jars, and 2 to 3 tablespoons salt per jar. Boil the water and salt. A little vinegar can also be added. Cool the liquid before pouring over garlic bulbs in the jar. Store at room temperature for two days. Continue the pickling process in the refrigerator for two to three months.

S. Y. Zenith

Notes:

April 20
Tuesday

1st ♋
☉ → ♉ 12:30 am

Color of the day: Scarlet
Incense of the day: Basil

Measure Personal Growth

When pursuing personal improvement, it helps to have a tangible manifestation of growth. Use this for such things as sticking to a meditation program, exercising, or practicing a new magical skill. For this spell, you'll need a large flowerpot full of potting soil and some small bulbs or seeds. Freesia, crocus, onion, lettuce, mint, and moss rose work well. Also choose a simple design or symbol representing your goal. Trace your symbol into the potting soil. Sow seeds or plant bulbs following the outline of the design. Concentrate on your goal as represented by the symbol. Then cover the seeds or bulbs, chanting:

> Down you go,
> Deep below.
> As you grow,
> So I grow.

Water carefully, and keep the soil barely damp until the plants sprout. When you need a boost toward your goal, visit your plants and repeat the chant.

Elizabeth Barrette

Notes:

April 21
Wednesday

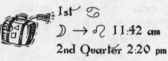

1st ♋
☽ → ♌ 11:42 am
2nd Quarter 2:20 pm

Color of the day: Topaz
Incense of the day: Marjoram

Air Magic

Air magic is especially powerful during the months of spring. Air is the realm of thoughts and visions, and because all magic begins with thought, air governs new beginnings. Ask the energies of air to assist you in any spells that deal with communication, education, travel, or creativity. Some symbols for air you might use in spellwork are feathers, bubbles, kites, wind chimes, smoke, and words. Use wind magic as an aspect of air. The cold north wind is a good time to deal with the physical details of your life. Use its energies to banish bad habits or any negative influences that are haunting you. The east wind is refreshing, a good wind for any spells for self-improvement. The hot,

dry south wind will aid you for spells to increase passion. The moist west wind is used for fertility spells and any workings where nurturing is wanted.

Lily Gardner

Notes:

April 22
Thursday
Earth Day

 2nd ♌

Color of the day: White
Incense of the day: Carnation

An Earth Day Ritual

It's Earth Day! Today is the day to realize and take full advantage of our symbiotic relationship with the Earth. Start your day with this simple ritual: Go outside with a piece of fruit, a bowl of water, and some organic fertilizer. Find a spot in your garden, window box, or nearby park and kneel before a plant. Tap into its green, generous energy. When you feel connected, acknowledge this being and all it gives to you by holding up the fruit and saying:

> *In all things I see your generosity, and I thank you.*

Eat the fruit, and tuck away any peels, seeds, or cores to compost later. Now hold your hands over the water and fertilizer and say:

> *In all my actions may I give back to you, most bountiful Mother Earth.*

Fertilize and water the plant, pouring your intentions for a healthy, whole planet into your actions.

Castiel

Notes:

April 23
Friday

2nd ♌
☽ → ♍ 2:24 pm

Color of the day: Rose
Incense of the day: Yarrow

Rite of the Evening Star

The evening star is attributed to Friday. She is the planet Venus who rules over love, money, and beauty. Long ago on this day in 215 BCE, a temple was erected on the highest hilltop of Rome in honor of the goddess Venus, making today a propitious day for creating a personal altar devoted to the goddess of love

and abundance. The Moon is in Leo so the mood is dramatic, theatrical. Wear velvet robes or a just a veil and stand naked if you wish as you invoke Venus, Aphrodite, Astarte, whoever you may call her and ask for her ear.

Hear me Venus Aphrodite

Graceful goddess of love!

Hear my prayer, hear my heart!

I honor you with this gift (give an offering)

And ask for your light and guidance!

State your prayer or request as you sit in attendance at her altar envisioning your desired outcome.

Igraine

Notes:

April 24
Saturday

2nd ♏

Color of the day: Brown
Incense of the day: Sandalwood

Communicate Cautiously

With Mercury deep in retrograde, here is a reminder of what that means and how it affects you. Mercury is the messenger god, and is most associated with all things that deal with communications—from casual discussions to important contracts. Retrograde is a retreating motion, moving backward, and like a card reversal in tarot, we see an opposition effect on all forms of communication. This is a time to be very aware of what you say, how you say it, and to whom you speak. Be prudent with your words and exercise caution when speaking with people. Do not engage in important discussions; keep contracts open until Mercury goes direct on May 11. Think before you speak and you should fare well during this confusing astrological period.

Boudica

Notes:

April 25
Sunday

 2nd ♍

☽ → ♎ 4:16 pm

Color of the day: Amber
Incense of the day: Heliotrope

honoring Earth Locally

Take the day to practice gratitude for the land. Think about your favorite local spots to visit—perhaps local parks, forests, rivers, or cemeteries speak to you on a soul level. If so, plan on visiting all of them today. Buy a number of good-sized quartz crystals or other sacred stone. The more locally mined, the better. (Also ensure that the crystals were not taken from the Earth in an unethical manner.) Go to the first sacred site on your list. When there, have a seat and charge the crystals by cupping them in your hands and saying something like:

> On this glorious April day, I charge and enchant these sacred stones. May these stones constantly draw vital energy from the Sun and Moon, and transfer their powers to the land. With gratitude and reverence, I leave these offerings on the beautiful Earth, both to connect me with the land and to honor the Mother in her multitude of forms. So mote it be.

Take one stone to each sacred spot, and bury it somewhere on the land.

Raven Digitalis

Notes:

April 26
Monday

2nd ♎

Color of the day: Silver
Incense of the day: Lily

A Spell to heal Inside

Sometimes our flaws go deeper than just bad habits, and if we want to change for the better, we first have to heal. Tonight, go outside with a cup of water, a few ounces of olive oil or grape-seed oil, and a bottle of jasmine oil. In the moonlight, invoke healing power and peace. Put five drops of the jasmine into both the water and the oil. Hold your hands over each mixture, first consecrating the water for cleansing the wounds of the past and then the oil for soothing them. Add the consecrated water to your bath that night, and as you soak, envision the empowered water washing away old hurts. If you feel like crying, let your tears fall. When you get out of the bath, rub yourself with the oil, imagining it relieving any lingering pain. Affirm that you are healed and ready to change.

Castiel

Notes:

answer our heart's most pressing questions. Hold the tea ball in your hands and think carefully about your question. Meditate on it fully and when you have reviewed all of your thoughts on the issue, brew the ball into a pot of tea and watch as it opens and reveals to you the shape, sign, or symbol that will answer your question.

Estha McNevin

Notes:

April 27
Tuesday

 2nd ♎
☽ → ♏ 6:28 pm

Color of the day: White
Incense of the day: Cinnamon

Blooming Tea Ball Divination

From a tea or coffee trader, procure one large hand-sewn tea ball. These are a traditional art form in China and are often hand sewn and infused with a variety of flavors, the most popular of which is jasmine. Each ball is constructed with delicate and youthful leaves and when warm water is added, the ball blooms in the teapot creating bouquets as they reveal flowers carefully sewn within the leaves. These treasures hold a world of exotic energy that can be lovingly observed and called on to

April 28
Wednesday

2nd ♏
Full Moon 8:19 am

Color of the day: Yellow
Incense of the day: Honeysuckle

Dream Fulfillment Ritual

The time of the Full Moon is traditionally a night for magic, so think of a wish or dream that you have and begin working toward its fulfillment. Start tonight by gathering as many white candles as you can find and arrange them in a circle on a safe surface. Next, write your wish on a piece of paper and fold it three times. Place the paper in the center of the circle. Set a piece of clear quartz on top of the paper and recite the following:

> Light of candles, light of Moon,
>
> Penetrate this humble room.
>
> Take this wish that I hold dear,
>
> Make it become crystal clear.
>
> Let this stone my wish hold fast,
>
> Grant it true, make it last.
>
> For good of all and harm to none,
>
> As I will so it be done.

Keep the stone in a special place to remind you of the dream or goal you are hoping to attain. Discard the paper—burn it or bury it if you like.

Ember

Notes:

April 29
Thursday

3rd ♏

☽ → ♐ 10:36 pm

Color of the day: Turquoise
Incense of the day: Balsam

Pagan Tree Day

Take some time today to plant a tree for the special gods and goddesses in your life. Because our spiritual practice is rooted in nature and the cycles of the Earth, we can plant a tree both to preserve the environment and as an intentional act of spiritual devotion. Research the trees associated with your gods and plant them if your area allows. Sometimes finding the deity's associated tree is as easy as looking into the myths. For example, the Buddha is associated with the Bodhi tree as it was the tree he sat under when he attained enlightenment. If you are planting seeds, you may wish to say something like:

> Goddesses and gods that I adore,
>
> I plant these seeds for what's in store.
>
> A deeper bond, a stronger love,
>
> The sacred song I'm part of.

May this act of devotion and
heart,

Ensure our love will
never part.

                    Abel R. Gomez

Notes:

glimmering light. Use the following
chant to complete the ritual:

May Eve fire, burn and glow,

Give life to everything we
sow—

Our gardens and our dreams
will grow,

As I will let it be so!

                    Ember

Notes:

April 30
Friday

3rd ♐

Color of the day: Purple
Incense of the day: Mint

May Eve

The night before May Day is
often celebrated with bonfires,
feasts, and general merrymaking.
Fires, one of the most popular traditions, are intended to frighten away
the darkness of winter and welcome
the life-giving Sun. Find a way to create your own May Eve bonfire. If you
can't actually create one outdoors,
use candles to represent a May Eve
fire. Light as many candles in your
home as you possibly can—red and
white ones if you can find them—
and spend the evening reveling in the

May's astrological sign is Taurus, the Bull (April 20–May 21), a fixed-earth sign ruled by Venus. Named for Maia, a Roman goddess of growth, May is a month of abundance and fertility. The Full Moon of May is appropriately called the Flower Moon, as the land rests fully in spring's fragrant embrace. Lush gardens are in bloom, roses are beginning to appear, and most grass and trees are a vibrant green. The breezes of May carry the scent of honeysuckle and black locust; this is a good time for tree magic and garden blessings. On the first day of May—May Day or Beltane—fertility festivals celebrate the union that creates life. Traditions include dancing around the Maypole and igniting sacred bonfires. Other new beginnings such as commencement celebrations also occur, and Mother's Day honors all who nurture. In ancient times throughout Europe, performers—dancers, musicians, and masked characters known as mummers—would create a procession through the streets, exchanging flowers and tree branches for gifts of food and money. This ritual brought the promise of a successful growing season. Gather flowers between sunset and sunrise on Beltane to make magical wreaths, garlands, and bouquets. Create a May Bough by decorating a small tree branch with colored ribbons to display as a centerpiece in your home.

May 1
Saturday

Beltane

 3rd ♐

Color of the day: Blue
Incense of the day: Pine

Spell for a Beautiful Dew

Today is Beltane, one of the eight sabbats marking the wheel of the year. Pagans celebrate this holiday with bonfires, feasting, and dancing around the Maypole. Associated colors include yellow, green, and sky blue. A traditional spell for beauty involved washing your face with dew gathered on Beltane morning. This updated version focuses not merely on physical beauty, but on a fresh approach to life. Go outside as early as you can—just before or after dawn is best—and wet your hands with dew from the grass or flowers. Touch your wet hands to your face, saying:

My face is as fresh as the Beltane dew

And so is my outlook on everything too.

As I wash my face and open my eyes

My heart becomes light as the wind in the skies.

Everything changes, and yet remains true:

Both true to itself and eternally new.

Elizabeth Barrette

Notes:

May 2
Sunday

 3rd ♐
☽ → ♑ 6:00 am

Color of the day: Gold
Incense of the day: Almond

Kite Flying Day

In the town of Hamamatsu in Japan there is a 400-year-old tradition of kite-flying, which began to honor the birth of a child. Today, teams dress in sixteenth-century costumes and "do battle" with their giant kites. Bits of glass are attached to the kite tails in an effort to sever opponents' strings. Spectators fly kites as well during the celebration that lasts several days. This would be a good day to get out and fly a kite of your own as a way to work with wind energy and the element of air. Here's a spell for using the air element to stir up change in your life. Do this while flying a kite, or simply go outside or open a window—find a way to feel the movement of air.

> *Winds of Change,*
> *swirling 'round,*
> *help to turn my life around.*
> *Winds of Change,*
> *guide my way,*
> *Come into my life today.*

Ember

Notes:

box or pot full of herbs will suffice. If the weather permits, put in your seeds and sprouts today; otherwise, feel free to bless what you've already planted, or the ground that you'll sow in.

> *From deep, dark earth the*
> *green shoots grow,*
>
> *And further down the roots*
> *do go.*
>
> *I'll tend them well, and meet*
> *their needs,*
>
> *Fertilized, watered, and free*
> *of weeds!*

Lupa

Notes:

May 3
Monday

3rd ♑

Color of the day: Gray
Incense of the day: Hyssop

Solar Success Spell

Today is the final day of the Roman festival of Floralia, goddess of flowers and vegetation; the festival was also one of pleasure and licentiousness, and prostitutes considered this their own special day. While you're more than welcome to have your own private celebrations of the latter sort, a more family-friendly celebration can include planting and blessing a garden. This need not be a huge urban farm; a small window

May 4
Tuesday

3rd ♑
☽ → ♒ 4:52 pm

Color of the day: Black
Incense of the day: Cedar

Control the Internal Blaze

To tame a fiery temper and use your passions to your advantage, bring together a small

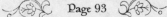

red candle for your fiery temple, a small piece of obsidian for its power to ground and transform, lavender incense, and a large blue candle for soothing peace. Light the incense in your sacred space and hold the red candle in your hands as you pour into it all the things that make you lose your temper or make you angry. Light it and place the obsidian next to it. As the candle burns your anger away, feel the obsidian transform that anger into passions that serve you well. As you breathe in that transformation, light the blue candle and breathe its energy to soothe you. Burn the red candle completely and dispose of it in the earth, bidding your uncontrollable temper farewell. Whenever you need soothing, light the blue candle!

Gail Wood

Notes:

May 5
Wednesday
Cinco de Mayo

 3rd ≈

Color of the day: Brown
Incense of the day: Lavender

A Spell to heal Another

Use the waning power of the Moon to banish disease and pain from a loved one today. Create an image of the person needing healing with cloth, clay, or paper. The closer it looks to the actual person, the better. Get that person's signature and add it to the image, energetically linking the two. In your ritual space, use your breath to cleanse and charge the image with your intention. Place a needle in the afflicted area of the body and chant something like:

> You are whole
> You are healthy
> You are well

As you chant, visualize the person's affliction becoming smaller and smaller until it disappears. Allow the pin to be a place of focus to direct the energy. When the spell is complete, hide the image in a dark place. Once the person is completely healed, bury the image in the earth.

Abel R. Gomez

Notes:

Holiday lore: Don't confuse Cinco de Mayo with Mexican Independence Day on September 16. Cinco de Mayo marks the victory of the brave Mexican army over the French at the Battle of Puebla. Although the Mexican army was eventually defeated, the *Batalla de Puebla* became a symbol of Mexican unity and patriotism. With this victory, the people of Mexico demonstrated to the world that Mexico and all of Latin America were willing to defend themselves against any foreign or imperialist intervention.

your seriousness. Light the candle and center. Show the candle flame both sides of the money, then fold the money three times and clip it to the back of your photo. Place your photo in the bottom of your earthenware dish and place the lodestone on top of it. Sprinkle salt around the photograph three times saying:

> *Orbiting Jupiter, thrice*
> *the Sun,*
> *Bring money on the run.*

Cover the dish and store it somewhere in the kitchen where it will remain unmolested.

Lily Gardner

Notes:

May 6
Thursday

 3rd ≈
4th Quarter 12:15 am

Color of the day: Crimson
Incense of the day: Myrrh

Spell for Prosperity

Thursdays are excellent days to cast spells for money and employment. Assemble your tools for this spell in the kitchen. You will need a covered earthenware dish, a bayberry candle, a lodestone (or substitute a magnet). You'll also need sea salt, a photograph of yourself, and paper money. Choose a bill as large as you can afford to demonstrate

May 7
Friday

 4th ≈
☽ → ♓ 5:34 am

Color of the day: Purple
Incense of the day: Violet

Rose Soul Mate Spell

Clean and sterilize a small, attractive jar with a cap. Set it upon a large, flat piece of stone. Put the jar in the center with rose petals, and

get some carrier oil such as almond, jojoba, and rose essential oil. Place two red candles on either side of the stone and light them. Sit down and fill the jar with rose petals. Pour some carrier oil into the jar—enough to cover the petals—and add rose essential oil. Secure the jar with the cap. While shaking it gently, recite:

> *Rose petals of north, east,*
> *   south, and west,*
> *Hereby a soul mate I request,*
> *As I will, so mote it be.*

Store the oil in a dark cupboard. This love oil can be used for anointing magical paraphernalia to do with love spells or dabbed over the body as a soft layering scent under your favorite perfume before going out.

S. Y. Zenith

Notes:

May 8
Saturday

4th ♓

Color of the day: Brown
Incense of the day: Patchouli

A Rejoicing Spell

Today is known as Flora Day in Helston, Cornwall, England. Locals dance the Fer dance, from the old Cornish word *fer*, which means "rejoicing." Celebrating the abundance of bright flowers and the full return of spring, locals rejoice and formally dance four times throughout the day, circling through their village, their footsteps bringing good luck. Today, use your footsteps to cast a spell for luck, rejoicing in the beauty of spring flowers in your area. Make time for a Saturday afternoon stroll, planning a route that will take you past flowerbeds or wildflowers blooming in spring's delight. With each step you rejoice. Let your heart lift and your spirit soar as your eyes devour the colorful riot of flowers. Celebrate their beauty and uplifting energy, knowing that winter is far behind and Flora has spread her magic around, rejoicing in color and fragrance.

Dallas Jennifer Cobb

Notes:

May 9
Sunday
Mother's Day

 4th ♓
☽ → ♈ 5:29 pm

Color of the day: Gold
Incense of the day: Marigold

honor the Great Mother

Today is Mother's Day. What better day to perform a ritual for our Mother Earth? She is the Great Mother of all life on this planet and is the sustainer of our very life force. It's good practice to frequently honor her. Today, think of a nice spot to visit in nature. Even if you have to travel to get there, be sure that the area is as energetically pure as possible, containing many trees, grasses, and plants. When you arrive, light a green candle and lay on the ground (nude, if possible, or with no blanket beneath you). Feel the glory of the season and contemplate the meaning of Mother's Day and how you can honor the Great Mother both inside and outside of ritual. How can you rearrange aspects of your life to be more environmentally friendly? After contemplating these types of questions, think about what it means to be Pagan—an Earth-worshipper—and what the Great Mother means to you. Perform meditative exercises, feel the trees and plants, leave an offering, and know that you, yourself, are part of the Great Mother.

Raven Digitalis

Notes:

May 10
Monday

 4th ♈

Color of the day: Lavender
Incense of the day: Rosemary

Rite of Spring for Ritual Robes

Each spring the moisture of the earth takes to beading itself on every living breath and the fresh mornings are made sweet with the drops of dew that linger. Having an early morning roll in the dew while in full ritual garb may draw a few strange looks from the neighbors, but it is awfully good fun. As the robe absorbs the fresh waters of life, try to imagine brand-new magical adventures and talents emerging from the rituals in which you will wear your robes. Feel the elements as they cradle you in the essence of life and draw that through the robes to your very flesh. Recognize the vital prana, or life force, in the small drops

of water. Each time you wear your robe, tap back into that energy and utilize it as you explore and observe the sacred.

Estha McNevin

Notes:

I can no longer stay the same,

Give me the courage to make a change.

When you have raised energy for your purpose, light the paper on fire, let it burn in the cauldron, and let the candle burn down in a safe place. Then, go out and get to it! What are you waiting for?

Castiel

Notes:

May 11
Tuesday

 4th ♈

Color of the day: Red
Incense of the day: Geranium

Risks for Rewards Spell

Ever just need to take a risk? Today is a great day for new ventures! To give yourself the courage to launch one of your ideas or just try something new, use this spell. Set up a small altar with a red cloth, a red candle, and fireproof dish or cauldron. All around the candle sprinkle oregano and black peppercorns. On a piece of paper, draw or write a brief description of what you want the courage to do. Light the candle and chant:

Nothing ventured, nothing gained,

May 12
Wednesday

 4th ♈
☽ → ♉ 2:48 am

Color of the day: Topaz
Incense of the day: Lilac

Dark Moon Tarot Ritual

At this dark Moon, our focus shifts from the inspirational force of Aries to solidifying, materializing, and actualizing what we initiated last month. The Moon in Taurus needs something tangible to come out of this darkness. We need to touch, smell, taste—physically experience! Taurus IS sensuality, so plunge your hands into the wet soil and revel in its heavy scent. Spend time in the kitchen and make something fabulous for dinner. Listen to classical music and drink a bottle of wine. Indulge in the simple pleasure of life, feeling no rush for the evening to end. Delight in the dark of the Moon! Now light a candle to illumine your way and using a tarot deck (or you can just listen for your own intuitive response), ask yourself these questions as you shuffle your cards, fan them out and draw four to move you through this dark Moon energy of Taurus Sun/Moon.

1. What am I resisting?
2. How can I break free?
3. What is my sensual delight?
4. How might I flourish?

Igraine

Notes:

May 13
Thursday

 4th ♉
New Moon 9:04 pm

Color of the day: Purple
Incense of the day: Clove

A home Decorating Spell

This New Moon falls when the Sun is in Taurus, an earth sign. This is the perfect time to begin home projects dealing with beauty, leisure, and decorating. These projects could be for the home itself, the garden, or landscaping. After you've chosen your decorating or remodeling project, cut out photographs from decorating magazines that inspire you and place them in a "wish" box. On the night of the New Moon, place several hawthorn leaves, pieces of bark, or thorns in the box with your photographs. The hawthorn tree, long associated with making wishes come true, blooms in May and will energize your wish. As you close your box, visualize your project completed and say:

> From ceiling to floor, from
>   door to door,
> My home is my haven, safe
>   and secure.
> As the Moon increases in
>   beauty and light,
> My decorating project will
>   take flight.

Put your wish box away and begin seeking sources that will help make your project a reality. These could include contractors, landscapers, and building supply companies. Attend house and garden tours or home-improvement shows; keep networking. You'll be surprised at how quickly your spell will begin to take form.

James Kambos

Notes:

piece of paper; put a big X through the name. The intent should be clear that you want nothing to do with this person. Anoint the paper with some "command and compel" oil and put the paper in an envelope. Write their name and "return to sender" on the front. Do not put your name anywhere on the envelope or on the paper; you want no association with this person. Burn the envelope in your cauldron or dig a hole and bury it in a place where it will be undisturbed.

Boudica

Notes:

May 14
Friday

 1st ♉
☽ → ♊ 9:18 am

Color of the day: Rose
Incense of the day: Alder

Return to Sender

Sometimes you receive unwanted attention from someone in your office, or a friend, or maybe a romantic flirtation that does not interest you. You may not want any attention, affection, or trust from this person. Rather, you just want them to get the feeling that you are not interested. Place the name of this person on a

May 15
Saturday

1st ♊

Color of the day: Gray
Incense of the day: Sandalwood

Armed Forces Day

Today is Armed Forces Day. Here is a candle spell that calls for protection for the women and men of our armed forces no matter where they may be called to duty. Light a white candle for your soldier.

Place a picture of that soldier in front of the candle. Take a few moments to ground and center. Visualize a deep purple-blue energy shield wrapped around them to keep them protected and safe from all harm. Now, repeat the spell.

> May the gods of your
> ancestors, keep watch over
> you I pray,
>
> I send protection and love
> to you, though you are far
> away.
>
> Feel my magic circle 'round,
> and create a shield.
>
> This loving protection for
> you, will never yield.
>
> By all the powers of Moon
> and Sun,
>
> As I will it, so shall it be
> done.

Allow the candle to burn out in a safe place.

Ellen Dugan

Notes:

May 16
Sunday

1st ♊

☽ → ♋ 1:46 pm

Color of the day: Yellow
Incense of the day: Juniper

Lakshmi Money Spell

In the Hindu tradition, Lakshmi is the epitome of love, abundance, and beauty. One of the treasures brought forth by the churning of the cosmic ocean, she brought forth *amrita*, the nectar of immortality that renewed the universe. Call upon the power of this goddess today to bring you financial abundance. This spell can work with a candle or a twelve-inch green cord. Whichever you choose to use, hold it in your hands and cleanse it with your breath. Burn some incense and create an altar space with an image of Lakshmi. Ground and center and invite Lakshmi to join your ritual space. Spend some time in prayer with Lakshmi before doing this working and allow yourself to receive the abundance you need.

> One, two, three,
>   money come to me,
> Four, five, six,
>   Lakshmi come to fix,
> Seven, eight, nine,
>   money now is mine.

Abel R. Gomez

Notes:

Green and brown
Death and birth
Rot it down
Into earth

Visualize the beneficial power of decay breaking down the material into crumbly black compost. Every two weeks, turn the pile with a shovel and repeat the chant. By the end of the summer your compost should be ready to use.

Elizabeth Barrette

Notes:

May 17
Monday

 1st ♋

Color of the day: White
Incense of the day: Lily

Enriched Recycling

Compost is made of decayed organic matter. By making your own compost, you can enrich your garden, lawn, or houseplants. It also gets rid of biodegradable kitchen and yard waste. To make a compost pile, alternate layers of "wet/green" and "dry/brown" materials. **Green**: grass clippings, overripe fruit, vegetable peels, etc. **Brown**: dead leaves, twigs, wood chips, shredded paper, etc. Water the pile to the consistency of a damp sponge. Encourage your compost pile to decay efficiently by using magic. Walk three times widdershins (counterclockwise) around the pile. With each circuit, chant:

May 18
Tuesday

 1st ♋
☽ → ♌ 5:06 pm

Color of the day: Gray
Incense of the day: Bayberry

Mustard Seed Protection Tactics

In the early days of the French Republic, a new calendar was designed based on the natural rhythms of nature. It dedicated each month to the season and each day to an animal, plant, mineral, or tool.

In the French Republic calendar, today is called The Flowering Wild Mustard. Use mustard seeds in this spell for protection. To protect yourself from a cold or headache, prepare a foot bath from crushed mustard seed and hot water. Visualize the pressure and congestion breaking up and evaporating. During the flu season, carry mustard seeds in a red flannel bag to protect against illness. Bury mustard seeds beneath your doorstep to keep negativity from entering your home. To protect your lover from harm, place his or her name, an agate, and mustard seed in a white flannel bag and keep it on your person during times of danger or distress.

Lily Gardner

Notes:

May 19
Wednesday
Shavuot

 1st ♌

Color of the day: White

Incense of the day: Marjoram

Get that Job Spell

A particular job caught your attention and you really want a chance to get in and interview for it. You know you can make that important impression and that you are the best person for that job. Make sure your résumé is up to date and follows the most current format. Do your homework; search résumé formats online and make sure you use spell-checker and grammar guides. On the back of the résumé, make a pentacle with your finger. You are protecting your résumé as well as making sure it outshines all the rest. You are making sure this résumé gets to the proper person, gets read, and gets proper consideration. A clear format, impeccable grammar and spelling, and the right qualifications will always get you noticed for that special job. And a little extra magic never hurts!

Boudica

Notes:

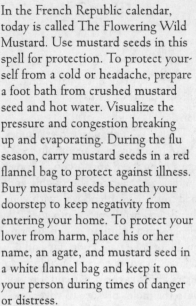

May 20
Thursday

1st ♌

2nd Quarter 7:43 pm

☽ → ♍ 7:58 pm

☉ → ♊ 11:34 pm

Color of the day: Crimson
Incense of the day: Nutmeg

Melt Away Debt

Most of us experience financial woes from time to time. If you have some debt that has exceeded your ability to handle or if you just want to become more financially stable, try this spell for success with money. And remember to pay your bills on time! Gather the following items: green votive candle, handmade if possible; a silver coin; a handful of sand or dirt; and a billing statement of some kind. Put the sand or dirt in the bottom of a glass candleholder. Place the coin on top of the sand and then put the candle on top of the coin. Draw an X across the bill or invoice with a black marker. Cut or tear it in half, then set the candleholder on top of the pieces. Visualize your debt being cut and melted away. Light the candle and allow it to burn completely.

Ember

Notes:

May 21
Friday

2nd ♍

Color of the day: Coral
Incense of the day: Rose

Birdseed Molds

Offer your thanks and gratitude to nature as you combine 2 cups of birdseed and ¼ cup of honey. Whisk 3 egg whites thoroughly and add to the mix. Blend well with your hands and firmly press into a wax paper–lined stainless steel bowl, ring-mold, or cake pan. Loop one end of a large, heavy-duty rope, making two extra knots at the other end. Press it into the mold. Be sure to cover one end of the rope well with seed; press the entire mold tightly. Take care to predict weight distribution. For full ring molds, it's best to lay the rope around the entire ring and leave excess for hanging; for bells and bars, a single top loop with two or three knots in the string will hold well. Cover the excess rope with tinfoil and place in a 200 degree F oven until solid (about 60 to 90 minutes). Let cool and peel away wax paper. Hang from a beloved tree.

Estha McNevin

Notes:

May 22
Saturday

2nd ♏

☽ → ♎ 10:50 pm

Color of the day: Blue
Incense of the day: Sage

Motorcycle Safety Spell

This is the time of the year when many motorcyclists begin taking to the road for travel and fun. But, safety should come first. After making sure your bike is road ready, a little magic isn't a bad idea as an extra safety precaution. A good friend of mine who rides swears by this magical tip. To keep away the gremlins, attach a small bell to your motorcycle. The sound of the bell is said to keep away any bad vibrations. There's just one catch—for the bell to work its magic, it must be given to you as a gift. These bells can usually be found at many motorcycle dealerships. Have a happy, safe season on the open road.

James Kambos

Notes:

May 23
Sunday

2nd ♎

Color of the day: Orange
Incense of the day: Frankincense

Solar Divinity Mirror

A solar divinity mirror is suitable as an additional tool for divination and ritual work. It can also be used as a base for tealights to widen the perimeter of reflection if more light is required. Another use is carrying it to deflect unknown psychic attacks and past-life exploration during the day. Obtain a few round mirrors and consecrate them on a bright Sunday noon when sunlight is at its strongest. Light some incense and a gold candle. Waft the mirror with the incense and pass it clockwise around the candle. Hold the mirror in front of you so that it reflects sunlight. Feel and know that the mirror is potently absorbing the solar energy. Recite a relevant rhyme or state:

Father Sun shining bright,
Bless my mirror with thy
*   might.*

Avoid exposing to moonlight at night. Recharge the mirrors once every two months on a Sunday at noon.

S. Y. Zenith

Notes:

Now, hold the paper up to the mirror and read the word you wrote backward, then forward, and feel that power to reveal meaning settling over you. Carry the paper with you to remind you of your ability to alleviate confusion.

Castiel

Notes:

May 24
Monday

2nd ♎

Color of the day: Silver
Incense of the day: Neroli

Un–Mumbo the Jumbo Spell

There's nothing more frustrating than not being able to get your message across. If you're having a hard time making yourself understood, here's something to help you communicate clearly and effectively. On a piece of paper write a word like *talk*, *speak*, *listen*, *voice*, or *understand* backward. Take your paper and go stand in front of a mirror—you can even use the bathroom mirror at work! Look directly into your eyes in the mirror and say:

> *Jibber-jabber*
> *Gobbledygook*
> *Change the form that my*
>   *thoughts took*
> *Let me make my meaning*
>   *plain*
> *Let them hear my voice again*

May 25
Tuesday

2nd ♎
☽ → ♏ 2:17 am

Color of the day: White
Incense of the day: Cinnamon

Kick Off Spring Cleaning

Spring cleaning is upon us! If you've been procrastinating, Tuesday is a wonderful day for getting a move on this. Pick a starting point, or make one of your own:
• The classic spring cleaning involves going through your home and removing clutter, chasing dust bunnies away, and otherwise making that place shine! Along with your physical activities, do a house-cleansing ritual.

• Go through your financial records, make a plan to tackle any debts, and decide whether it's time to look for a more fulfilling job.

• Meditate on things in your life you'd like to change. Make a list, then pick one to concentrate on. Research ways other people have kicked the same habit and find what works for you.

If you don't get it all done in a day, don't feel bad—let today kick off your spring cleaning, however long it needs to be.

Lupa

Notes:

move, your favorite dance music, a piece of parchment paper, and a pen with red ink to represent your passion for your dream. Wear your favorite party clothes or the clothes you will wear when your dream is realized. Write your dream on one side of your paper, using as many words as you want. Breathing deeply, read those words and bring it into your body. Fold the paper in half with the writing inside. On the blank side, write your dream in one sentence. Then fold the paper so it is as small as possible. On the top, write your dream in one word. Wear the paper next to your heart. Turn on the music and dance, knowing that your body remembers your dream. As you will it, so it will be.

Gail Wood

Notes:

May 26
Wednesday

 2nd ♏

Color of the day: Brown
Incense of the day: Lilac

A Spell for Your Wildest Dreams

Today in 1951, Sally Ride, the first American woman in space, was born. To realize your wildest dreams, you need a large space to

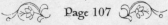

May 27
Thursday

2nd ♏

☽ → ♐ 7:15 am

Full Moon 7:07 pm

Color of the day: Turquoise
Incense of the day: Carnation

Unfurl that Goddess Energy

Happy Full Moon! For this spell, you will need nine different fresh flowers and a white candle. When picking the flowers, leave a little offering of cornmeal or sugar at the base of each plant. When selecting the candle, inscribe the symbol of the Triple Moon on the wax nine times in various places. Light the candle on your altar. Focus on what the Great Goddess means to you and how she has blessed your life with abundance. Think about the various ways in which others perceive the Goddess and compare your own experiences and perceptions to those around you. Where do you agree in opinion? Where do you contrast? This spell is designed to draw you closer to the energy of the Goddess and ask her to reveal her deeper nature to you over time. Lay each flower at the base of the candle. Use your intuition to determine which to lay first, second, and so on. As you lay each flower, say the corresponding line of this chant. Be sure to meditate after speaking each line, and make sure the candle safely burns all the way down at the end.

> By the placing of one, the spell's begun.
>
> By the placing of two, align me with you.
>
> By the placing of three, I call unto thee.
>
> By the placing of four, your wisdom I implore.
>
> By the placing of five, make my senses come alive.
>
> By the placing of six, I declare myself a servant and Witch.
>
> By the placing of seven, I seek the knowledge of Hades and heaven.
>
> By the placing of eight, reveal your beauty great.
>
> By the placing of nine, let the truth of your existence be mine.

Raven Digitalis

Notes:

May 28
Friday

3rd ♐

Color of the day: White
Incense of the day: Orchid

Freya's Smooth Magic

riday is sacred to the Norse goddess of magic, beauty, and love, Freya. After all, the day took its name from her, Freya's-day. Since we are in a waning Moon, let's push away any relationship troubles you might be dealing with. Things not so romantic at home? Is there a silly misunderstanding between you and your sweetie? Here's just the spell to smooth things out. Oh, and before you start wondering, the individual that you will be casting on is . . . yourself.

> May the goddess Freya hear
> my plea on this Friday night,
>
> Help me to banish all hurt
> feelings, and to remove strife.
>
> May my actions and words
> be caring, kind, and true,
>
> Your love shines through me
> in all that I say and do.
>
> For the good of all with
> harm to none,
>
> By Freya's magic, this spell
> is done!

Ellen Dugan

Holiday lore: Opinions are divided concerning the origins of the holiday of Memorial Day in the United States. This is a day set aside for honoring the graves of American war dead. While most historians credit the origins of the custom to Southern women, there is also a rumor, historically speaking, of an anonymous German who fought in the American Civil War (no one is sure on which side). At the end of the war, this soldier was allegedly overheard commenting that in the Old World people scattered flowers on the graves of dead soldiers. In May 1868, a Union army general suggested to Commander John A. Logan that a day be set aside each year to decorate Union graves. Logan agreed, and he set aside May 30 for this ritual. His proclamation acknowledged those "who died in defense of their country" and "whose bodies now lie in almost every city, village, or hamlet churchyard in the land." This patriotic holiday was later amended to include all the dead from all the wars, and its date was shifted to a convenient Monday late in May.

May 29
Saturday

 3rd ♐
☽ → ♑ 2:44 pm

Color of the day: Brown
Incense of the day: Pine

Oak Apple Day

Today is celebrated in the British Isles as Oak Apple Day commemorating the return of King Charles the Second after the restoration of the monarchy in 1660. It is said that he hid in the boughs of an oak tree to escape his pursuers as he made his way back into the city. But the celebration may actually date back to pre-Christian nature worship—to an ancient Pagan rite in celebration of the Garland King or Green Man. In this ritual, sprigs of oak leaves are worn or garlands of leaves gathered from the oak grove. You could create a headpiece or mask using fresh oak leaves in homage to the Garland King. You might also purchase a garland of oak leaves at the local craft store to hang in your home on this day, symbolizing the end of winter, the restoration of the king! Celebrate this ancient holiday with a draught beer and some plum pudding. But be forewarned! It is rumored if you are spotted not wearing a sprig of oak pinned to your lapel, then someone will pinch your bum! Oddly enough, Oak Apple Day is now celebrated as Pinch Your Bum Day!

Igraine

Notes:

May 30
Sunday

3rd ⅏

Color of the day: Yellow
Incense of the day: Eucalyptus

A Light Spell

Sunday, is Sun day, a day for a light spell. As the days lengthen toward solstice, we leave the darkness behind, enjoying more sunlight and brightness. In the middle of the day, find a spot where there is some shadow and some direct sunlight close together. If it's cloudy or rainy where you are, go inside and use a bright light to create shadow and light. Stand in the shadow, and see yourself shrouded in darkness. Feel the cold and foreboding. Know that very little grows, thrives, or survives in darkness. Take a big step forward, stepping into the light. Feel the radiant energy on your skin. With your eyes closed, turn your face toward the Sun (or lamp) and affirm:

> Light within me, light
> around,
>
> Light becomes me, light
> abound.

Symbolically affirm that you stand in the light, and work for the light, for the goodness of all.

Dallas Jennifer Cobb

Notes:

May 31
Monday
Memorial Day (observed)

3rd ⅏

Color of the day: Lavender
Incense of the day: Clary sage

On Respecting Religions Equally

Walt Whitman, American poet, was born on this day in 1819. A deist, Whitman considered all religions to be equal, and in his famous "Song of Myself," he speaks numerous times of the equality of religions and people:

> I do not call one greater and
> one smaller,
>
> That which fills its period
> and place is equal to any.

In "With Antecedents," he says:

> I adopt each theory, myth,
> god, and demigod,
>
> I see that the old accounts,
> bibles, genealogies, are true,
> without exception.

Since it is also Memorial Day in the United States, this is a good day to resolve conflicts and to examine and criticize our prejudices and biases (no matter how justified we may feel they are). Take time today—and after today—to meditate on the idea that while we may differ in culture, religion, and circumstances of birth, we are all equally deserving of respect and consideration.

Lupa

Notes:

June is the sixth month of the year. Its astrological sign is Gemini, the Twins (May 21–June 21), a mutable-air sign ruled by Mercury. The month is named for Juno, the principal goddess of the Roman pantheon, and wife of Jupiter. She is the patroness of marriage and the well-being of women. This is one reason June is the most popular month for weddings. June brings the magic of midsummer—the Summer Solstice, longest day of the year. Summer is ripe now with bird song and the pleasant buzz of evening insects. The gentleness of spring has given way to the powerful heat of summer—the Full Moon of June is called the Strong Sun Moon. Various cultures pay homage to Sun gods this time of year. In some places summer is just getting started and the hottest months are yet to come, yet after the solstice we don't even notice the days beginning to get slightly shorter. This is the time for enjoying the splendor of summer: playful picnics and hikes through the woods, long nights beneath the stars, and tending gardens and flowerbeds. Roadsides are a riot of color, and herbs such as St. John's wort, vervain, and yarrow can be used in herbal amulets. This is the time of year to honor the faeries—leave offerings of ale, milk, fruit, or bread before cutting flowers or herbs and they may help your garden grow.

June 1
Tuesday

3rd ♑

☽ → ♒ 1:08 am

Color of the day: Black
Incense of the day: Bayberry

Toward True health

The Romans celebrated the goddess Carna, who presided over internal organs, particularly the heart, liver, and lungs. Carna is also associated with general vitality and health, the conversion of food to energy, and the building blocks of the body. If you've been considering starting a diet and exercise plan for the purpose of better health (not just to lose weight in order to fit the media's depiction of "beauty"), this is a good day to start, especially because fresh produce is now more abundant both in gardens and stores. It's also an auspicious day for making medical appointments, especially with nutritionists and internists. Celebrate with a feast of healthy food, perhaps with a vow to give up junk food or other bad culinary habits. Ask Carna to bless you in your quest for greater health, and to help you notice when you are becoming ill or developing an injury over time.

Lupa

Notes:

June 2
Wednesday

3rd ♒

Color of the day: Yellow
Incense of the day: Bay laurel

Unleashing Creativity

Today we are in a waning Moon phase, and we have the planetary correspondence of Mercury—it's Wednesday. So, let's remove any issues you may have with creativity. Maybe you are trying to finish an arts and crafts project? Perhaps you are stuck and having trouble finishing a writing assignment? Be it writing a ritual or spell, a mundane report, or even a school paper, it is beyond frustrating dealing with mental blocks to your creativity. Here is a spell designed to help remove those artistic blocks and to get your creativity flowing again.

*Today is the day that is
sacred to Mercury,*

*May this clever, nimble god
bring creativity.*

*With a bit of guile and a
whole lot of fun,*

*Remove all blocks and grant
me inspiration.*

*For the good of all bringing
harm to none,*

By Mercury's magic, this spell is done!

Ellen Dugan

Notes:

June 3
Thursday

3rd ♒

☽ → ♓ 1:34 pm

Color of the day: White
Incense of the day: Clove

The Gossip-Stopper

To help stop unnecessary or slanderous gossip by those around you, take a walk around 7:30 pm. Find the leaf of a plant that resembles (even slightly) a human tongue. At precisely 8:00 pm, pick this leaf from the plant and leave a small offering at its base. That evening, put some honey on your right index finger and spread it on the upper side of the leaf. While you are doing this, say something like:

By the power of Mercury, I affirm that [name] can only speak sweetly of me . . .

Now, sprinkle a pinch of slippery elm on the leaf, which should stick to the honey. Roll up the leaf and tie it with a natural jute or hemp string, saying:

. . . or you shall speak of me not at all. [Name]'s tongue is tied.

Take this little spell to a public park and bury it in the ground. For more extreme situations, bury this little spell on the property of the person in question (if you are brave enough). Note: this spell also requires that you must be mindful not to speak slanderous gossip of the other person either.

Raven Digitalis

Notes:

June 4
Friday

 3rd ♓
4th Quarter 6:13 pm

Color of the day: Coral
Incense of the day: Yarrow

A Love Spell

Ruled by Venus, Friday is a fortuitous day for a love spell. Whether you're seeking a mate, want

to strengthen existing bonds, or heal love within an important relationship, this spell can contribute to the energy of love between two beings. Place two candles—one white for purity of intention, one red for passion and romance—together on a fireproof surface. A bowl or small plate is good. Anoint the candles with a suitable essential oil—jasmine for emotional healing, rose for growing love, or patchouli for earthy passion—while envisioning the manifestation of love. Light the candles, invoking:

> I light this match so love
> burns bright,
>
> Glows warm and strong
> within my life,
>
> Passion, commitment, and
> trust I tether,
>
> Love be strengthened as these
> melt together.

As the candles burn and the melting waxes commingle, know that the bonds of love grow.

Dallas Jennifer Cobb

Notes:

June 5
Saturday

 4th ♓

Color of the day: Brown
Incense of the day: Pine

Animal Guardian Meditation

If you have discovered your animal guardian, then you know what a silly sense of humor they have. Part of the pleasure of their company is laughter and innocent joy. How do you know who your animal guardian is? It's so simple! You just ask. In the book, *The Golden Compass*, your guardian is referred to as your daemon. We are born with one and they are our guardians, differing from a totem or medicine animal. One of the easiest ways to make contact is through a meditation or dream. Before going to sleep, state aloud and very clearly that you are ready to meet your animal guardian. You may need to do this more than once. If he/she appears in a dream, don't forget to ask its name. This is like a cosmic ignition key that activates your relationship. You will begin to experience their presence wherever you go. If your guardian doesn't make an obvious appearance, then look for signs as you go about your day. If you are attentive, you will be rewarded. Your guardian loves attention!

Igraine

Notes:

your interview. Place the candle in the glass and light it. After it burns completely, fold your résumé, put it in the envelope, and mail it.

Gail Wood

Notes:

June 6
Sunday

 4th ♓
☽ → ♈ 1:50 am

Color of the day: Amber
Incense of the day: Hyacinth

Recharge Your Résumé Ritual

To empower your résumé to get an interview, collect a copy of your résumé, an addressed and stamped envelope, sugar, a white cloth, a small green candle, a glass candleholder, a sharp knife, symbols of job success, and frankincense incense to draw positive vibrations. On top of the white cloth, place the résumé in the center with the envelope to the right. Light the incense and smudge the résumé and envelope. With the knife, carve the candle with symbols of success; on the bottom carve a square for manifestation. Taste the sugar and put some in the bottom of the glass for sweet success. Hold the candle and envision the résumé being opened, read, and a call being placed to you to schedule

June 7
Monday

4th ♈

Color of the day: White
Incense of the day: Hyssop

National Trails Day

This is National Trails Day. America has many miles of hiking, biking, and equestrian trails. Some trails cross several states, such as the famous Appalachian Trail. Other countries have their own trail systems. Trail activities offer benefits such as exercise and enjoying outdoor scenery. Use a recreation map to identify trails near your home or distant ones you'd like to visit. Today is a good day to learn walking meditation. Not all meditation has to involve sitting motionless and thinking of nothing! Choose a quiet, safe trail to walk. Dress comfortably and carry water. As you walk, set aside the everyday worries and chatter filling your head. Let your mind drift a little. If intrusive thoughts return, acknowledge them and gently push them away. Rest your eyes on the blue sky, the flowers and trees, and any animals you might pass. Relax. This, too, is meditation.

Elizabeth Barrette

Notes:

movie. You should get into the habit of always making some time during your busy week for yourself. Time to relax, leave the day's worries behind you and just think about nothing. It can be as little as half an hour or as much as a day at a spa. Be nice to yourself; give yourself a break.

Boudica

Notes:

June 8
Tuesday

4th ♈
☽ → ♉ 11:41 am

Color of the day: Gray
Incense of the day: Ginger

I'm Pooped: Energy Time Out

Been doing too much? Just finished school? Running around with the kids to all their events and activities? The school year is almost over and it's that last stretch to make it to summer. Take time this evening to find a place where you can take a deep breath and spend some time on yourself. I suggest a hot bath, candlelight, relaxing oils and incense, a hot cuppa tea, and a good book or

June 9
Wednesday

4th ♉

Color of the day: Brown
Incense of the day: Lilac

Vesta's Meal

As the "house" of Vesta, the goddess of hearth fire, the Temple of Vesta was the symbolic hearth of all of Rome and played a large role in the empire's protection and fortune. Every year on this day, the vestal virgins would open their temple to all the women of Rome, who came in barefoot, dressed in simple clothes, and bearing offerings of everyday food. Ensure fortune, health, and happiness for your family today. Honor Vesta by making a hearty home-cooked meal. Pick comfort foods that everyone can enjoy. Set some bread, a small dish of water, and a few pinches of salt in the middle of the dinner table as an offering to the goddess, then light a white candle to represent her fire and say the following blessing:

> Wherever a home is tended,
> Vesta makes a sanctuary.
> Preserve our home and family,
> In love, health, and safety.

Castiel

Notes:

protects the property from negativity, and being ruled by Venus, it is also useful in love magic. A feverfew potion is easy to make and has many magical uses. Begin by cutting a few stems of feverfew—include flowers, stems, and leaves. Cut stems into small pieces and add to a cup of boiling water. Turn off the heat and allow this brew to steep for five minutes. When cool, strain liquid into a spray bottle, then discard the plant material. Use this magical potion to cleanse magical tools such as a magic mirror, or to purify a space of negativity. And for some love magic, mist a love letter before sending.

James Kambos

Notes:

June 10
Thursday

 4th ♉
)) → ♊ 6:11 pm

Color of the day: Turquoise
Incense of the day: Jasmine

A Feverfew Potion

In June, feverfew is at its peak in my herb garden. Its tiny white flowers add a casual charm to the border. Although used as a medicinal plant, feverfew also has many magical qualities. Planted near the home, it

June 11
Friday

 4th ♊

Color of the day: Rose
Incense of the day: Thyme

Basil Money Spell

Conjure forth the power of basil today to bring you abundance and wealth. Basil is associated with Mars, the element of fire, and several

Pagan deities including Vishnu and Ezulie. Cast a simple spell today by gathering five pinches of basil and bringing them to your ritual space. Breathe deeply. Ask the spirits of the herb for their blessings and assistance. Hold your hands over the herb and say something like:

> Powerful herb of wealth
>   and fire,
> Bring forth my true magical
>   desire.
> By the powers of above and
>   below,
> Come to me, money flow.

Chant the spell five times. As you do this, visualize yourself surrounded by abundance and wealth. Complete the spell by gathering the blessed and empowered herb and sprinkling it in your wallet to attract money. Offer some to friends and loved ones and invite them to do the same.

Abel R. Gomez

Notes:

June 12
Saturday

4th ♊
New Moon 7:15 am
☽ → ♋ 9:50 pm

Color of the day: Blue
Incense of the day: Patchouli

New Moon Love Spell

Sometimes called the Lover's Moon, this New Moon is a perfect time to bring love into your life. Prepare a bath into which you mix a potion of 3 tablespoons of honey, 9 drops of rose oil, and 3 drops of lemon verbena oil. Honey, symbolizing love and sweetness, was given to a newly married couple and is the origin of "honeymoon." The rose is so synonymous with love that each color of rose has its own magical properties. June is the month when the rose is at its height of potency. Lemon verbena is used to make you attractive to the opposite sex. These ingredients combined with water, the realm of emotions, will dissolve any resistance you may harbor toward a love relationship. Before slowly sliding into the water, light some new red candles around the tub. Breathe deeply and soft focus your eyes as you gaze into the candlelight. Feel yourself opening emotionally to the possibility of a new love. Stay with that process until you feel confident that your heart is open. Then say:

As I bathe by candlelight
I draw new love to me
tonight.

By the New Moon next month, a new lover should have entered your life.

Lily Gardner

Notes:

June 13
Sunday

1st ♋

Color of the day: Orange
Incense of the day: Frankincense

Gnome Invocation

The spirits of the Earth love nothing more than the lush soil of the gardening season. Their playful energy and devotion to hard work can be an inspiration to us as we begin to twiddle our fingers in the mud again. To draw in these delightful beings, this simple call (best given to a likeness of a gnome along with some milk, honey, and graham crackers) can be repeated each day that work is done in the garden.

Oh keepers of the soil,
Spirits of nature's sweet
kingdom;

I do call on you to aid me,
As I work my hands within
the earth;
Be with me,
That my aches and pains
may diminish;
Guide me as I make my beds
in spring,
And protect me as I turn
them in at the fall;
Fill my garden with your
abundant productivity,
Let love and light flow
actively around thee!

Estha McNevin

Notes:

June 14
Monday
Flag Day

1st ♋
☽ → ♌ 11:54 pm

Color of the day: Lavender
Incense of the day: Clary sage

Minerva honored Today

Ovid described Minerva as "the goddess of a thousand works." Patroness of the arts, she is said to have invented music. Her name translated means "mind" and she is called upon for any creative or intellectual endeavor. For this spell, prepare an altar with yellow cloth, candles, and flowers. Place at the center of your altar the tools of your artistic medium and a cauldron. You're going to burn an offering to the goddess, so be sure your cauldron is situated such that you're able to contain the fire. Now write on a sheet of paper your artistic or creative wish. Fold it such that you can place it in the cauldron. Light your candles and center. When you feel focused, light the paper with your wish and sprinkle the herbs, mustard, caraway, and rosemary over the fire. Focus on your wish and watch it rise on the smoke to the heavens. Thank Minerva as if your wish had already been granted.

Lily Gardner

Notes:

Holiday lore: It was on June 14, 1777, that Congress standardized the flag of the United States with 13 stripes in alternating red and white and 13 white stars on a blue background. Forty-one years later, in 1818, Congress voted to keep the number of stripes at 13 representing the 13 original colonies, but to add a new star for each new state. A star's addition becomes official on the Fourth of July following the state's admission. The current flag of 13 stripes and 50 stars has been in use since July 4, 1960, following Hawaii's 1959 statehood.

June 15
Tuesday

1st ♌

Color of the day: Black
Incense of the day: Cedar

Mudra Magic

A mudra is a mysterious gesture or posture used in ritual throughout the world. The raising of the arms skyward to invoke the gods can be considered a mudra. In the Hindu religion, mudras are a familiar practice frequently witnessed in ritual dance as well as yoga. There

are many types of mudras and their intention is quite magical. They are used in the healing of mind, body, and spirit. As in the art of palmistry, areas of the hand have specific correspondences. By creating energetic links with these hand gestures or poses we can align ourselves to a specific intention. Begin your mudra magic by sitting quietly. Place your hands, palms up on your knees with the tips of your thumb, middle, and ring finger all connecting in a circle and your index and pinkie fingers extending straight. This is an energy mudra that promotes the ability to envision and shape your future like the planting of a garden. Choose to sow the seeds for your future harvest as you project your intention through this magical mudra.

Igraine

Notes:

June 16
Wednesday

 1st ♌

Color of the day: Brown
Incense of the day: Lavender

Isis Rite to Remove Ovarian Cysts

The Egyptian goddess Isis is the goddess of rebirth, magic, and giver of life. Isis was also worshipped as the goddess of medicine and wisdom. Isis taught reading skills and agriculture. A ritual petitioning Isis to remove ovarian cysts can be tried if all else seems impossible. Draw a magic circle and consecrate a picture or statue of Isis with rose essential oil. Light a candle and some incense. Offer fruits, flowers, honey, candy, and rose water. On a piece of parchment paper, write your petition using words close to your heart or improvise with:

> I plead with you blessed Isis,
> From my ovaries may cysts be
> forever released.

Visualize the cysts being absorbed by a black hole and yourself being given a clean bill of health by the doctor. When ready, give thanks and close the circle. Continue to worship Isis on the altar by lighting incense and candles every day.

S. Y. Zenith

Notes:

June 17
Thursday

1st ♌
☽ → ♍ 1:41 am

Color of the day: White
Incense of the day: Nutmeg

Stash Your Cash Ritual

Whether or not it's in your nature to save for a rainy day, we've all run across a situation where we needed to squirrel away our pennies for something we really wanted. To encourage a cash stash to increase faster, I use this spell. Take some money you want to put aside and put it in an envelope. Add a piece of malachite and a piece of citrine, then sprinkle in dried, crushed mint, and add a cinnamon stick. On the front of the envelope, draw symbols for prosperity, perhaps the rune *fehu* or even dollar signs. Now tie the envelope shut with three cords or ribbons—one gold, one green, and one purple. Charge the package with your intention to save for whatever it is, and keep it in your sacred space. Each time you add to the envelope, charge the packet before you put it away.

Castiel

Notes:

June 18
Friday

1st ♍

Color of the day: Pink
Incense of the day: Rose

Relationship Woes

Since the Moon is waning today, use this day to remove any barriers you may have in your personal life regarding relationships. This can be for love, friendship, or family. Remove all the petals from a pale pink rose. Place the petals in a bowl. Next, write a description of the relationship problem on a small piece of paper. Tear the paper into small pieces and mix the shreds of paper with the rose petals using your fingers. As you mix, recite the following:

> *Goddess Freya, hear this plea,*
>
> *Help solve this problem gracefully.*
>
> *By your gentle love I ask,*
>
> *Guide me in this special task.*

Visualize the issue you need help with as a wall or boundary and then imagine a rain of rose petals falling on the wall and dissolving it. Bury the mixture in your yard or in a potted plant.

Ember

Notes:

And remember, if things are not going as well as you like, visualization can examine the issues and help you correct these as well.

Boudica

Notes:

June 19
Saturday

1st ♍
2nd Quarter 12:30 am
☽ → ♎ 4:13 am

Color of the day: Gray
Incense of the day: Ivy

Strengthen Your Position

If you find yourself in a good job, you are in a good relationship, or you have the best family relationship you have had in a while, you may want to reinforce this streak of good fortune by strengthening your position. Be shrewd; know why the position you are in right now is working. What is making this situation work? Visualize maintaining this situation with more of the same. Are the right people in the right jobs and is communication open? Visualize continued good communications and employee satisfaction. Is it because you and your partner are working toward the same goals? Then visualize the projects as a couple with common interests. Visualization is the best tool a Witch can use to assure continued success in any situation.

June 20
Sunday
Father's Day

2nd ♎

Color of the day: Gold
Incense of the day: Marigold

Reflecting on Father

Today is Father's Day. Many of us will honor our biological fathers with a visit, a phone call, a gift, or something else to mark this occasion. For some of us, the person who has acted as a father to us may not necessarily be our biological father; some men may also act as father figures to those to whom they are not related by blood. Additionally, some may have strained relationships with their fathers—or none at all. And for some, "Father" isn't a human being, but a deity.

Regardless of who your father is and what your relationship may be, take some time today to observe that relationship; the same goes if you are a father yourself. You may be celebrating the presence of a wonderful person in your life, or you may take time to heal and mourn. Either way, may this day be blessed.

Lupa

Notes:

June 21
Monday
Litha –
Summer Solstice

2nd ♎

☉ → ♋ 7:28 am

☽ → ♏ 8:14 am

Color of the day: Silver
Incense of the day: Lily

Solstice Changeover Spell

This is the night when the reign of the Oak King gives way to the Holly King—a sort of changing of the guard. Tonight, decorate your altar or other special place with oak

leaves, flowers, and holly leaves. Use silk ones if you can't get the real plants. In addition, this night is a good time to honor faeries. Make a gift for them and leave it outside and they'll help your garden grow. Slice an apple horizontally so the star pattern inside is revealed. Make several thin slices and leave them beneath a tree or in a flowerbed with these words:

> Longest night, a time
> to play,
>
> I leave this gift to honor
> the Fey.
>
> Frolic and dance from
> dusk 'til day,
>
> Then with goodwill be on
> your way.

Ember

Notes:

June 22
Tuesday

2nd ♏

Color of the day: White
Incense of the day: Basil

Welcome in Summer Spell

Summer is a time of relaxation, energetic pursuits, and pleasure. Even when we have jobs and many other responsibilities, we can still enjoy the playground of summer's delight. You will need a lemon, some sugar, water, and a spoon. Hold the lemon in your hands and envision a refreshing, energetic, joyful summer. Cut the lemon in half as you double your vision and squeeze the juice into the glass. Put a teaspoon of sugar to sweeten the other parts of your life. Add water, envisioning the wonderful, soothing qualities of water all summer long. Stir the mixture clockwise and chant three times:

> Welcome summer, welcome
> Sun, my work is done, the
> fun's begun.

Taste, and then sweeten to your taste. If you need to stir the lemonade again, stir counterclockwise and use the chant. Add ice and drink the lemonade to your pleasure and delight. Have a fabulous, fun summer!

Gail Wood

Notes:

June 23
Wednesday

2nd ♏
☽ → ♐ 2:10 pm

Color of the day: Topaz
Incense of the day: Honeysuckle

Honoring Your Body

Today is sacred to both Ishtar and Venus, goddesses of love and sexuality. In their honor, spend some time alone or with a partner to honor the sanctity of your body and sexuality. Bless a cup of salted water and disrobe in front of a mirror. Allow your gaze to see every part of yourself. Touch your body and know that you are stroking the skin of the divine. When ready, begin anointing your body, starting with your head and ending with your feet. As you touch the water to your skin say:

> I bless my _____. There is
> no part of me that is not of
> the gods.

Take a deep breath and look at yourself in the mirror once more. See the beauty in all of your parts. Bow to

your God-self. You are human. You are divine. You are beautiful. There is no part of you that is not of the gods. Blessed be.

Abel R. Gomez

Notes:

June 24
Thursday

2nd ♐

Color of the day: Purple
Incense of the day: Apricot

Old Midsummer's Day

In the British Isles, this day was celebrated as Midsummer's Day. Not to be confused with the astrological date of the Summer Solstice, this day also has quite a bit of legend and lore surrounding it. This is a classic time to work with the faeries. Here is a spell designed to both celebrate and work with the faeries in your garden. Before you begin, take a moment to plant some pretty flowers in the garden, just for the faeries. (Keep in mind that fragrant blossoms are well loved by the Fey.) Then leave a small tumbled stone for them as a sign of your intentions. Now repeat the spell.

June twenty-fourth is the old Midsummer's Day,

Faeries gather around and hear me, I pray.

Bless my life and garden with your loving energy,

No tricks, just joy, and a friendship between you and me.

Ellen Dugan

Notes:

June 25
Friday

2nd ♐
☽ → ♑ 10:21 pm

Color of the day: Pink
Incense of the day: Cypress

Create Your Path

It's almost the Full Moon! It's the ideal time to do some manifesting magic. Try doing this very nifty spell with an egg yolk. First, buy a carton of all-natural, eco-friendly, eggs. (Better yet, get some from a local farmer.) Enter a sacred state of mind and crack the egg in a bowl or dish.

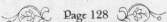 Page 128

Focus on positive things you wish to bloom in your life—those things that you wish to be reborn and strengthened in your path. Sprinkle some herbs, flowers, or leaves (aligned to your purpose) on the cracked egg and, with your left index finger, puncture the yolk while focusing on your intention. This will release the sacred (re)birth energies inherent in the yolk, and will lend power to your manifestation. Thank the universe and put your herb/egg mixture in flowing water at the end of the spell. Continue to focus on those things you wish to manifest in your life, and frequently petition the Divine for assistance in your life's path.

Raven Digitalis

Notes:

June 26
Saturday

 2nd ♑
☽ Full Moon 7:30 am

Color of the day: Indigo
Incense of the day: Rue

Celebrate Leadership

The Full Moon of June is associated with the goddess Juno (Greek Hera). Juno presides over marriage, hence the popularity of June weddings. Her other areas of influence are women and leadership. Her stones include pearl and moonstone. Honor Juno with an esbat celebrating leadership, especially female leaders. Decorate the altar in royal purple, with pictures of queens and goddesses. Add a rod, scepter, crown, or other symbol of power. Read this invocation:

> Hail Juno, queen of the gods!
>
> Your might holds up the heavens;
>
> Your grace shines down upon the Earth.
>
> Bless me, that I might see your face
>
> In the face of every woman I meet
>
> And show them respect in your honor.

Hear me as I give thanks

*To those who have
    guided me.*

You men can talk about the strong women you've known in your life. You women can do the same; you may also acknowledge your own strength. When you are through, thank Juno and close your ritual. If possible, find time today to do a favor for a woman in a leadership position or send a thank-you card to one who has helped you in the past.

Elizabeth Barrette

Notes:

spell, give your porch a good sweeping, plant a window box or pots with seasonal flowers, and keep them watered. Add a wind chime, a comfy chair or two, and a cool drink. Now grab a book and sit! Smell the scents of summer: flowers, freshly mown lawns, or the sweet dampness after a rain. Take time to see what you've been missing: butterflies, the flash of a hummingbird, or the drowsy movements of a bumblebee. End this spell by making eye contact with a passerby—give them a smile and a wave. Repeat this spell as often as possible.

James Kambos

Notes:

June 27
Sunday

3rd ♑

Color of the day: Yellow
Incense of the day: Almond

A Front Porch Spell

Porches are magical places. In the art of feng shui, porches have special significance, serving as a transitional space between the outside world and our private space. As we settle into summer, treat yourself to some front-porch magic. For this

June 28
Monday

3rd ♑
☽ → ♒ 8:52 am

Color of the day: Gray
Incense of the day: Rosemary

Blessed Fruit

Gather a piece of fresh fruit in your hand. Take a moment to meditate on the journey that this piece of fruit has taken to reach you.

Envision its development on the bough or vine. Imagine its dew-sodden flesh at dawn and the firm hand that plucked it. See the distance that this piece of fruit has traveled and all of the interactions it's had along the way, until you find yourself right back to the moment that it came to you and was cradled within your own hands. Feel the life force of the seed hidden within and imagine a great fruit tree sprouting from that seed. Envision a wealth of fruit growing on the tree and let this picture of bounty and stability guide you through the day!

Estha McNevin

Notes:

June 29
Tuesday

3rd ≈

Color of the day: Red
Incense of the day: Cinnamon

Possibilities Day

Today, let go of your usual way of doing things. Let go of who you've become, and how you are in the world. Forget what you've been told about how you should be; today, envision all you could be. Let the fullness of summer suffuse you with possibility. Spend the day imagining possibilities, dreaming and scheming. Dress differently and eat things you've never tried. Open up the abundance of summer and let it into your life. Carry a notebook and make lists of all the possibilities—things to learn, places to go, foods to eat, and fun to have. Write down everything you think of, even if it seems silly. Let your subconscious speak through this list, and when you write it, really listen. There are endless possibilities, the thing of dreams, and the fertile material for you to grow a summery new look, new project, or new you.

Dallas Jennifer Cobb

Notes:

June 30
Wednesday

 3rd ♒
☽ → ♓ 9:10 pm

Color of the day: White
Incense of the day: Bay laurel

human Rite for Safe Travel

When in doubt or anxious about traveling to certain places, prayers can be made to Lord Hanuman, Hinduism's beloved monkey god. He traveled great distances swiftly and fearlessly to rescue the goddess Sita from her captor, the King of Lanka, and deliver her back to her husband Lord Rama. Pictures or idols of Lord Hanuman are available from Internet stores by mail order if they can't be found locally. Before traveling, offer bananas, incense, milk, fresh water, honey, yogurt, unsalted nuts, and a candle to Hanuman. Speak your wish and ask for protection, safety, and a smooth journey to the destination and a smooth return home. Recite his mantra 108 times on Tuesdays and Saturdays. During free time while away from home, continue to chant the mantra "Om Sri Hanumate Namaha." This mantra should also be recited under the breath when feeling insecure or frightened while outdoors or when entering eerie places.

S. Y. Zenith

Notes:

July is the seventh month of the year. Its astrological sign is Cancer, the Crab (June 21–July 22), a cardinal-water sign ruled by the Moon. Named for Julius Caesar, July brings a time of ripening and fulfillment. The ancient Celts were attuned to the cycles of Sun and Moon, and now, during the height of summer, is a perfect time to study the night sky and take camping trips to enjoy star-gazing away from city lights—take advantage of connecting with the natural world. Outdoor activities are in full swing now and Independence Day, July 4, is the major holiday this month—a time when many people enjoy barbeques and vacations. Since July's astrological sign is associated with water, this is a good time to practice water magic or visit lakes, rivers, and oceans. Enjoy the splendid flowers of these warm, sunny days: purple liatris (blazing stars), coneflowers, orange daylilies, and the glow of blue chickory along roadsides. This time of year is referred to as the "dog days of summer." Sirius, the "dog star" rises and sets in conjunction with the Sun. The heat of July can be oppressive, so relax in the shade or enjoy the sultry nights by taking a magical, moonlight swim. The Full Moon of July is sometimes called the Blessing Moon.

July 1
Thursday

3rd ♓

Color of the day: Green
Incense of the day: Jasmine

Stretching Time Spell

Today marks the halfway point of the year. Where are you in terms of everything you wanted to accomplish? A little behind, maybe? Time hard to find? Whenever you need some extra time to finish a project, gather together a yellow candle, a purple thread, and some bergamot oil. Anoint the candle with the oil and set in a holder somewhere it can burn down safely. Run the purple thread between your hands and say the following:

> As a spider spins her web
> Eternally she'll stretch her
>   thread.
> As that thread, let this
>   time be
> Stretched as long as I
>   shall need.
> By Arachne and Ariadne
> And by my will, so mote
>   it be!

Wind the thread around the candle, tie it off, and light the candle. Get to work, and note how much you can get done before the flame goes out!

Castiel

Notes:

Holiday lore: Today is the first day of the season for climbing Mt. Fuji in Yamabiraki, Japan. Mt. Fuji is the highest peak in Japan and is revered in Japanese culture. Considered the foremother or grandmother of Japan, Fuji is an ancient fire goddess of the indigenous Ainu people. In modern times, the Ainu mostly resided on the northern island of Hokkaido. The name *Fuji* was derived from an Ainu word that means "fire" or "deity of fire." Each year since the Meiji era, a summer festival has been held to proclaim the beginning of the climbing season and to pray for the safety of local inhabitants and visitors or pilgrims to the sacred mountain. The two-month climbing season begins today and ends on August 30.

July 2
Friday

3rd ♓

Color of the day: Coral
Incense of the day: Vanilla

The Feast of Expectant Mothers

Today is the Feast of Expectant Mothers. Honor the life force that allows the human species to continue and the women who manifest it. If you know someone who is pregnant, visit her today—take her out to dinner, go shopping, or do something else festive. Otherwise you could donate some of your time and resources to an organization that caters to pregnant women. Here is a blessing you can say privately or write in a card if you know someone who would appreciate it:

> Blessed be the life-bearers
> Who bring new souls into
>   the world.
> Blessed be the babies
> Who are our hope for
>   the future.
> Blessed be the mothers and
>   fathers
> Who raise them to be good
>   people.
> Blessed be the pregnant
>   women
> For they are precious beyond
>   price.

          Elizabeth Barrette

July 3
Saturday

3rd ♓
☽ → ♈ 9:44 am

Color of the day: Blue
Incense of the day: Pine

Spell to Shine Bright

One of the most important qualities of a good priest or priestess of the Craft is self-love. Part of our work as Witches is not only to see divinity in the world, but also to see it within ourselves. Call upon Isis, the Egyptian goddess of magic, this day to shine bright. No icon is more evocative of this sense of self-love as the image of Isis with her wings outstretched in the fullness of her power, beauty, and glory. Find a copy of this image—a statue, piece of jewelry, or just a printout—then hold the image to your heart and say something like:

> Isis, Goddess, Queen of
> Wonder,
>
> You who are mistress of all
> enchantment.

With your blessings this day,

*May I shine with the
radiance of a million stars.*

*May my truest, most
beautiful divine self*

*Shine brightly, that I may see
the beauty within.*

Abel R. Gomez

Notes:

July 4
Sunday

Independence Day

 3rd ♈
4th Quarter 10:35 am

Color of the day: Yellow
Incense of the day: Juniper

Celebrate Personal Freedoms

Happy Independence Day! Tonight, as you head out to go see the local fireworks, consider using the energy and light of the fireworks display in a creative type of fire magic. When the fireworks begin, look up and focus on the colors, the sounds, and the reaction of the people around you. Tap into this festive mood and channel this energy into a spell that celebrates your right to religious freedom. I suggest writing down the following charm ahead of time. Then take it along with you and work it while you enjoy the fireworks!

*I celebrate tonight, my right
to live free,*

*To follow my magical faith
openly.*

*By fire and color, this
freedom spell is begun,*

*May it open both hearts and
minds, bringing harm to
none.*

Ellen Dugan

Notes:

Holiday notes: On July 4, 1776, the Second Continental Congress adopted the Declaration of Independence. Philadelphians were first to mark the anniversary of American independence with a celebration, but Independence Day became commonplace only after the War of 1812. By the 1870s, the

Fourth of July was the most important secular holiday in the United States, celebrated even in far-flung communities on the western frontier of the country.

July 5
Monday

 4th ♈
))→ ♉ 8:29 pm

Color of the day: Ivory
Incense of the day: Rosemary

A Yarrow Dream Spell

Now in the garden and along the roadside you'll see the magical yarrow blooming. Its silvery-green foliage and stems are topped with flat yellow flower heads. When dried and crushed, it releases a pungent scent. Herbalists have used yarrow for healing, love magic, and dreamwork. Yarrow's scent can trigger deep memories and is useful in past-life dream spells. To do this, crumble the dried flowers and leaves from three yarrow stems. Place them on a cloth or in a pouch you use for magic. Before bedtime, inhale the scent, clear your mind, and say:

> My past lives are with me
> now and forever,
>
> All time—past, present, and
> future

Are like a river that flows
together.

Leave the yarrow on your nightstand and drift to sleep. Your dreams may run together. If you awaken during the night, write down your dreams. Repeat as needed.

James Kambos

Notes:

July 6
Tuesday

 4th ♉

Color of the day: Maroon
Incense of the day: Ylang-ylang

Turn Pain into Art

Mexican artist Frida Kahlo was born today in 1907. Her life was vibrant, yet full of tumult—childhood illness, a serious bus accident that caused serious injuries and lifelong pain, and a stormy relationship with fellow artist Diego Rivera all left their mark. Yet she was able to turn her experiences into an incredible collection of paintings. Creative pursuits can offer us an outlet for our own pain, if not a cure. Today, think of something that bothers you, perhaps something you wish you

could change but may not have the means to at this time. Take your feelings about this issue and focus them into some act of creativity; this can be artwork, music, dance, writing, or even volunteering. Turn that creativity into a ritualized action focused on easing the pain and finding solutions for its cause. Let it be a cathartic conduit for what you feel.

Lupa

Notes:

July 7
Wednesday

 4th ♉

Color of the day: White
Incense of the day: Lilac

Lucky Seven

On the goddesses' magic wheel of time, odd numbers were sacred. Sacred scriptures from many cultures link the number seven with sacred beings: The Pleiades or Seven Sisters in early Greece, The Seven Mothers of the World in pre-vedic India, The Seven Midwives in Egypt, or the Seven Sages of Arabia. Both Artemis and Aphrodite were associated with the ancient cult of the Seven Pillars

of Wisdom. Today, the seventh day of the seventh month, perform a powerful luck spell. Take seven coins in your hand and stack them with the largest value on the bottom, the smallest on top forming a small pillar. Wrap the pillar in a scrap of red or purple cloth. Tie a knot to secure the cloth and invoke Lady Luck—Roman triple goddess Fortuna.

Fortuna, bless this charm,
make it lucky indeed.

Leave the charm at a crossroads as an offering. As it leaves your hand, know luck flows freely to you seven-fold.

Dallas Jennifer Cobb

Notes:

July 8
Thursday

4th ♉
☽ → ♊ 3:51 am

Color of the day: Turquoise
Incense of the day: Nutmeg

Financial Planning

You should always be aware of your financial situation; your income vs. your expenditures. All sorts of things get in the way of the plans you would like to make and you should be prepared with a backup plan for such circumstances. Were you planning on a trip this summer? Did you want to go someplace special? Would you like to go on a vacation but didn't quite find the money to do it? Did you start a vacation fund for this trip? Maybe this is the time to start a vacation fund for next year or to start budgeting your money so you can take a trip later this year. Always be aware of your finances and make sure you plan ahead for those eagerly anticipated travel arrangements.

Boudica

Notes:

feelings or use a photo to represent what you need help to heal. If it's a broken relationship, you can use other symbols as well, such as a ring. Put the item(s) inside the circle. Imagine the circle of candles like an embrace—surrounding you with peace and comfort. Speak these words three times:

> Love is lost and love is
>   gained,
> Bringing solace; sometimes
>   pain.
> Comfort me from loss I feel,
> Guide my heart; help me to
>   heal.

Ember

Notes:

July 9
Friday

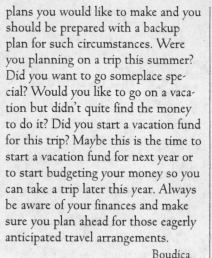

4th ♊

Color of the day: Pink
Incense of the day: Cypress

heal a Broken heart

Anyone who has ever experienced loss knows how hard it can be to move on. Use this spell any time you need comfort. Arrange any number of pink candles in a circle on a safe surface. Write out your

July 10
Saturday

4th ♊
☽ → ♋ 7:38 am

Color of the day: Indigo
Incense of the day: Rue

Switch It Up Ritual

The definition of ritual is "a detailed method of procedure faithfully or regularly followed."

Sometimes our self-enforced rituals can block our progress. Habitual patterns create boredom and each day becomes the same. Switch up your daily ritual by moving through your day making different choices. If you normally wake up at eight in the morning with the alarm clock abuzz, change your awareness to your body's natural rhythm, allowing yourself to wake with the rising Sun. If you usually reach for a cup of coffee and read your morning e-mail, make a soothing mug of tea and go outside, breathing in the possibility of the day. Go the gym every morning? Take a yoga class and experience your body as a sacred temple. Changing up our most basic rites that we adhere to without question fosters expansion and growth, allowing for fresh perspectives to move us forward in our lives. Create simple magic by being receptive to a new experience every day.

Igraine

Notes:

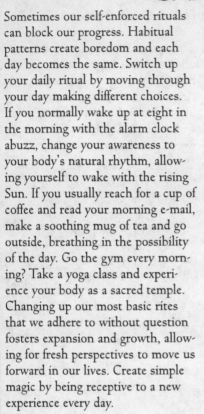

July 11
Sunday

4th ♋
New Moon 3:40 pm

Color of the day: Gold
Incense of the day: Eucalyptus

Charge Up New Studies

New Moons are a good time to start a new course of study, magical or otherwise. To invigorate your study, gather three yellow candles, three almonds for wisdom, a white cloth, a pen, and a new tablet or notebook. Spread out the white cloth and arrange the closed notebook and pen in front of you. Place the three almonds on top of the notebook. Arrange the three candles across from you. Light the left-most candle and call forth intellectual ability, light the second candle and call forth clarity, and light the third candle and call forth knowledge retention. Pick up the pen as if ready to write and open the notebook to the first page. Eat the almonds and envision the knowledge transforming into wisdom. Pick up the pen and write an invocation to the gods asking them to bless this notebook to your study and your wisdom.

Gail Wood

Notes:

July 12
Monday

 1st ♋

☽ → ♌ 8:53 am

Color of the day: Lavender
Incense of the day: Lily

A Prosperity Spell

Hey, do you know what day it is? (Of course you do, you're a Witch!) It's the day after the New Moon. The Moon is experiencing her third day of "darkness," (just as the Moon is "full for three days") and there is no better time, in terms of the phases of the Moon, to work some prosperity magic. Who doesn't need a few extra bucks—or a few thousand? Take a walk with an empty chalice in hand, and gather as many types of fresh green leaves as there are in your general vicinity. If you have dried herbs like patchouli and peppermint, or green stones like jade or aventurine, add them to the mix. When you arrive home, light a green candle, enter a meditative state, and pour fresh spring water into the chalice, saying something like:

As this sacred water dries,
so the properties of these
glorious plants are released.
I charge the spell as one of
prosperity, abundance, and
financial growth; may the
powers of water and earth
assist me in drawing all the
finances I need—and much
more. So mote it be.

Repeat the words every day until the water is fully evaporated.

Raven Digitalis

Notes:

July 13
Tuesday

 1st ♌

Color of the day: Red
Incense of the day: Ginger

A Creativity Spell

Invoke Ixchel, the Moon and snake goddess of the Maya, who ruled weaving, magic, health, fertility, sexuality, and creativity. Ixchel's familiar was the dragonfly, the intricate creature of myth and garden, whose luminescent wings glitter as they flutter. Let the dragonfly flutter through your life. What do you want to create? Is it a painting, piece of music, or a poem? Or do you want to create a new life for yourself, peeling off the old like a snake shedding its skin? With Ixchel, the magic of the dragonfly is yours. Let luminescent colors brighten your imagination,

inspiring creativity. Paint your life with the brush of change, let the thrum of hummingbird wings inspire. Even tiny things can be mighty. Go now, and create. Take up your pen or brush, imagination, and creativity. Bring your visions to life, with Ixchel.

Dallas Jennifer Cobb

Notes:

July 14
Wednesday

1st ♌
☽ → ♍ 9:15 am

Color of the day: Yellow
Incense of the day: Honeysuckle

Black Obsidian Psychic Shield

When confronted by an aggressive person on the telephone or someone who is by nature negative and who drains your energy, use three black obsidian–charged tumbled stones in a pouch to shield off negativity and keep your nerves intact. Holding a pouch containing black obsidian during uncomfortable telephone calls or in the pocket during quarrels prevents the other party's ill wishes from manifesting. After obtaining the stones, wash them in

salt water. Dry them and pass over a candle and some incense. Visualize them emitting protective energies. Take each stone and repeat:

> Protect me from harm,
> Send all ill charm,
> Under solid ground,
> By God's grace it is there
> forever bound!

Put the black obsidian into a pouch and carry in your handbag, briefcase, or pocket. For breaking hexes, the pouch should be carried on the person continuously for ninety days to remove all traces of evil malevolent attacks.

S. Y. Zenith

Notes:

July 15
Thursday

 1st ♍

Color of the day: Crimson
Incense of the day: Myrrh

Magical Activism

Witchcraft is about engagement with the world. This engagement can come in many forms, one of which is political activism. One of the easiest and most effective forms is leafletting. Infuse your activism today with magical energy. Gather leaflets you wish to distribute and hold them in your hands. Breathe deeply and connect to earth and sky. Visualize the leaflets surrounded by the symbol of Venus, attracting people to take them. Enchant the leaflets by saying something like:

> Spirits of justice and truth,
>
> May all who see this paper be awakened.
>
> May their eyes be open to truth,
>
> May this cause bring peace and love,
>
> I offer this work to the God and Goddess.
>
> So mote it be.

Take another breath, and bless the leaflets with your own power and dedication to your cause. Hold them before you and allow the gods to bestow the blessings. Go out and be the change you wish to see in the world.

Abel R. Gomez

Notes:

July 16
Friday

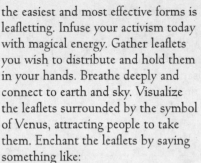

1st ♏
☽ → ♎ 10:24 am

Color of the day: White
Incense of the day: Orchid

Friendship Stones

Fridays are a great magical time for attracting new people into your life. Here is a waxing Moon spell designed to draw new friends or even a group of new magical friends to you. Surround a picture of yourself with four rose quartz stones. Then repeat the spell.

> With the rose quartz stones and a wish so true,
>
> May the gods bless me in all that I do.
>
> Into the astral realm I send out a magical request,
>
> May I attract new friends, ones who will suit me the best.
>
> They will come into my life in the best possible way,
>
> Bringing friendship and fun, for many happy days.
>
> For the good of all, bringing harm to none,
>
> By the power of earth, this spell is done.

Keep the stones with you. As your new friends come into your life, offer them a stone as a token of your friendship.

Ellen Dugan

Notes:

penny heads up each time you find yourself inspired to. As you do so, will an essence of luck and wealth into the coin and envision this being sent into others as they pick the coin up. When you're all done, make your wish!

Estha McNevin

Notes:

July 17
Saturday

1st ♎

Color of the day: Black
Incense of the day: Magnolia

Wealth-Drawing Coin Spell

The number 777 is often related with manifestation and luck. It is a principal number of many deities, namely that of Ganesha and is heavily associated with Venusian wealth and agriculture as well. The lush and fertile gardens of the Earth are the esoteric foundation for luxury as all of our goods and needs are manufactured with elements, which we collect from nature. A wonderful way of drawing wealth is to put it out there and this spell spreads luck to others as well as the self. Go to the bank and get $7.77 worth of pennies. For the entire day, place a

July 18
Sunday

1st ♎
2nd Quarter 6:11 am
☽ → ♏ 1:42 pm

Color of the day: Orange
Incense of the day: Hyacinth

Magically Banish Illnesses

The elemental powers of fire can be tapped for magical uses. A simple method is using a fluid condenser—a magically charged infusion of herbs for implementing in rituals and spellwork. Tinctures, extracts, oils, and resins are fluid condensers. Fire rules the banishing of illness and good health. For ridding illness, obtain some herbs of your choice, such as angelica, basil, cinnamon, juniper, pennyroyal, or rosemary. Put a handful of herbs in a pot, cover it with water, and boil for twenty-five minutes. Let cool without removing lid. Strain liquid and return to boil until it is half in quantity. Cool, strain, and pour into a dark bottle with vodka. Shake the bottle and store in a dark place for two weeks. Use for anointing healing candles, petitions, and sachets or decant into a spray bottle for spraying a sick room at least twice a day.

S. Y. Zenith

Notes:

July 19
Monday

 2nd ♏

Color of the day: Gray
Incense of the day: Hyssop

A Human-Rights Prayer

Two notable events occurred on this day: in 1692, five women were hanged in Salem, Massachusetts, accused of being Witches; and in 1848, the Women's Rights Convention began in Seneca Falls, New York. This is a healthy reminder of how far human rights in general have come—and how far they have yet to go even today. It's also a reminder that change for the better is possible—and not just through magic. Today, pick a human-rights issue or other cause that you may not know a lot about and research it. Then determine what you can do to make the situation better, and make plans to take action. Say this brief prayer before you begin:

> Libertas et Iustitia, Liberty
>   and Justice,
> Witness my act in favor of
>   you both.
> Add your strength to my
>   will,
> Your voice to my words,
> And guide me ever along
>   your path.

Lupa

Notes:

July 20
Tuesday

2nd ♏

☽ → ♐ 7:48 pm

Color of the day: Scarlet
Incense of the day: Geranium

A Summer Morning Spell

Where I live, summer mornings begin without haste. Mist veils some of the hills and hollows. The sunrise is slow and deliberate. And, the dew shimmers on fern and grass. It is a new day, a new beginning. This day never existed before, and never will again. Before you rush into the day and gulp your morning coffee, ease into the day with this spell. Stretch and yawn. Touch your toes and feel your body become limber. Draw back the drapes or raise the blinds. Visualize that you're raising the curtain on the first act of a play, and in effect you are. Look into your mirror and say, "A new day. A new me!" Now brew your morning coffee and savor the aroma. And please don't skip breakfast. Give yourself some extra time to connect with nature. Snip a small bouquet from your garden or just water a houseplant.

James Kambos

Notes:

July 21
Wednesday

2nd ♐

Color of the day: White
Incense of the day: Bay laurel

Cow Appreciation Day

This is Cow Appreciation Day. Many cultures consider the cow a sacred animal, including Hindu, Celtic, and Egyptian traditions. The cow is associated with various goddesses including Brigid, Bubona, Hathor, and Ninsun the Wise. Her qualities include contentment, motherhood, nurturing, and wealth. Her element is earth. Honor the cow today by eating dairy products and abstaining from beef. Remember that you are what you eat—happy, healthy cows give good food, but cows trapped in miserable conditions give less wholesome food. Take care of yourself and the cows by promoting free-range livestock. Join community-supported agriculture and you may visit "your" cows during an open house! Here is a Cow Appreciation blessing:

> Hail, Sacred Cow
> Mother of plenty,
> Giver of good milk!
> We bow to your abundance
> And praise your perfection.
> Bless us with wealth and
>   health

As we bless your patience
And your generosity.
So mote it be!

Elizabeth Barrette

Notes:

Inspire giving for the
good of all,
Start with me, hear this call.
Giving will enrich our lives,
Giving will strengthen
our ties.

Ember

Notes:

July 22
Thursday

2nd ♐

☉ → ♌ 6:21 pm

Color of the day: Green
Incense of the day: Mulberry

Generosity

There is a widely held belief in the Craft that what you do comes back to you. Generosity is something we can never have too much of in the world. Today, be generous. Use this spell to increase the spirit of generosity within you—that it may spread outward and inspire others. Donate something today— money or goods to charity, or donate your time as a volunteer. The good you do will come back to you. Light a purple or white candle and recite the following:

July 23
Friday

2nd ♐

☽ → ♑ 4:39 am

Color of the day: Rose
Incense of the day: Alder

Neptunalia Spell for Fertility

Neptune holds dominion over the seas and all sources of fresh water. He is the lord of fertility because his rains nourish and fertilize the Earth. His festival, Neptunalia, is celebrated outdoors. When praying to the gods or goddesses, it is important not only to create an altar that is pleasing to him/her, but also to make a sacrifice. Neptune is partial to both bulls and horses, so perhaps a grilled steak would be a good offering. Another might be a bottle of fine

Italian wine. For your altar, carve a trident into a fine blue pillar candle. Dress the altar in shades of blue and adorn it with shells, horses, pieces of coral, and little boats. Pray:

> Hail Neptune!
> Ruler of the waters,
> Holder of the earth,
> Dark-haired lord!
> Blessed one, be kindly
>   in heart
> And grant me (name your
>   wish for fertility).

Lily Gardner

Notes:

July 24
Saturday

2nd ♑

Color of the day: Brown
Incense of the day: Sandalwood

Love Yourself Today

Loving yourself is one of the most important things a person can do. Unfortunately, many of us forget to practice self-love—the feeling of total acceptance, compassion, and love for all that you are. Think about ways you beat yourself up mentally. Many of these self-imposed stresses are borne of the desire to fit in and feel loved by others. However, if it weren't for life's diversity—including diversity in physical forms, mental processing, and individual expressions—life would be bland. To help cultivate self-love, light a red (or pink) candle and meditate on reasons why you, and others, should accept and love you as you are. While none of us are perfect, we mustn't hate ourselves in the moment. Spend the day loving and adoring yourself. Take a bath, watch a movie, pig out on sweets, walk around naked, drink some wine (if you are of age), and cultivate a greater sense of self-worth and appreciation. Every one of us is sacred and has our own special gifts, abilities, and pieces of the Puzzle of Life.

Raven Digitalis

Notes:

July 25
Sunday

2nd ♑

☽ → ♒ 3:38 pm

Full Moon 9:37 pm

Color of the day: Amber
Incense of the day: Almond

Embracing Your Shadow Exercise

Witches are adept at embracing their shadow. They innately understand there is no division in our human nature. We are complex and yet divine in our whole being. Part of our soul's journey is to no longer deny those aspects of ourselves that we label negative. As an artful exercise to encourage and integrate your shadow self, spread on the floor a roll of paper large enough for you to lie upon. You will need a friend to assist you. Lying on your back, have your partner trace the outline of your silhouette with a black marker. Stand up and then draw a vertical line down the center of your shadow body. Choose crayons, pastels, or colored markers and, working through the seven chakras, draw some aspect of yourself that is hidden or unacknowledged on the left side and then a complementary or balancing quality that you own on the right-hand side. Create a rainbow-bridge phrase or affirmation to connect these two polarities bringing them into harmony, creating unity and embracing your shadow.

Igraine

Notes:

July 26
Monday

 3rd ♒

Color of the day: Silver
Incense of the day: Narcissus

Solar Spell Bag

In a gold or yellow sachet combine the following:

Frankincense
Myrrh
Orange peel
Marigold
1 gold coin
6 drops of frankincense oil
1 drop sweet orange oil

Sit in the full sunlight at noon and allow the light to penetrate your entire being. Let the bag sit in front of you absorbing the energy of the Sun. Charge it with your own energy, absorbed from the Sun. Let light and warmth fill you and radiate entirely around the bag. Feel yourself ruled

by this force of life and let it recharge the spark of life within your soul. Let this charm remind you of your eternal link with the Sun and use it as a tool to help you focus on your goals and aspirations. In times of confusion or depression, meditate with this bag and reconnect to the Sun. Go back to that moment in time. Let it fill you all over again!

Estha McNevin

Notes:

known software authorities. Use the Internet to find the best software you can afford. Be sure all the security updates are loaded as soon as you notice the icon alert in your tool tray. Make sure your virus protection is up to date. Always be looking for security downloads for your software and make sure you install them in a timely manner. Never open an attachment to an e-mail that you are not expecting. And finally, always ask the blessings of the Great Motherboard for protection for your hardware.

Boudica

Notes:

July 27
Tuesday

 3rd ≈
Color of the day: Black
Incense of the day: Cedar

Computer Protection

The best way to protect your computer is not really with spells, but with good software that stops virus intrusion and prevents malware or spyware from entering your machine. There are several programs out there that come highly recommended and an Internet search for virus protection programs will yield recommendations from well-

July 28
Wednesday

 3rd ≈
☽ → ♓ 4:00 am

Color of the day: Brown
Incense of the day: Lavender

Financial health

It's Wednesday, a day of the week associated with Mercury. The Romans attributed commerce and wealth to this god, so you may be tempted to do a quick money spell to bring in enough cash to cover this month's bills—but what about next month? Instead, look toward working with Mercury to create healthier financial habits. This may involve buying some Finance 101 books that are aimed at a general audience, exploring relevant Web sites, and perhaps even seeking out a financial adviser for help improving your situation. Ask Mercury to help you find the resources you need at the best time possible:

> Mercury, Hermes, god of wealth,
>
> Help me gain financial health.
>
> I'll take the time to learn things well,
>
> Explore beyond the money spell.
>
> Wise god, guide me in the right direction
>
> And help me take the proper actions.

Lupa

Notes:

July 29
Thursday

3rd ♓

Color of the day: Purple
Incense of the day: Apricot

Parents' Day

Today is Parents' Day. We are all parents to our inner child. To connect with your inner parent, find a quiet place and take three centering breaths. As you breathe deeply, go deep inside yourself to your heart center. Look around and connect with its loving energy. You will see your own child spirit here and send energy from your heart to this child; feel the vibrant energy between you. From your left walks your inner mother. Send her energy from your heart and feel the vibrant connection. From your right walks your inner father. Send him energy from your heart and feel the vibrant connection. You are enveloped in a hug. Know that you can come to them for guidance when you need the loving hand of a mother or father or both. Return now to the here and now by taking three centering breaths and opening your eyes.

Gail Wood

Notes:

July 30
Friday

3rd ♓

☽ → ♈ 4:42 pm

Color of the day: White
Incense of the day: Yarrow

Nostalgia Now!

While no one should live in the past, moments of nostalgia are sweet, and the time of the waning Moon and the waning summer is the perfect time to indulge. Get yourself the type of soda you loved as a kid. As the Sun begins to set, take it outside with you on the porch, stoop, or front steps. Listen for sounds that remind you of wonderful summer moments—the ice cream truck, leaves in the breeze, a car radio. Recall a happy summer evening and hold it in your mind as vividly as you can. Whisper to yourself:

> The times gone by
> Now time's stood still
> Let me relive this moment's
>   thrill
> Then bid it goodbye.

Close your eyes and feel the magic of a bygone summer moment flowing through you. Enjoy your soda to bring yourself back into the magic of the present.

Castiel

Notes:

July 31
Saturday

3rd ♈

Color of the day: Blue
Incense of the day: Sage

Spell for Transformation

It is traditional to bake man-shaped breads with the first harvest of grain on this date. The loaf-man symbolizes the transformation from the Green Man into John Barleycorn, the harvest sacrifice. Begin with the desire to transform some part of your life that you're less than happy with. Transform the problem area into an affirmation, a present-tense, one sentence, positive statement of the outcome you desire. Now light a new orange candle and gather ingredients to make your favorite bread recipe. If you've never tried making bread before, you may wish to buy frozen bread dough from your market. Incorporate ingredients with magical properties into the bread dough before you shape it. Some suggestions would be almonds for well-being, allspice for health, anise or apple for love, vanilla for power, and cinnamon for prosperity. Spend fifteen minutes every night before sleep saying your affirmation.

Lily Gardner

Notes:

August is the eighth month of the year and is named for Augustus Caesar. Its astrological sign is Leo, the Lion (July 22–August 23), a fixed-fire sign ruled by the Sun. This is the time of "first fruits" the beginning of the harvest season. The month begins with the ancient festival of Lughnasadh, when the Irish honored Lugh, the many-skilled god, and celebrated with games and feasting. The Anglo-Saxons called this Lammas, or "loaf mass." A loaf of bread was baked with the first harvested grain and blessed at mass. This is a good time to share a homemade loaf with family and friends. This is the midpoint of the light half of the year. In many places, August means "back to school"—time to prepare for fall and, in some cases, more work and less relaxation time. We begin to harvest our gardens now and reap what we sowed in the spring—the Full Moon of August is often called the Corn Moon. The landscape begins to hint at the autumn to come—fields and gardens turn yellow with goldenrod, sunflowers, and black-eyed Susans. Daylight wanes more quickly now, and the evening music of cicadas serenades us gently into cooler nights. We can sense that summer is drawing to a close as we prepare to enjoy a bountiful harvest.

August 1
Sunday
Lammas

3rd ♈

Color of the day: Gold
Incense of the day: Eucalyptus

Corn Dollies for Spellcraft

Corn on the cob can be offered at the altar to the Corn Mother for fertility and nourishment. With cornhusks and wheat straws, corn dollies can be made for employing in spellcraft when needed. The dollies can be carried on the person as charms, talismans, or amulets. They can be consecrated for hanging on the rafters of the home to protect the property and its residents. A pair of similar dollies can be made to represent two lovers. The pair can also represent a single person seeking a soul mate. They can be used for numerous magical purposes so use your imagination and experiment with them. For scenting a room, a dolly or two can be dabbed with essential oil and hung in strategic places. Create several dollies for different uses. Use only one or two dollies for each magical purpose. Never re-use the same dolly for another matter. If it helps, the shape of a dolly can be drawn over two pieces of cloth, cut out for stuffing with dried corn, and sewn up. Rituals and spells in which corn dollies can be utilized are success, self-confidence, motivation, career improvement, courage, good health, inner strength, and companionship.

S. Y. Zenith

Notes:

Holiday lore: Lammas is a bittersweet holiday, mingling joy at the current high season's harvest with the knowledge that summer is soon at an end. Many cultures have "first fruit" rituals on this day—the Celt's version is called Lughnasadh; the Anglo-Saxon version called Hlaf-masse. In the Middle Ages, the holiday settled on August 1, taking its current form for the most part, with sheaves of wheat and corn blessed on this day.

August 2
Monday

3rd ♈
☽ → ♉ 4:13 am

Color of the day: Gray
Incense of the day: Hyssop

Hummingbird Blessing

The summer garden, alive with bright colors, attracts magical visitors. Take time today to be outside in nature and receive magical blessings. Whether you live in the countryside with your own spacious garden, have a home in the city with a cozy front yard, or dwell in an inner-city apartment, find a spot where flowers grow. Pause, and let your attention be drawn to the flowers. See the small universe that exists within each blossom. Whether it's sunflowers that attract bees, coneflowers (echinacea) that summon the butterflies, or bee balm (Monarda) that welcomes the tiny hummingbird, these flowers are the source of sustenance for small creatures. They sustain diverse species and attract magic to the garden. As the insects, bees, and birds visit the flowers, know your life is blessed by diversity, joy, and abundance. Earth's garden is in full bloom and blessed by hummingbirds.

Dallas Jennifer Cobb

Notes:

August 3
Tuesday

3rd ♉
4th Quarter 12:59 am

Color of the day: Red
Incense of the day: Bayberry

Drawing Energy to Yourself

Sometimes we spend so much time sending energy to people who ask for some help that we may forget that, even though we may not be ill or have serious issues, we still need some for ourselves. In Reiki, we learn to lay hands on ourselves and draw universal energy down through our chakras to augment our personal energy. You can do the same kind of meditative practice on yourself. Sit in a comfortable place, lay your hands across your chest and concentrate on drawing energy from the elements down through your crown chakra to parts of your body that feel tired or stressed. You can also draw from the universal energies to help heal your heart or your soul. And, of course, there is always Deity to lend a helping hand. Remember to take time for yourself to allow healing for your own needs.

Boudica

Notes:

August 4
Wednesday

 4th ♉
☽ → ♊ 12:54 pm

Color of the day: Topaz
Incense of the day: Honeysuckle

A Zinnia Spell

August wouldn't be August without zinnias. Their bright cheery colors contain the warmth of the August Sun and echo the region of their origin, Mexico and the American Southwest. When Cortez found them growing in Mexico, the Aztecs already held them in high esteem for their beauty. Use them in spells for strength, health, endurance, or abundance. This spell for health combines them with another late-summer flower, goldenrod. Cut a stem of a red or yellow zinnia and a goldenrod. Tie them together to dry in a dark, airy space. When dry, raise them toward the Sun and say:

> Flowers bright as the Sun,
> Protect me from winter's grief
> When summer's done.

Crush them and place them in an envelope as a symbol of their protection. Keep them until next Midsummer, then burn them in a ritual fire. Repeat again when the zinnias and goldenrod bloom.

James Kambos

Notes:

August 5
Thursday

 4th ♊

Color of the day: Crimson
Incense of the day: Balsam

Augury of the Birds

As you walk beside the river's edge, a hawk flies alongside you and perches in an old pine. You approach cautiously so as not to unsettle him, but he remains quite still and stares directly into your eyes. Outside your window, a robin gathers dry grasses in its beak while preparing to build its nest. A goldfinch lands on a yellow rose bush outside the kitchen door. A bald eagle flies directly overhead as you stand in awe. Awakening you in the night, you hear the owl hoot. The cat brings in a baby wren barely fledged. It dies as you watch hopeless. In the light of day, a barn owl is terrified, trapped in the garage. Swallowtails build their nest in the rafters of your porch. This is the augury of the birds. Take note of their color, their

sightings, and their actions. What is the significance of a murder of crows calling as they fly past, a thunderstorm approaching? What do they tell us? That is for us to decipher.

Igraine

Notes:

August 6
Friday

4th ♊
☽ → ♋ 5:50 pm

Color of the day: Purple
Incense of the day: Mint

A Prayer for Peace

The United States dropped the atomic bomb on Hiroshima, Japan 65 years ago today, ending World War II. The blast killed 75,000 people and many thousands died afterward from fire and radiation poisoning. We must pray that such a thing never happens again. In a quiet room, light a blue candle for peace. Center by focusing on your breath and say this Metta Sutta from the Buddhists:

In safety and in bliss

May all creatures be of a blissful heart.

Let no one work another's undoing

Or even slight him at all anywhere;

And never let them wish another ill

Through provocation or resentful thought.

And just as might a mother with her life

Protect the son that was her only child,

So let him then for every living thing

Maintain unbounded consciousness in being

Above, below, and all 'round in between,

Untroubled, with no enemy or foe.

Let him resolve upon this mindfulness.

This is Divine Abiding here, they say.

Lily Gardner

Notes:

to gaze until you feel the strength of your allure. Go forth and be fabulous!

Gail Wood

Notes:

August 7
Saturday

4th ♋

Color of the day: Brown
Incense of the day: Ivy

An Alluring, Exotic Spell

Today is the birthday of Mata Hari (1876–1917), a sensational, notorious, and exotic woman executed for spying during World War I. All of us want to be beautiful, alluring, and mysterious sometimes. For a spell to bring forth your inner exotic nature, collect a length of sheer fabric, like chiffon, in your favorite color, glitter, a mirror, catnip for beauty, and a silver candle. In a darkened room, place the glitter and catnip in the candleholder and then light the candle. Sprinkle your chiffon veil with catnip and glitter. Hold the mirror and soften your eyes. Gaze into the mirror and call forth your alluring self. When your beautiful self is present, put the veil on and breathe in the mysterious wonder of your marvelous, exotic self. Continue

August 8
Sunday

4th ♋
☽ → ♌ 7:23 pm

Color of the day: Gold
Incense of the day: Frankincense

Summon the Sandman

They say that sleep is the brother of death. If you have problems falling asleep, staying asleep, or feeling rested after having awoken, try the following: Procure a number of dried poppy pods. Place these in a vase by your bed or hang them upside down from the ceiling above where your head rests. The energy of poppy helps invoke dreamtime energies. Taking the poppies and a tea mixture, say the following incantation:

I summon thee, Sandman.
I summon thee, Sandman.
I summon thee, Sandman!
Hear my calls, oh Lord of

Slumber. I am experiencing difficulty within your world of dreams and rejuvenation, and ask for your assistance. Please bless me with the ability to fall asleep and stay asleep easily, and only when desired. I love and respect the realms of sleep and dreaming, and humbly ask to be taken there when I desire. Thank you, Sandman, oh Lord of Sleep. Blessed be. Shhhh.

Finish by taking one of the dried poppy pods and leaving it outside (ideally on a quiet, undisturbed piece of land) as an offering to the Sandman.

Raven Digitalis

Notes:

August 9
Monday

4th ♌
New Moon 11:08 pm

Color of the day: White
Incense of the day: Neroli

The Bat and Path

The nighttime is darkest at the New Moon; similarly, when we experience new beginnings in our lives, we may have trouble seeing ahead to the future. The bat is an excellent animal to call on during the New Moon; even when visibility is low, bat uses echolocation as an alternative. Bat's emergence from a cave or other shelter every evening also parallels the motif of death and rebirth, and therefore new beginnings. As such, Bat is a great guide to help you find different perspectives on recent changes in your life.

If you have someplace safe near you where bats fly at night, you may wish to contact Bat there. Do be aware that in some areas bats are common carriers of rabies; do not touch any bat you may find on the ground or elsewhere, even if it looks healthy. Otherwise, any place where you can see the night sky will work. Call Bat to guide you:

> It's dark! And I can't see
> The way that lies before me.
> Bat, you are loved well by the
> night

*Help me find the way that's
right!*

You may then ask Bat for advice about specific situations, and inspiration to find creative solutions to your problems.

Lupa

Notes:

your beads and cord. String the beads with the intention of deepening your devotion. Bless the completed rosary with your breath and present to the four sacred directions. Hold it before you and allow the gods to cast their blessings. Use your newly created rosary as a meditation tool that helps you focus on your magical connections. Allow the rosary to be a simple reminder of what you hold sacred in the world.

Abel R. Gomez

Notes:

August 10
Tuesday

 1st ♌
☽ → ♍ 7:01 pm

Color of the day: Black
Incense of the day: Ylang-ylang

Pagan Rosary

Rosaries are deeply useful and practical tools for spiritual devotion and alignment with the elements, spirit totems, guides, and the gods you work with. Create your own personalized rosary today. It can be any size or style you desire. Do you want a necklace, or something you can wear around your wrist? Take a trip to the craft store and pick out beads that remind you of the element, spirit allies, and gods you connect with. Cast a circle and bless

August 11
Wednesday
Ramadan begins

1st ♍

Color of the day: Topaz
Incense of the day: Bay laurel

Charity Begins here

Today begins Ramadan, the most blessed month in the Islamic calendar, observed by fasting and acts of charity. Charity in Pagan life helps us remember that we are all part of the universal energy of giving and receiving. For a spell to help us express our charity, gather a small box, green ribbon, pieces of paper, and a large bowl. On the paper, write all things for which you are grateful and place them in the box. Tie the box with the green ribbon, knotting it three times. With each knot, give thanks for the bounty in your life. Place it in the bowl. Place the bowl on your altar or a shelf where you can't see the contents. At each New Moon for a year, put a percentage of the cash in your wallet in the bowl. At the end of the year, donate the money to a charity of your choice.

Gail Wood

Notes:

bringing in the harvest. To honor the Dog Star, find a quiet place for clear stargazing and call out to the light of this neighboring solar system. Its two suns (one equal in size to our own Sun and blue, the other twice as large as our own and white) unite as one from our earthly vantage. With arms extended, voice your presence to Sirius; encompass images and symbols of the things that you are harvesting for the fall and allow the light of the Dog Star to filter through you; feel it preparing you for winter and the changes to come!

Estha McNevin

Notes:

August 12
Thursday

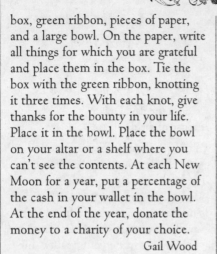

1st ♍
☽ → ♎ 6:43 pm

Color of the day: Green
Incense of the day: Carnation

Wish Upon the Dog Star

As the last days of summer draw the heat and sap of the season to the surface, the Dog Star hangs in the sky. One of the brightest stars of the night sky, our ancestors saw Sirius as a sign of the hunt and of

August 13
Friday

1st ♎

Color of the day: Pink
Incense of the day: Rose

A Lucky Spell

It's Friday the thirteenth! A good-luck day for magical people everywhere, this is traditionally a powerful day for witchery. Today is Freya's day and as the number 13 is a magical number, this is a perfect time to work with the Norse mistress of mystery and magic. Cats were sacred to Freya, so if you are owned by a feline, add a few loose strands of cat hair to this candle spell. (Check their brush or your furniture for the loose cat hair.) Pick out a votive candle and put it inside of a votive cup, then add the loose hairs on top. Lastly, light the candle and repeat this spell.

> Freya, Fridays are your
> sacred day,
>
> Lend your magic to mine, as
> I pray.
>
> By cat magic and candlelight
> I work this spell,
>
> For good luck, joy, and
> success, may it turn out well.

Ellen Dugan

Notes:

August 14
Saturday

 1st ♎

☽ → ♏ 8:26 pm

Color of the day: Gray
Incense of the day: Sage

Let Your Beauty Shine

While not everyone can win a beauty contest (the first one was held on this day in 1908), there is no one who isn't beautiful in some way. Today, empower an amulet that will help you bring your beauty shining to the surface. Set up your altar with jasmine incense for the beauty of the Moon, a golden candle for the Sun, lovely flowers for the earth, and water in a crystal bowl for the sea. Select a piece of jewelry you think is beautiful, and lay it on a hand mirror on your altar. Cast your circle, and invoke the elements and deities by speaking them fair. Hold your hands over the amulet, directing power into it, and chant:

> Charms that I have, come
> forth and show,
>
> Let all who see, my beauty
> know.

Put on the jewelry, take up the mirror, and see how beautiful you are!

Castiel

Notes:

August 15
Sunday

1st ♏

Color of the day: Yellow
Incense of the day: Juniper

World Reiki Day

Today is World Day of Reiki. Reiki is an ancient Japanese technique of energy healing made public by Dr. Mikao Usui. A form of "laying on hands," it entails the Reiki master channeling universal energy into the recipient. It promotes health and soothes many ailments. Reiki is taught in three levels. The master attunes new students using ancient symbols and sounds, enabling them to channel this life force. You can do Reiki for yourself, other people, animals, or even plants. Consider taking a Reiki course or getting a Reiki treatment from an experienced practitioner. Here is a basic exercise in energy work: Sit comfortably and calm your mind. Cup your hands together as if holding a ball. Imagine a sphere of energy forming between your hands. Concentrate on making it stronger and brighter. You may feel a warmth or tingling as it builds. Finally, release the power into the ground.

Elizabeth Barrette

Notes:

August 16
Monday

1st ♏
2nd Quarter 2:14 pm

Color of the day: Silver
Incense of the day: Lily

Spicy Chickpea Soup for health

The famous healer, Saint Roch, braved the bubonic plague to help those in need. He is celebrated in rural Italy today with a festival featuring spicy chickpea soup. Light a new green candle and make this soup for good health:

1 package dried chickpeas, soaked overnight, rinsed and drained
2 diced carrots
1 medium onion, diced
1 clove garlic, minced
1 tsp. grated ginger root
¼ cup chopped cilantro
1 tsp. garam masala
2 cups chicken broth
1 can coconut milk
¼ cup apple juice
Salt and pepper

Bring chickpeas to a boil in a large pot of salted water. Boil hard for 10 minutes and drain. Sauté carrots, onion, and garlic until soft. Add ginger and seasonings. Combine chickpeas and sautéed vegetables in a food processor or blender and puree. Combine pureed vegetables

with chicken broth and bring to a boil. Cover and simmer 35 minutes. Add coconut milk and apple juice, then heat through. Salt and pepper to taste.

Lily Gardner

Notes:

you need fuel: in your heart for emotions, in your head for thoughts, or in your core to fuel you physically. Say:

> I am brilliant, golden, and bright,
>
> My mind, body, and spirit are light.

As the days shorten and cool, return in meditation to this stored light, using it to warm and fuel you. Sunlight also helps the body create much-needed vitamin D.

Dallas Jennifer Cobb

Notes:

August 17
Tuesday

 2nd ♏

☽ → ♐ 1:34 am

Color of the day: Gray
Incense of the day: Ginger

harvest the Sun

Tuesday, ruled by Mars, is characterized by heat and metal. Now is the time to harvest the Sun's energy. Lay sacred metal objects and jewelry in a sunny spot to charge and collect energy. Or do some reverential sunbathing, storing the radiant energy within. Enjoy the sunlight before 11 am or after 3 pm to avoid the most harmful UV rays. In a safe space, lay as fully exposed as you can. Breathe and envision the Sun's energy seeping into your skin. Draw it, and store it as a golden orb where

August 18
Wednesday

 2nd ♐

Color of the day: Brown
Incense of the day: Lilac

Weather Magic

It's late summer. The weather is hot and still. In many areas, this time of the year can bring withering droughts. The harvest is ripening, but not yet complete. Some crops still need water to finish developing their seeds or fruit. A bad drought can diminish the harvest. Weather magic requires careful thought and a steady touch. First you should study the basics of weather science to understand how the mundane processes work. Observe weather in your area to see how it normally behaves. A good beginner's exercise in this field is to summon a storm to your location when conditions call for "scattered showers." Stand outside and chant:

> Storm call
> Cloud come
> Rain fall
> Earth drum

Raise your hands on "storm call" and lower them on "rain fall." Let the chant speed up as the energy builds. Finally, fling the energy skyward and let it go. Ground any remaining energy.

Elizabeth Barrette

Notes:

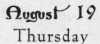

August 19
Thursday

2nd ♐

☽ → ♑ 10:17 am

Color of the day: Purple
Incense of the day: Clove

Vinalia (Roman)

Today is one of the two dates that the Romans celebrated Vinalia—the dedication of libations to Jupiter. In honor of Vinalia, find a way to enjoy your favorite wine or fruit juice. Share with friends, and pour some on the ground as an offering to the deity of your choice. A toast can be a kind of spell—be aware of your intent and then drink to it. Here's one you can try, since drinking to good health is a popular toast:

> Health, wealth, happiness,
> May this drink be blessed—
> Peace, love, good fortune's
>   kiss,
> May our lives be blessed.

This can be done to ask for a good harvest in the fall if you grow, or if you make your own wine or juice, why not start a batch today? Raise a glass and make a toast. As they say in Italian, *salute!*

Ember

Notes:

August 20
Friday

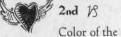

2nd ⅋

Color of the day: Coral
Incense of the day: Thyme

Love Your Furkids

I have six cats. Most Pagans have furkids of some kind or another. You should know the name of the protector of your furkids. With me, it is most definitely Bast. Be sure your pets see the vet regularly because the best medicine is prevention. If they are outdoor pets, make sure they have their rabies shots. Check for fleas regularly and use a flea product to keep those nasty little bugs off your pet and out of your house. Be sure to have your outside pet spayed or neutered. And most of all, take care of your pets. Fresh water daily, feed them a balanced diet and remember that junk food affects them much in the same way junk food affects us. Take good care of your furkids and the gods and goddesses will smile on their continued good health.

Boudica

Notes:

August 21
Saturday

2nd ⅋

☽ → ♒ 9:37 pm

Color of the day: Indigo
Incense of the day: Patchouli

Natural Growing Pains

August is a time of transition for many animals born in the spring. Short-lived insects will most likely not survive (or even get to) the coming winter. Other young animals are in the process of preparing for when they'll be turned out on their own. For many species this is a crucial time of learning and developing important skills. Humans go through growing pains, too; if spring is the time of new beginnings, autumn often heralds growth—but not necessarily without trouble. This is a good time to study up on techniques and information you'll need to get through tough times. Even if you aren't facing any pressing issues right now, you very well may in the future. Young animals are good teachers; research what those in your area are learning to prepare for the months ahead, and see if these lessons can help you.

Lupa

Notes:

August 22
Sunday

 2nd ♒

Color of the day: Amber
Incense of the day: Heliotrope

Pepper Protection Spell

Cast a spell today to surround yourself with protective energy or to protect someone you love. You'll need a piece of paper, some black pepper, and a black pen. In your ritual area, create a sacred space by welcoming the presence of the elements and the gods. Begin the spell by writing the name of the person who needs protection in the center of the paper. Draw five circles around the person's name. Take the pepper and sprinkle it over the circles and say something like:

> Surrounded by protection,
> Surrounded by love,
> (name) is protected
> below as above.
> So mote it be.

As you speak these words, visualize the person named surrounded by protective circles. Place it on your altar for a Moon cycle. After twenty-eight days, release it back to nature by burning it or burying it in the earth.

Abel R. Gomez

Notes:

August 23
Monday

 2nd ♒

☉ → ♍ 1:27 am

Color of the day: Ivory
Incense of the day: Narcissus

Remember the Slave Trade

Today is the International Day for the Remembrance of the Slave Trade and its Abolition. It's a long title, yes, and its meaning is just as big. We are all at least somewhat familiar with the American slave trade. Today, take a good amount of time to research the slave trade. Use the Internet, encyclopedias, history books, or talk to people who are very informed about its history. You will begin to feel—and strongly feel—the energy of injustice rise within you. How could such cruelty and evil be inflicted by one group of people to another group? As you feel this anger, also feel sorrow and compassion for those brutalized and enslaved during that dark period of American history. On the candle, inscribe the word "FREEDOM" on the wax in capital letters. Ignite it, saying:

> I light this candle to commemorate all those mistreated in the slave trade.
> Oh, Mighty Ancestors who suffered at the hands of cruelty and evil, be free! Be free! Be free! Gone forever

*injustice shall be, and in a
state of Unity the Earth shall
become. I thank you for your
sacrifices for the human race.
You are never forgotten, and
are forever free.*

Raven Digitalis

Notes:

us, plow our fields, and pull our
loads changed history. Even today,
we reckon the power of an engine in
horsepower. When someone is off on
a trip, bless and present them with a
picture of small figurine of a horse,
and bid them keep it with them as
they travel. As you say good-bye, or
head out yourself, envision a herd of
horses running on ahead, ensuring
both security and excitement.

Castiel

Notes:

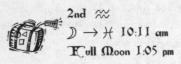

August 24
Tuesday

2nd ♒︎
☽ → ♓︎ 10:11 am
Full Moon 1:05 pm

Color of the day: Red
Incense of the day: Cinnamon

horse-Powered Travel Spell

It's one of the last weeks of summer, and many will be returning
from vacations, heading off to college,
or off seeking one last summer adven-
ture. To protect your own favorite
travelers, including yourself, call
upon the power of the horse. Many
cultures, not the least of which are
the ancient Celts and the American
Indians of the Plains, revered the
horse as an animal of power, whose
willingness to convey us, fight with

August 25
Wednesday

 3rd ♓︎

Color of the day: Yellow
Incense of the day: Lavender

Opiconsivia (Roman)

Today is one of the days Romans
honored the goddess Ops, Earth
Mother (the other day is Opalia,
December 19). Ops came to be associated with abundance and prosperity.
She made vegetation grow, and was
sometimes invoked by sitting and
placing hands on the ground. This is
an appropriate day to celebrate our

Page 168

connection to the Earth and to be mindful of the natural world. Find a way to get outside if you can; if not, sit on the floor. Visualize yourself connecting with the Earth. Imagine your fingers reaching down, touching the roots of trees and plants. Feel the connection. Honor Mother Earth today by purchasing some locally grown or organic produce and preparing a special meal—or set up a birdfeeder in your yard. Think of other ways you can care for Mother Earth and show appreciation for nature.

Ember

Notes:

piece you pull from the loaf chant:

> *The fallen Sun will rise again; from his flesh does life begin.*

See yourself as part of the life cycle for the animals in the park and contemplate all the elements that came together to create the moment. As you observe and interact with nature, feel the rhythm of life as it flows freely from your selfless exchange; try to draw inspiration from this moment or repeat this offering anytime you are feeling removed from nature. Giving freely to nature is a liberating way to slow down and take stock of the amazing world around us!

Estha McNevin

Notes:

August 26
Thursday

3rd ♓
☽ → ♈ 10:49 pm

Color of the day: White
Incense of the day: Jasmine

Bread and Bones

Make or purchase a loaf of bread from a baker and visit a body of water where birds or other animals are present. Feed the entire loaf to the animals in the park and with each

August 27
Friday

3rd ♈

Color of the day: Purple
Incense of the day: Vanilla

Rose Love Spell

Gather two roses, a bowl, some spring water, two small pink candles with candleholders, a piece of

paper, red ink, and two tablespoons rosemary. Charge the roses with love, then the candles, spring water, and rosemary. Light the candles. Make sure there are no fire hazards such as wind blowing in through the window. Sprinkle rosemary around the base of the candleholders clockwise. Fill the bowl with spring water and place the roses in it. Sprinkle rosemary around the bowl clockwise. Write your magical need on paper with ink. Be specific about what you want. When ready, place the paper beneath the bowl and recite:

> I want love,
> As a pair like the roses in
> the bowl,
> I draw love from above,
> My partner will I soon
> behold!

Visualize your wish being fulfilled and that you are happily sharing life with a suitable partner. Let the candles burn down.

S. Y. Zenith

Notes:

August 28
Saturday

3rd ♈

Color of the day: Black
Incense of the day: Sage

Basil Harvest Ritual

Basil is one of the most magical and purifying of all herbs. To the Orthodox Christians, basil is among the holiest of plants. A sunny morning in late August is the perfect time to harvest basil. As you cut the basil, say a silent thank you to Mother Earth for sharing this gift with you. As a symbol of gratitude, leave a few stems uncut. When done, rinse the basil in cool water and let it drain. In simple ritual, place one sprig of basil on your altar as an offering to the Goddess and God. Tie the rest of the basil in small bunches to dry. Chop a few of the fresh leaves and toss with sliced tomato and feta cheese. Dress with olive oil and red wine vinegar. Eat slowly; enjoy, and savor the taste of this magical herb.

James Kambos

Notes:

August 29
Sunday

 3rd ♈
☽ → ♉ 10:35 am

Color of the day: Orange
Incense of the day: Almond

Three of Cups

In France on this day the wine-growers gather to celebrate the grape harvest. It is a festival of sharing in the abundance Mother Earth has to offer. Summer is waning and the crops are fruitful. To show your appreciation for the simple joy of today, place the Three of Cups from your tarot deck or perhaps a bundle of fresh grapes on your altar. Spontaneously invite a few friends over to share a nice glass of wine or white grape juice. If the mood is fitting gather together joining hands. Begin to weave like the grapevine in a spiral dance creating a sense of communion. Then raise your glass in a salute to joy and simply say:

> To you our Mother
> Each other
> Sister, brother
> May our hearts be open
> To laughter and loving
> Sharing our blessings
> Saluting our becoming
> Full of life's riches
> Salute!

Igraine

Notes:

August 30
Monday

 3rd ♉

Color of the day: Lavender
Incense of the day: Clary sage

Sweet Dreams

Monday has the astrological influence of the Moon. Since we are in a waning Moon phase, let's conjure up a good night's sleep. This spell calls on Selene, the Greco-Roman goddess of the Moon. A much-loved deity of Witches, Selene brings no-nonsense solutions to magical and mundane problems. To start this spell, brew a cup of chamomile tea. As it steeps, enchant it to help you to sleep easily and peacefully. Hold the mug or teacup in your hands and focus your intent on the tea. Then repeat the verse.

> Lady Selene, goddess of the Moon,
>
> Now hear my call and grant me a boon.

*Enchant this tea, may it
bring rest and sweet dreams,*

*A good night's sleep, sent
from you, on a moonbeam.*

*By an August waning
Moon's light,*

*May this spell turn out just
right!*

Now drink your tea and sweet
dreams!

Ellen Dugan

Notes:

*I greet the East,
the Sun will rise,
the power of air,
the breath of skies;*

*I greet the South,
warm and bright,
the power of fire,
to pierce the night;*

*I greet the West,
rain and sea,
the power of water,
to comfort me;*

*I greet the North,
tree and stone,
the power of earth,
I'm not alone.*

Ember

Notes:

August 31
Tuesday

 3rd ♉
☽ → ♊ 8:19 pm

Color of the day: White
Incense of the day: Basil

Invoke the Elements

This can be used and repeated
during circle casting to invoke
the elements, or simply as a way
to meditate on their properties.
Although this begins with east, it can
be changed since some traditions pre-
fer to begin with north.

September is the ninth month of the year. Its name is derived from the Latin word *septum*, which means "seventh," as it was the seventh month of the Roman calendar. Its astrological sign is Virgo, the Maiden (August 23–September 23), a mutable-earth sign ruled by Mercury. This is the month autumn begins. Change is in the air—first noticed by the slanting angle of sunlight. We return now to a time of balance, the equinox, when day and night are equal in length. The days will soon begin to get noticeably shorter and, by the end of the month, temperatures start to cool. Chrysanthemums in every color begin blooming in neighborhoods and fall colors just begin to hint at their arrival. At the Fall Equinox, also called Mabon, we celebrate the second harvest as we enter the dark half of the year. Decorate your home and altar with clusters of grapes, apples, pumpkins, and acorns. Wine and cider are in season now and birds and butterflies begin to migrate. Woodland creatures begin storing food and preparing their nests for the winter—look for squirrels and chipmunks hiding nuts and seeds. Watch for monarch butterflies as they embark on their long journey south. The magnificent Harvest Moon is the Full Moon of September.

September 1
Wednesday

 3rd ♊
4th Quarter 1:22 pm

Color of the day: Brown
Incense of the day: Bay laurel

The Breath of Fall Tea

To drink in the best aspects of autumn, combine the following:

1 T. cinnamon
1 tsp. clove
1 tsp. dill
½ tsp. basil
Peel from 1 orange finely diced
1 cup oolong tea

This tea needs a lot of room to steep so it's best brewed loose in a mug or in a large tea ball. Charge the mixture with the following blessing nine times:

> Here I command the warmth
> of all life; the light within
> me; the Sun's supreme might.
> Quicken the pulse, as the
> season is undone. Cradle the
> sweet seeds of lust just begun.
> Foster our hopes as they stir
> in the womb; harbor the
> breath of life, beneath earth's
> silken tomb. Awaken within
> me the embers of might; the
> pulsing beacon of will and of
> sight. For here I imbue the
> glimmering fragments of fate,

> which expand to eternity and
> guide me through the gate.

Estha McNevin

Notes:

Holiday lore: Many Greeks consider this their New Year's Day. This day marks the beginning of the sowing season, a time of promise and hope. On this day, people fashion wreaths of pomegranates, quinces, grapes, and garlic bulbs—all traditional symbols of abundance. Just before dawn on September 1, children submerge the wreaths in the ocean waters for luck. They carry seawater and pebbles home with them in small jars to serve as protection in the coming year. Tradition calls for them to gather exactly forty pebbles and water from exactly forty waves.

September 2
Thursday

 4th ♊

Color of the day: Purple
Incense of the day: Apricot

Whisk Away Financial Woes

Thursday's are perfect for prosperity spells, but as we are in a waning Moon, this is actually a good time to banish any financial problems you may be having. This spell calls on Jupiter and Jove, the old gods associated with this day of the week. Go outside and find an oak tree, which is sacred to them. Select a perfect oak leaf. Then hold the leaf in your hands and repeat the spell.

> By Jupiter and Jove, I banish
> poverty,
> In its place, I now call for
> prosperity!
> The oak leaf is a natural
> symbol and sign,
> That my fortune will increase
> come rain or shine.
> For the good of all, with
> harm to none,
> By Thursday's magic, it will
> be done.

Keep the oak leaf as a token of your spell. Carry it with you until the Moon becomes full again. Then return the leaf to nature.

Ellen Dugan

Notes:

September 3
Friday

4th ♊
☽ → ♋ 2:50 am

Color of the day: White
Incense of the day: Rose

Clear Your Path to Love

Friday is a day to attract love, although the waning Moon does not make this Friday ideal. But you can always interpret a Moon phase to your advantage—instead of calling for love today, try banishing obstacles to love. Think about the things that stand in the way of having a good relationship. Are you shy? Does your lifestyle allow you to meet new people? Are you still fixated on a love that was never meant to be? Write these obstacles down on a piece of paper, roll it up, and tie it with black thread. Light a red candle, and have a cauldron or fireproof dish handy. Light the paper in the candle, and drop it into the dish to burn, chanting:

> Obstacles to love, I banish
> thee; by my will, so mote it be!

Finally, light some rose incense to seal the spell with love's promise.

Castiel

Notes:

September 4
Saturday

4th ♋

Color of the day: Blue
Incense of the day: Sandalwood

A Subconscious Writing Spell

Perform a divinatory spell using your creative and artistic talents—or lack thereof! Begin by thinking of something you wish to gain insight on. Next, pick up a piece of paper and a writing instrument. Put yourself in a meditative state of consciousness and shift your mind's focus to only the question at hand. Clear your mind of other thoughts to allow your higher, subconscious mind to deliver messages during the exercise. When you feel that your mind has sufficiently shifted into a meditative and highly focused state, begin drawing. Sketch any symbols, patterns, words, or shapes that come to mind. Don't worry about it making

sense. You must shut off your rational mind for this exercise, allowing yourself to completely immerse in the power of intuition. Take as long as you like. When finished, return to "normal," or grounded, consciousness and try to interpret what you've just drawn. This "automatic writing" of sorts should be able to be interpreted symbolically, and will help shed insight on the question at hand. Experiment with this regularly to further hone your abilities and uncover your natural skill of divination.

Raven Digitalis

Notes:

September 5
Sunday

4th ♋
☽ → ♌ 5:45 am

Color of the day: Amber
Incense of the day: Frankincense

Honoring Jupiter

Now through September 19 the ancient Romans honored Jupiter, the greatest of their great gods. This is the time to ask Jupiter to help make a wish come true. This is the one time to ask for something big because Jupiter, the father of the gods and the Supreme Roman deity, usually responds in a big way. Cover your altar with royal blue fabric, and decorate with flowers of the season in colors associated with him such as purple asters and yellow mums. In a dish, place symbols sacred to him—an oak leaf and a pinch each of nutmeg and clove. Ask if he will honor you with his presence, then announce your wish to him. Meditate on your request. In a gesture of gratitude, leave the oak leaf and spices at the base of an oak tree.

James Kambos

Notes:

September 6
Monday
Labor Day

4th ♌

Color of the day: Silver
Incense of the day: Rosemary

Offering to the Land Spirits
In shamanic cosmology, the world is an interconnected interplay of spirit beings. All things that exist have a spirit. Begin to get to know

the spirits around you by giving an offering to the spirits of your land. Traditional offerings include fruits, cakes, cookies, or juices. If you have a ritual space outside near your home, give an offering there. If not, use your intuition and find a place outdoors that calls to you. The base of a tree is one idea. Breathe deeply and bow before the spirits of the land. Speak to them. Give them your offerings. Say something like:

> Spirits of this land,
> Guardians of this place,
> Accept these offerings.
> May our partnership grow
> With gratitude and love.

Invite these spirits to your ceremonies and spells. Allow them to teach you the magic of the land. Return to this place once a month and refresh the offerings.

Abel R. Gomez

Notes:

September 7
Tuesday

 4th ♌
♌ → ♍ 5:53 am

Color of the day: Gray
Incense of the day: Cedar

harvest Basket Spell

Find a large basket or cornucopia and fill it with a variety of fresh fruits and vegetables. As you wash and prepare them for your basket, imagine the life cycle of the bounty before you. Think of the brave farmers who work the land, and the pickers, packers, and produce clerks who have helped this food make its way to you. Strive to appreciate this cycle and imbue your basket with honor and gratitude. When you entertain visitors at your home or prepare meals for family and friends, use the fruits and vegetables from your harvest basket to help share your wealth with those around you. Let this spell remind you of the true bounty of generosity.

Estha McNevin

Notes:

September 8
Wednesday

 4th ♍
New Moon 6:30 am

Color of the day: Yellow
Incense of the day: Lavender

Embrace Your Inner Student

September is upon us, and around the world people of all ages are headed to a new school year, from grade school to grad school. As the weather cools, we tend to stay indoors more, which makes this a good time to concentrate on reading, studying, and other sedentary pursuits. Of course, we can still practice indoors, too! If you're like many Pagans, you have some subject or another that you've been meaning to look into more, but just haven't made the time. It may be something directly related to magic and spirituality or it may be an auxiliary topic such as history, mythology, or psychology, among others. Or you may have a new magical paradigm you want to try out. There might even be a deity or spirit who's been trying to get your attention. Any of these can be a suitable focus for the coming months; take today to start planning your studies. Make a list of what you've been meaning to get around to, then pick a topic and run with it. Hit the library and the Internet, and perhaps even find relevant groups online or in person. Make the most of your winter hibernation!

Lupa

Notes:

September 9
Thursday
Rosh hashanah

1st ♏

☽ → ♎ 5:01 am

Color of the day: Green
Incense of the day: Nutmeg

Japanese Chrysanthemum Festival

In honor of this annual event, do some magic involving this lovely flower. Mums have become symbolic with the season of autumn in the United States and are sold in stores and nurseries around this time. Find a bouquet of mums or purchase a potted plant. Use these color correspondences for mums—red for love, passion, and courage; orange for success; yellow for confidence; pink for friendship; purple for spirituality; and white for peace. Choose the color that suits your need and write your goal or purpose on a piece of paper. Cut one mum flower from your plant

or bouquet and wrap your paper around it. Say the following words:

> *Nine times nine,*
> *This need is mine.*
> *With harm to none,*
> *So it be done.*

Bury or burn the paper and flower.

Ember

Notes:

September 10
Friday
Ramadan ends

1st ♎

Color of the day: Pink
Incense of the day: Mint

Sew Be It

Today is the anniversary of the 1846 patent on the sewing machine and is celebrated as Sew Be It Day! Sacred to the goddess Athena, needle arts are a way to do subtle and powerful magic. Even the simplest act of repair can be strong magic. A basic basket of needles, pins, thread, and scissors can be found in almost every household. To bless your sewing tools, place them on your altar. Light a blue candle and use lavender incense. Call in the blessings of each element to the tools, the basket, and your sewing. Call in Athena and present your sewing tools to her for blessing. Then say:

> By spool and thread, my wishes are spread; with magic and pins, my magic begins. As I will it so mote it be with your blessings three times three.

Thank Athena and the elements.

Gail Wood

Notes:

there. We may know someone who worked in the recovery process. I have a friend who lost his son, a fire-fighter, in the collapse. Such bravery should not go unnoticed or unacknowledged. On this day, we join people everywhere in remembering those who were lost and those brave souls who worked to help to save what could be saved on that fateful day. We remember what was done and we pray to the gods that this will never happen to anyone ever again. We also pray that our governments realize why this happened, and work toward world peace. So mote it be.

Boudica

Notes:

September 11
Saturday

 1st ♎
☽ → ♏ 5:21 am

Color of the day: Gray
Incense of the day: Ivy

A Day of Remembrance

September 11, 2001, touched us all. For those of us who live in New York City, we probably know someone who was involved. We may have had a loved one or friend who was part of the disaster, who died

September 12
Sunday

1st ♏
Color of the day: Gold
Incense of the day: Juniper

Child Protection Spell

It's back to school, which may be both a relief and a worry for parents of school-age children. Of course, we need to talk to our children about safety issues, but what can we do magically? Gather a piece of red coral, amber, and malachite. Beads made from these stones would work perfectly. Light a white candle for fire and a stick of lavender incense for air. Use salt to represent earth and the element water should be contained in a shell. These representations of the elements are all used in protection magic. Pass the stones over or through each element as you ask the powers of the elements to bless and protect your child. Now carry the stones next to your skin for three days and three nights. Tuck the stones in a pocket of your child's backpack with instructions to carry it always for good luck.

Lily Gardner

Notes:

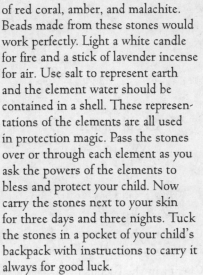

September 13
Monday

 1st ♏

☽ → ♐ 8:52 am

Color of the day: Lavender
Incense of the day: Clary sage

The Epulum Jovis Banquet

According to old Roman lore, today is the Epulum Jovis, a banquet day for a triad of deities: Juno, the protector of the Roman

State; Minerva, the goddess of war, wisdom, and arts; and Jupiter, the thunder god and warrior. On this day, a big celebratory meal was held in the wake of the summer battle season. Here is a mealtime prayer to honor this triad of deities and to celebrate all the blessings you have in your life.

> Under this enchanted September evening's waxing Moon,
>
> May Juno, Minerva, and Jupiter, now hear my tune.
>
> Please, bless my home and my family with your grace.
>
> May we always be happy, strong, healthy, and safe.
>
> By all the powers of three times three,
>
> As I will it, then so must it be.

Ellen Dugan

Notes:

September 14
Tuesday

 1st ♐

Color of the day: Red
Incense of the day: Ginger

The Sacred Chest of Rebirth

In ancient Greece this was the first day of rites involving initiation into the cult of Demeter and Persephone, known as the Eleusinian Mysteries. On this first day of ritual, sacred objects were brought from Athens to Eleusis, where the temple of Demeter stood at the base of the Acropolis. These arcane artifacts played a part in the secret rites that promised union between the initiate and the divine goddess. One of these mysterious articles was a *kiste* or "sacred chest" that contained objects symbolic of death and rebirth. No one knows for certain what these chests contained, but it is suggested that its contents might have included an egg, a phallus, a golden snake, and the seeds of a pomegranate. You can create your own sacred chest, mindful of the myth of Demeter and her daughter Persephone, who each winter descends into the underworld to live with her husband Hades and returns again each spring to join with her mother Demeter, symbolizing the annual cycle of death and rebirth.

Igraine

Notes:

September 15
Wednesday

1st ♐
2nd Quarter 1:50 am
☽ → ♑ 4:30 pm

Color of the day: Topaz
Incense of the day: Honeysuckle

Clarity in the Clouds

Nephomancy is divination by means of clouds. The shape and color of clouds can send subtle messages from the Universe. Go outside and observe the clouds for a hint of things to come. Here are a few sample interpretations for colors: **Red clouds**: passion and intense energy. **Purple clouds**: spirituality and connection with higher powers. **Gray clouds**: mixed messages or balance. **Black clouds**: storm coming, metaphysical or mundane. **White clouds**: all is well. **Silver clouds**: hope, wishes, or blessings. Here are some interpretations based on the shape of a cloud: **Bird**: air energy or flight. **Boat**: water energy or travel on water. **Car**: travel on land. **Crescent Moon**: magic. **Dog**: loyalty or friendship. **Fist**: conflict. **Heart**: love and romance. **Mare's tails**: freedom or speed. **Teardrop**: sorrow or regret. **Tree**: earth energy and grounding. **Triangle**: fire energy or transformation. **Waves**: forward motion, water energy, or cycles.

Elizabeth Barrette

Notes:

Holiday lore: Keirou no Hi, or Respect for the Aged Day, has been a national holiday in Japan since 1966. On this day, the Japanese show respect to elderly citizens, celebrate their longevity, and pray for their health. Although there are no traditional customs specifically associated with this day, cultural programs are usually held in various communities. Schoolchildren draw pictures or make handicraft gifts for their grandparents and elderly family friends or neighbors. Some groups visit retirement or nursing homes to present gifts to residents.

September 16
Thursday

 2nd ℣

Color of the day: Green
Incense of the day: Myrrh

Citrine Money Spell

Cleanse and consecrate seven citrine tumbled stones and one small citrine pyramid. Put them in a steel cashbox along with a hundred dollar bill and some gold and silver coins. Other notes of lesser denominations than a hundred can be used as well. On Thursday, when in a positive state of mind and wishing to draw money luck, take the cashbox to the altar. Light a yellow candle. Arrange citrine tumbled stones in a circle. Place the candle and pyramid in the center. On a piece of parchment paper, write your wish for financial abundance. Meditate and see in your mind's eye that money is flowing freely to you. When ready, light some incense, state your wish, and pray to Kuber, the Hindu god of wealth by reciting "Om Sri Kuberaye Namaha." Chant the mantra 18 times, 27, 54, or 108 times daily for thirty days or up to ninety days.

S. Y. Zenith

Notes:

September 17
Friday

2nd ♑

Color of the day: Purple
Incense of the day: Orchid

Energy Clearing Spell

Friday is ruled by Venus and was a traditional day for cleaning the home. Even if you don't have time to undertake a major house cleaning, take twenty minutes to transform it. Use Venus' influence to clear old energy in your home, opening it to harmony, prosperity, love, and friendship. Walk through your home and quickly clear the clutter, moving from room to room. As you leave each room, open the windows. Visually clear of clutter, feel the fresh air flow in and through your home. Now go to the front door, cast it open wide, and welcome Venus to enter:

> Venus now that the clutter
> is gone,
>
> I bade you enter into my
> home,
>
> Your harmony, love, and
> prosperity,
>
> Bless me, my home, and
> community.

Close the doors and windows in the opposite order, consciously containing the new, clear energy within the space.

Dallas Jennifer Cobb

Notes:

September 18
Saturday
Yom Kippur

2nd ♑
☽ → ♒ 3:35 am

Color of the day: Brown
Incense of the day: Rue

Reconcile Past Wrongs

Today is Yom Kippur, a traditional Jewish holiday meaning "Day of Atonement." At this time, Jews seek God's forgiveness for their sins; wrongs against other people are supposed to be repaired prior to this holiday. They also fast and refrain from doing any work. It is customary to wear white clothes, symbolizing purity. Paganism does not have a concept of "sin," but does offer behavioral guidelines. So today is a good time to consider your relationship to the gods and to other people. Have you broken any important rules? Have you harmed anyone (including yourself) during the past year? If so, what could you do to reconcile these wrongs? You may also want to perform some kind of purification ceremony. One good option is taking a bath with sea salt or other bath salts. Light some white candles in the bathroom and visualize all impurities washing away from you.

Elizabeth Barrette

Notes:

September 19
Sunday

 2nd ♒

Color of the day: Orange
Incense of the day: Eucalyptus

Feng Shui Magic

In the ancient art of feng shui, practitioners use a map or house system known as a Bagua to determine localities of influence around the living space. Using an astrological mandala as your Bagua, you can easily divide your dwelling into twelve specific areas that you can energize with the use of crystals, water, or personal objects. Visualize a horoscope chart and place it atop your living space, the front door or position of honor would be Capricorn. You would then follow the natural procession of the zodiac moving counterclockwise. Aquarius is next and this area immediately to the left of the front door would be the location of innovation. You might want to put your computer here. The Pisces area would be a great place for a meditation room or a place to practice yoga. Aries is next. This area would be very energized and so you might place an object here that you want to activate or bring to life. Place a green gemstone in the next section, Taurus, to encourage the flow of money. Next up is Gemini. Energize this area when you need to study or it could be a place where you socialize. The back of the house is where the hearth is and this is the domain of Cancer. This is the best place for your kitchen. The Leo area might be a game room; for Virgo, a workspace; Libra for coupling, along with Scorpio for sex. Sagittarius might reflect symbols of faith. You could set up an altar here to the right of the front door. This is a fun and easy way to play with feng shui.

Igraine

Notes:

September 20
Monday

2nd ♒

☽ → ♓ 4:15 pm

Color of the day: White
Incense of the day: Lily

Offering to Time

Time has assumed semidivine status, even in our seemingly secular society. We make sacrifices to time. When we're not careful, we become victims of time. Most people probably wish they had more control over time. Give an offering to Time today to become an ally. Call upon Maa Kali, whose name means "Time" and who dances the cycles of all things into existence. Go to a crossroads in the dark of night and offer three red flowers, preferably a hibiscus, or three drops of your blood. As you do, say something like:

> Great Mother Kali,
>
> You who hold the secret power of Time,
>
> Please accept this offering.
>
> May I gain a deeper knowledge of your mysteries,
>
> May I become an ally to time, and not a victim,
>
> Hail, sweet mother.
>
> Jai Maa.

Take a breath and bow to her, allowing your forehead to touch the ground. It is done.

Abel R. Gomez

Notes:

September 21
Tuesday

2nd ♓

Color of the day: White
Incense of the day: Bayberry

Bless the Peace-Seekers

Happy International Day of Peace! Today, light a white candle in honor of Eirene, the Greek goddess of peace and one of the Horae, three deities who promoted order. Her Roman counterpart is Pax. Ask for Eirene's blessing upon those who seek to bring peace to the world, whether locally or globally, and ask how you may add your own efforts effectively and ethically:

> On this day, when war still rages,
>
> I dedicate my time to peaceful ages.

Where none need fear Ares'
blade,

Eirene, I ask you for your
aid.

You may also wish to honor St. Francis of Assisi. In addition to being the patron saint of animals, the famous "Prayer of St. Francis" attributed to him includes the line "where there is hatred, let me sow love." While some Pagans may feel residual animosity toward Christianity, peace begins with critiquing one's own prejudices.

Lupa

Notes:

September 22
Wednesday

Mabon – Fall Equinox

2nd ♓

☉ → ♎ 11:09 pm

Color of the day: Brown
Incense of the day: Lilac

Mabon Spell of Gratitude

Mabon, the Witches' version of Thanksgiving, is the second of the three harvest sabbats and a time to reflect on what blessings we've received. It's probably instinct to always want more in our lives: more money, more love, more friends, a better job, a fitter body, a house in the country. We rarely rest having realized one goal before we eagerly pursue the next. This striving makes for a full and rich life, but for real happiness, we must practice the art of gratitude. As Lao Tzu said:

Be content with what you
have;

Rejoice in the way things are.

When you realize there is
nothing lacking,

The whole world belongs to
you.

Begin this on Mabon and continue a practice of gratitude throughout the year. Every morning, light a stick of incense on your altar and take a few minutes to thank the Spirit for the multitude of blessings you enjoy each day.

Lily Gardner

Notes:

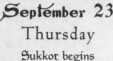

September 23
Thursday
Sukkot begins

2nd ♓
☽ → ♈ 4:47 am
Full Moon 5:17 am

Color of the day: Crimson
Incense of the day: Carnation

Boost Your Financial Bounty

September is Harvest Moon, celebrating the end of the harvest and gratitude for the bounty of nature. To bring a financial boon into your life, place a bowl of unsalted nuts that includes cashews, almonds, and pecans (no peanuts) on your altar. Underneath it, place some play money. Decorate your altar with the harvest color. Cast your circle, calling in the direction and the Harvest Mother. Thank her for all that you have harvested in this season. Commemorate with your voice the things that were well and plentiful and honor the things that did not flourish. Ask her for her blessings and ask her to increase your financial bounty. Raise energy by toning and send the energy into the universe for the blessings of abundant financial resources. Eat some of each nut and prepare a libation of nuts for the nature spirits and leave it outdoors. Say farewell to the Goddess, the directions, and take up your circle. Put the play money in your wallet to draw more money to you. Each day, eat some of the nuts, replenishing the bowl with more. Maintain this magic for as long as you need it or until the next Full Moon.

Gail Wood

Notes:

September 24
Friday

3rd ♈

Color of the day: White
Incense of the day: Yarrow

A Spell to Balance Energy

On this post–Full Moon day, the Sun is in Libra. One of Libra's characteristics is balance, so you can utilize this solar energy to weave your spell. Begin by taking two sheets of parchment paper and, with black ink, draw a large "plus" sign on one, and a large "minus" sign on the other. This represents the yin and the yang: the positive and negative currents of energy flowing through reality and upholding all of existence. This is the dualistic principle of reality (e.g., up/down, light/dark, god/goddess, etc.). Stand and position your legs together with your arms at your sides. Look to the heavens, close your eyes, and raise both arms at the elbows, cupping your hands. In each hand, hold one of the sheets of paper. This position represents the scales of Libra. Chant:

> *I summon thee, energy and spirits of Libra, oh great scales of balance! Hear my prayer. I invoke the power of absolute balance, and ask you to balance my mind, my heart, my body, and soul. Ever toward spiritual wholeness I grow, and forever shall I be balanced in life. This I ask, this I pray. So mote it be.*

Raven Digitalis

Notes:

September 25
Saturday

 3rd ♈
☽ → ♉ 4:17 pm

Color of the day: Black
Incense of the day: Pine

Letting Go Spell

The waning Moon supports culling, releasing, and letting go. We all face loss: a pet dies, a relationship changes, a job ends, or a cherished friend is gone. We also experience sadness as the seasons shift. Summer's gone, and with it the expansive, fertile energy of the Mother goddess. In autumn, the energy of the Crone is upon us—goddess of decay, death, and rebirth. Acknowledging death and decay opens you to the powerful energy of rebirth. Get a leaf that has fallen to the ground. Say:

> *I knew you maiden, young and shining,*
>
> *Saw you ripen, mother of all,*
>
> *Now you age and return to the earth,*
>
> *Nourishes as you compost,*
>
> *Matter of rebirth.*

As the leaf falls from your hand to the ground, know it will compost, producing matter to nourish and sustain spring's new life. Be at peace with the ancient cycle: Birth, life, death, rebirth.

Dallas Jennifer Cobb

Notes:

September 26
Sunday

3rd ♉

Color of the day: Yellow
Incense of the day: Marigold

A Time to Connect Spell

Where did summer go? Are the summers shorter than they used to be? Where I live, autumn is already creeping down the valley. Early morning mist lays heavy over the hills, the dogwood trees blaze with color, and chipmunks are filling their dens with grain. Time hasn't changed, we have. In our day-to-day rush to achieve success, we've lost track of time. The eternal rhythm of time hasn't stopped. The seasons still turn, the wild geese still own the sky as they fly south, and farmers still plant and harvest. This is the season for thinking about the eternal cycles and our place in the cosmos. Today, try to go without a clock or a cell phone. Do something you love. Connect with a friend and have a meaningful conversation. And tonight, connect with the most ancient clock of all—take a walk beneath the stars.

James Kambos

Notes:

September 27
Monday

3rd ♉

Color of the day: Gray
Incense of the day: Neroli

Quality Family Time

The kids are back in school and your spouse hasn't seen you in days; you are working, driving the kids to sports practice, possibly cooking, helping with homework, making sure the bills are paid and the garbage is taken out, and you need to stop for a second and touch base with your family. Yes, you are always with them, but how much are you talking? What are you sharing? When was the last time you actually sat down at the kitchen table and all ate together? Try to spend some quality time with everyone in your home, grabbing time whenever you can. It is not how much time you spend, it's what you spend it doing. Sit down together, watch a movie, laugh, make popcorn, start a pillow fight, or just relax a bit and kick off your shoes.

Boudica

Notes:

September 28
Tuesday

3rd ♉
☽ → ♊ 2:10 am

Color of the day: Scarlet
Incense of the day: Cinnamon

Banish Fear

We all have fears of various types. Today, identify one or more of your fears that you wish to banish. It could be public speaking or fear of spiders—anything that bothers you. Use a red or white votive candle and find a clear quartz point. Using the crystal point, carve your fear into the candle—in symbol or words. Light the candle and place the crystal near it. Study the candle flame for a while and visualize your fear melting with the wax. When the candle is burned down, your fear will be diminished as well. After the candle burns down, keep the crystal with you if you like, or place it on your altar or other special place where you can see it often—it will serve as a reminder of your courage.

Ember

Notes:

September 29
Wednesday
Sukkot ends

3rd ♊

Color of the day: White
Incense of the day: Marjoram

Motivation Ritual

The year wanes in earnest, and any projects for the year are wrapping up. It's easy, when you've spent a long time on a venture, to lose interest or want to give up. If that's the case, try this ritual for motivation: gather three white candles, and anoint one with rosemary oil, one with bergamot oil, and one with clary sage oil. Arrange the candles around a quartz crystal. Make a circle around the candles with yarrow, mint, sage, and a few acorns. Cast your circle and light the candles. Stare into the flames and say:

> By my own two hands,
> By flame, rain, wind, and the
>   power of the land,
> May my power and true
>   potential
> Rise up from within.
> May I seek to finish
> All that I begin.
> By the God, and Goddess
>   Sacred Three,
> And by my will so mote it be.

Castiel

Notes:

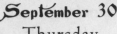

September 30
Thursday

3rd ♊

☽ → ♋ 9:46 am

4th Quarter 11:52 pm

Color of the day: Turquoise
Incense of the day: Jasmine

Coin Grass Money Spell

Also known as "ground ivy," coin grass is said to attract money to the bearer when used in spellwork. Cut out a square pouch from green cotton or flannel cloth. Place it on a clean table or on the altar. Anoint a green candle with cinquefoil or five finger grass oil. Cinquefoil bestows the "five lucks" of love, money, health, power, and wisdom. Set the candle in a candleholder and light it. Take some silver coins and dollar bills and insert them into the pouch with some coin grass. Tie the pouch. Pass it over the candle and touch it to your forehead, heart, knees, genitals, and feet. Hold it with both hands and speak your wish for financial luck so you can pay off some bills. Carry the pouch wherever you go. When the money eventually comes and if there is surplus, donate a portion to charity.

S. Y. Zenith

Notes:

October is the tenth month of the year. Its name is derived from the Latin word *octo* meaning "eight," as it was the eighth month of the Roman calendar. Its astrological sign is Libra, the Scales (September 23–October 23), a cardinal-air sign ruled by Venus. October is autumn's promise fulfilled. The resplendent colored leaves dazzle us in hues of gold, crimson, and orange, blazing throughout forests and neighborhoods. This is truly a magical month, with its climactic major holiday, Samhain (which means "summer's end") on the 31st. This is the last harvest festival of the year, the night when it's said the veil between the worlds is thin—a night to honor our ancestors and the souls of the departed. This night came to be called All Hallows Eve since the Christians named the next day All Saints' Day—this is the origin of the name Halloween. Decorations for this night abound on nearly every doorstep. Jack-o'-lanterns light the darkness and the crisp, cool air seems filled with enchantment. Leave an apple outside for wandering spirits and light a candle in the window to guide them on their journey. October's Full Moon is called the Blood Moon in honor of the sacrficed livestock that would feed families through the winter.

October 1
Friday

4th ♋

Color of the day: Pink
Incense of the day: Alder

To Rid Yourself of a Bad Habit

The October waning Moon is a great time to do a little house-keeping on your psyche. What habits would you love to be free of? It's always best to focus on one change at a time. Remember that most bad habits serve to comfort you, so think of a more positive way to comfort yourself. When you've decided what you want to work on, go outdoors and collect two fall leaves—one for the bad habit and one for the activity you will use to replace the bad habit. Write your bad habit on one leaf and your good replacement on another leaf. Go outdoors with your bad habit leaf. Let it fall away from you. When it has fallen to the ground, grind it beneath your heel. You're finished with it forever. Press the leaf of comfort in your Book of Shadows.

Lily Gardner

Notes:

Holiday lore: According to Shinto belief, during the month of October the gods gather to hold their annual convention. All of the *kami* converge on the great temple of Isumo in western Honshu, and there they relax, compare notes on crucial god business, and make decisions about humankind. At the end of this month, all over Japan, people make visits to their local Shinto shrines to welcome the regular resident gods back home. But until then, all through the month, the gods are missing—as a Japanese poet once wrote:

> The god is absent;
> the dead leaves are
>   piling up,
> and all is deserted.

October 2
Saturday

4th ♋

☽ → ♌ 2:21 pm

Color of the day: Blue
Incense of the day: Sage

Home Cleansing Spell

In a clean spray bottle, combine the following ingredients for a refreshing room mist: water, a pinch of salt, a few tablespoons of lemon juice, and several pinches of dried rosemary. Spray the mist throughout your home. Open windows if you wish to help dispel any negative energy.

> Cleanse this home,
> make it well,
> as I carry out this spell.
> Salt and herbs,
> clear the air,
> purify it everywhere.
> For good of all,
> and harm to none,
> as I will so it be done.

                                    Ember

Notes:

licorice-twist candy, and a pink paper cutout heart. Place the licorice twists on top of the paper heart and place it on your altar. Call in Venus. Place your hands over the licorice and the heart and tell Venus of your concerns and your desire for a return to honesty. Cut the licorice and cut through the dishonesty and eat it, saying:

> Dear Venus, I cannot do this
> unassisted, away from truth
> my love has twisted, bring
> back honesty and the truth;
> please give our love a fresh
> new youth.

                                    Gail Wood

Notes:

October 3
Sunday

 4th ♌

Color of the day: Gold
Incense of the day: Hyacinth

Revisit the First Blush of Love

Sometimes the truth in our love relationships can get twisted and finding our way back to honesty can be a challenge. A spell to augment real-world strategies can help if you are sure you can handle the truth. Decorate your altar in deference to Venus and include pink and red candles, rose quartz, and rose incense. Add a sharp knife, two pieces of

October 4
Monday

4th ♌
☽ → ♍ 4:00 pm

Color of the day: Ivory
Incense of the day: Hyssop

Invisible for a Day

Want to know how to cast a glamour for invisibility, or to have your actions go unnoticed? As long as your actions are honorable, this spell works out well. Therefore, if things are crazy at work or school and you need to lie low for a day to let things settle down, this is a fine spell to keep you "under the radar," as it were.

> Today I'll conjure a little
> personal magical fog,
>
> As I use the Moon's waning
> light to devise some
> camouflage.
>
> So my actions may go
> unnoticed for a short time,
>
> I seal this glamour up with
> the sound of a rhyme.
>
> My vow to harm none with
> this clever Witches' spell.
>
> This spell holds for just one
> day, and all will be well.

This spell will last twenty-four hours. No moping if you feel ignored! After all, you are trying to be invisible.

Ellen Dugan

Notes:

October 5
Tuesday

 4th ♏

Color of the day: Maroon
Incense of the day: Ginger

Take a Timeout

In 1582, when the Georgian calendar was implemented, this day did not exist. The ancient Celts, in order to balance their way of reckoning the year, had a day that was "time out of time." Even now, every four years, and every year that ends in "oo," we have a day that occurs at no other time, and keeps our calendar on track. It may be that, sometimes, everybody needs a little time out of time. Can you take a little time today to disappear, to retreat and hide away? Even if you slip out for just an hour, or turn off the phone and lock the door, enter that time with the intent to be without attachment, obligation, or meaning. Try burning a black candle to invoke the peace of the void. When you return, observe how your time out of time helped you to feel refreshed and reset.

Castiel

Notes:

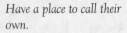

October 6
Wednesday

 4th ♏
☽ → ♎ 3:52 pm

Color of the day: Yellow
Incense of the day: Marjoram

World habitat Day

This is World Habitat Day.
Consider the state of human
habitat—urban, suburban, and
rural—as well as wildlife habitat. Do
people in your area have adequate
shelter? Do animals have space to live
too? What areas allow humans and
wildlife to share the space safely?
Take responsibility for helping
maintain the habitat in your area.
You might volunteer at Habitat for
Humanity or in a city park. If you
have a yard, offer suitable food, water,
and nesting sites for wildlife. Include
a statue of any deity associated with
plants or animals. Here is a prayer
for habitat:

> May all the green-growing
> ones
>
> Have earth and sunlight and
> water.
>
> May all the running and
> crawling ones
>
> Have food to eat and nests
> to sleep.
>
> May all the two-legged ones

> Have a place to call their
> own.
>
> May we all live in harmony,
>
> And learn to share the Earth.
>
> Elizabeth Barrette

Notes:

October 7
Thursday

 4th ♎
New Moon 2:45 pm

Color of the day: Purple
Incense of the day: Jasmine

Prayers to Ganesha

One of the cornerstone practices
of Hinduism is the repetition
of mantras, Sanskrit prayers. It is
believed that the consistency of the
repetition allows the true power of
the mantra to unfold. Typically a
mantra is chanted 108 times over a
forty-day period to allow the magic to
manifest in one's life. It's almost like
repeating a spell over and over again,
allowing its energy to build. Start a
practice of chanting to Ganesha today.
Ganesha is the elephant-headed god
of the Hindu tradition that removes

obstacles, grants protection, and bestows blessings. His mantra is "Om Ganapatayea Namaha." *Om* is the vibration of the universe, containing all potentials and possibilities. *Ganapatayea* is another name for Ganesha. *Namaha* literally means, "I bow to you." When we chant this prayer, we surrender to the God and Goddess and allow for the obstacles blocking our path to be removed. May your day be blessed.

Abel R. Gomez

Notes:

October 8
Friday

 1st ♎
☽ → ♏ 3:52 pm

Color of the day: Coral
Incense of the day: Cypress

Ritual for Dispelling Darkness
The darkest card in the tarot is the Nine of Swords. It depicts someone who is sitting upright in bed holding their head in their hands as if waking from a bad dream. Nine swords hover overhead, perhaps to pierce through the thoughts or

images held in our minds. The card expresses anxiety, sleeplessness, and haunting dreams. The key is in altering our perceptions around situations that are disruptive to our peace. Dispel these dark and ominous swords by performing this simple ritual. On paper, write nine negative thoughts that you are holding. Cut each one into a single strip. Place a small cauldron at your feet with lit incense or, if possible, stand before a burning fire. Toss each negative thought into the flames as you say:

> *By the element of fire*
> *I burn away my fear*
> *Releasing it to the flames*
> *Dispelling the darkness*
> *Entrusting the God*
> *and Goddess*
> *To show me the light.*

Igraine

Notes:

October 9
Saturday

 1st ♏

Color of the day: Gray
Incense of the day: Ivy

hard Work Spell

Saturday, ruled by Saturn, is traditionally a day of hard work. Saturn was known as the Lord of Death, his domain death and atonement. The changing weather mirrors the Saturnine energies of somberness, heaviness, and darkness, and demands we bundle up to atone (be "at one") with winter. Use Saturn's influence to power a spell of hard work. Whether storing summer clothes, preserving vegetables, or preparing machinery and tools for winter, today is the day for a tough job. Choose one task. Set a time limit of three hours, and dive in. Work hard, then reward yourself with something stimulating—ginger and lemon tea to warm, or dark chocolate to inspire.

                    Dallas Jennifer Cobb

Notes:

October 10
Sunday

1st ♏

☽ → ♐ 6:09 pm

Color of the day: Amber
Incense of the day: Heliotrope

To Your Mental health

Today is World Mental Health Day. To utilize the power of this modern holiday, think about your own mental state. Are you prone to mood swings? Are you emotionally balanced for the most part? Do you let things get to you more than they should? Have you been diagnosed with a mental illness or know someone who has? Light one black candle and one white candle. Set them on the floor and lie between them. Be sure that the candles are somewhat far apart from each other, and that your head is situated between the two pillars. Enter a meditative state and contemplate the power of the two extremes—lightness and darkness—on either side of your head. Think about the ways in which you err to one side more than the other. For example, do you frequently enter unhealthy states of depression or anger? Or give too much of your own energy to other people? Or sometimes forget to love yourself? When you have meditated on your general mental state, jot notes and keep the list in your pocket or purse. Look at it frequently and think about how you can enter a more balanced state of mind regularly.

Raven Digitalis

Notes:

and security as a nation are founded on the genocide of over 500,000 natives. When we make offerings born of our own shame, we learn to commune as elements of nature and we begin to heal our own negative karma. We become aligned to the cure rather than mindlessly choosing to continue on as the disease!

Estha McNevin

Notes:

October 11
Monday
Columbus Day (observed)

 1st ♐

Color of the day: Lavender
Incense of the day: Rosemary

Offerings to our Ancestors
For many, this day is a celebration of the triumph of the human spirit. In historical reality, it commemorates little more than the beginning of the grand theft of this nation and our abject control of it. Offering our national native ancestors all-natural tobacco, corn, honey, sage, and sweet grass is one small way that we can attempt to heal a racial and cultural rift that leaves many natives feeling violated by the mere celebration of this holiday. This humble act of acknowledgment is the very least that we can do! Our modern wealth

October 12
Tuesday

 1st ♐

Color of the day: Black
Incense of the day: Geranium

Safe Return from Military Service
If you have a partner or any loved ones serving in the army, navy, or the air force who has been stationed overseas, pray to the Roman goddess Fortuna Redux for her protection and safe guidance home after duty is completed. This ritual can be shared with other military husbands, wives, and adult children. Before the journey abroad, gather everyone in the altar

room. If space is not big enough, perform the ritual outdoors on a night when it is not windy. Have everyone write the names of those who are serving. Draw and consecrate a big circle with everyone and everything they brought inside it. On a makeshift altar, light incense and tealight candles. Call to goddess Fortuna Redux in turns and offer flowers, fruit, sweets, mead, and honey. Spell verses are always more potent when you pen them yourself, so prepare a short verse before attending.

S. Y. Zenith

Notes:

October 13
Wednesday

 1st ♐
)) → ♑ 12:17 am

Color of the day: White
Incense of the day: Lavender

The Drink of Life

Today is the Fontinalia, sacred to Fontus, the Roman deity of fountains and springs. What might Fontus think of the condition of the water today? The present state of industrial pollution, agricultural runoff, and an enormous island in the Pacific made of old cell phones, shopping bags, and other garbage is hardly a fitting honor for a deity who helps ensure that life continues here! After all, without water to drink, no living being would last long. Take time today to study your relationship with the element of water—not just the esoteric, abstract meanings, but physical H_2O itself. What's your water use like? When you call to the spirits of the west (and water), do your actions outside the circle match your respect for them in ritual? How might you honor Fontus and his allies today, tomorrow, and every day after?

Lupa

Notes:

October 14
Thursday

1st ♑
2nd Quarter 5:27 pm

Color of the day: White
Incense of the day: Myrrh

heal a Broken heart Spell

Now as the trees begin to lose their leaves, this spell will help you let go of the pain caused by a broken heart. Time is the best cure for a broken heart, but to begin the healing process, try this spell. As the natural world is beginning to prepare for its winter rest, this charm draws upon these seasonal energies to help dissolve your pain. To begin, go to a quiet area and find a stone that you are drawn to. Hold the stone tightly, feel your hurt entering the stone, and follow the instructions in this verse:

> When wild geese are flying,
> And the fields are dying,
> When frost lies white upon
>   the ground,
> Go to a grove, where ancient
>   trees can be found.
> And there, bury your stone
>   beneath the fallen leaves.
> Release the pain, and the
>   Earth will consume your
>   grief.
> It is done.

James Kambos

October 15
Friday

2nd ♑
☽ → ♒ 10:24 am

Color of the day: Purple
Incense of the day: Orchid

Spread the Love

This is the time of year when we start to prepare for the holidays. At the office, at school, or within your local group, many institutions and community members are looking to help families make it through the coming season. The needs include blood for hospitals, food and clothing for those less fortunate, and Yule presents for those unable to afford them. Others need help with heating bills that eat up families' earnings each week, leaving only money for immediate essentials. It's time to start spreading some of that Pagan holiday spirit we are so fond of reminding everyone we have. Many Pagan communities pool together to help their own or to help the greater community depending on need. It is time to put back into your community the love that the Goddess is famous for. It starts with you—share some.

Boudica

Notes:

October 16
Saturday

 2nd ≈

Color of the day: Indigo
Incense of the day: Pine

A Spell for a Sweetie

Today is Sweetest Day! Originally a holiday celebrated locally in the northeastern United States, this sweet holiday is growing in popularity. This is a day to celebrate your friends, lovers, and loved ones. So with that thought in mind, here is a spell for your sweetie. We have a waxing Moon today so this is a perfect time to work for increasing love and romance. Place a pink candle in a holder and arrange a few rose quartz stones around the candle. Light the candle, visualizing your love, and then repeat the charm:

> May the gods smile down on us both this day,

> May our partnership be blessed, come what may.

> The color pink for my sweetheart and rose-colored stones

> Will gently strengthen our love, no matter where we roam.

> For the good of all with harm to none,

> By fire and earth, this charm is done.

Ellen Dugan

Notes:

October 17
Sunday

 2nd ≈
☽ → ♓ 10:52 pm

Color of the day: Yellow
Incense of the day: Frankincense

Personal Poppet Magic

Poppets aren't a widely used spell method because people think they are only used to represent others. But they can represent you, too, and to great effect. Make a poppet to

represent your own happiness. Cut the shape of a person out of a colored cloth (folded over so you cut two) that appeals to you. Sew the shapes together all around, but leave a space open for filling. Stuff your poppet with dried rose petals, lavender, calendula, St. John's wort, and basil. You may also add some rose quartz, sunstone, and fluorite if you like. Tuck in a strand of your own hair. Sew the poppet closed, then hold it against your heart, infusing it with your energy and your wishes for happiness. Set your poppet up in a special place, surrounded by items and pictures that make you happy. Now there will always be a part of you that is in a "happy place."

Castiel

Notes:

October 18
Monday

2nd ♓

Color of the day: Silver
Incense of the day: Clary sage

Rescue Remedy Ritual

This is a wonderful ritual for a Monday morning or anytime you might feel a sense of anticipation that feels uncentering. Begin by filling a basin with cool water. A few drops of essential oil is a nice addition. Cup the water in your hands and splash your face while you visualize the number 7 encircling yourself with white light. Splash again, seeing violet at your brow whispering the number 6. As you envision a blue orb at your throat see 5. Keep bathing your face with the cool, scented water working your way down through each chakra center, witnessing the corresponding color as you count backwards. Heart is 4 and green. Solar plexus is 3 and yellow. Sacral chakra is orange and 2, and the root chakra or base of the spine is red and the number 1. When you've completed the chakra countdown, sit in a straight-backed chair holding with both hands a tall staff or pole between your legs, firmly planted on the ground. Close your eyes and experience the grounding of the staff as you breathe deep into

the belly. With each breath, begin to count back up to seven and then state:

I am rooted like an oak,

As deep as I am tall,

My guardian angel I invoke,

To hold me as I call ____
_____. (State your
purpose for needing to be
grounded and centered.)

Igraine

Notes:

him. You may make offerings for him or ask him for aid in issues involving competition and conflict in which you need the upper hand. If you are interested in training in a martial art, this is also a good day to start your quest for a dojo, or even take your first lesson. Others may want to look at the motif of putting away weaponry. If you know someone currently in a war zone or at risk of being sent to one, or if you simply wish for all troops to return home safely, emphasize the retiring of the weapons with prayers for peace.

Lupa

Notes:

October 19
Tuesday

 2nd ♓

Color of the day: Gray
Incense of the day: Basil

Armilustrium (Roman)

Armilustrium was a Roman festival in honor of Mars, the god of war. During this time, the Roman legions would clean and store their weapons for the winter, and festivities were held to celebrate the homecoming of the troops. If you are a devotee of Mars, set aside this day for

October 20
Wednesday

 2nd ♓
☽ → ♈ 11:23 am

Color of the day: Brown
Incense of the day: Bay laurel

Time in the Dark

Darkness is a potent magical force. It is mystery, fear, wonder, and enigma. As the wheel turns closer to Samhain, we are reminded of its profound power and mystique in nature, and in turn, our lives. Darkness represents a deep fear of the unknown in the collective psyche of our society. Take a step to transcend this fear tonight. Spend some time alone in a dark place. Find an area where you can be in complete silence and darkness. Sit in a comfortable position and breathe. Are you afraid? What sorts of thoughts does it bring up for you? Keep breathing and allow yourself to be held in the caress of the Dark Mother. Allow any fear or nervousness to simply be. Breathe deeply. Surrender to the experience. What blessings do you find in this abyss? Enfold thy innermost self in the Rapture of the Infinite.

                              Abel R. Gomez

Notes:

October 21
Thursday

 2nd ♈

Color of the day: Crimson
Incense of the day: Nutmeg

Knotted Love Spell

St. Ursula, the Christianized version of the Teutonic Moon goddess, is celebrated today. It was said that St. Ursula sailed down the Rhine River with 11,000 virgins in attendance. Her retinue was hijacked and slaughtered by the Huns, and St. Ursula became the patron of single women. If you're tired of being single, take a red candle, a picture of yourself, a photo of your potential love, and a length of red ribbon 22 inches long. Light the candle and center. Tell St. Ursula about your love. Sell her on the idea of the two of you as a committed couple. When you've made your case, place the pictures of you and your love face to face and seal them together with melted wax from your candle. Now take the red ribbon and wrap it around your pictures, knotting it 11 times. Thank St. Ursula and leave her an offering of a croissant at the foot of a tree.

                              Lily Gardner

Notes:

October 22
Friday

 2nd ♈
Full Moon 9:37 pm
☽ → ♉ 10:30 pm

Color of the day: Pink
Incense of the day: Thyme

Broom Magic

Leaping around the yard on a broomstick may not get you to the Moon, but it does have its own invigorating advantages. A full sweeping of the home and yard can clear away excess negative or stagnant energy. Following this energetic and physical cleaning regimen with consistency can help to prevent seasonal depression and illness by limiting the amount of dust and rotting leaf or food particles in your environment. Without these emblems of stagnation and disease, leaping through the yard on a broomstick brings about a sense of liberation from the death and decay of the season. As this liveliness quickens the blood and helps to lift your mood, remember to draw in the luck and favor of the Witches who have come before you. Above all, have a right good laugh and a hardy cackle.

Estha McNevin

Notes:

October 23
Saturday

 3rd ♉
☉ → ♏ 8:35 am

Color of the day: Brown
Incense of the day: Magnolia

home Protection Spell

Make or buy an item to display in your home that you can charge with protective energy. This could be a wreath, ornamental plaque, a painting or statue—anything you can display. Before you hang it or put it in view, place the item in a circle of salt. Sprinkle the salt clockwise as you say:

Salt of earth,
Guard this home,
While I'm here
Or when I roam.
Keep it safe,
And all within,
For good of all—
This bond begins.

Ember

Notes:

October 24
Sunday

 3rd ♉

Color of the day: Orange
Incense of the day: Almond

Ease a Transition

Change may sometimes be good, but it's rare that it isn't hard. If you're having a difficult time with change in your life, try calling upon the Goddess in her aspects as mother and midwife, the one who brings forth and the one who ushers in. Find a moonstone and a piece of obsidian, and hold one in each hand as you sit in meditation. Burn incense with hyacinth or saffron to aid you. Review your situation in your mind, and then call to the Great Mother and Midwife. Open yourself to receive their message, which may be anything from a feeling of comfort to words of advice. Carry the stones in a pouch, and add thyme, black cohosh, borage, or columbine for courage, to remind you of the Goddess' message.

Castiel

Notes:

October 25
Monday

3rd ♉
☽ → ♊ 7:47 am

Color of the day: Ivory
Incense of the day: Lily

Believe in Tomorrow Spell

This is an autumn planting ritual that will renew your spirit. Spring-flowering bulbs are always planted in the autumn; in so doing, you're reaffirming your belief that there will be a tomorrow. For this spell, the soil will serve as your altar and your garden tools will be your magical tools. Prepare your planting area; it needn't be large. Smell the rich earth as you turn the soil and visualize it bursting with color next spring. Select your bulbs. These could be crocus and daffodils to bring luck. Hyacinths will draw protection and happiness with their fragrance. And tulips are known to attract love. Or you may select other bulbs. As you plant, handle your bulbs with reverence. The bulbs will appear to be dry and lifeless, but each bulb contains the mystery of life renewed. In essence, you're holding tomorrow in your hands. After planting, leave a coin in the soil as a sign of thanks.

James Kambos

Notes:

October 26
Tuesday

 3rd ♊

Color of the day: Black
Incense of the day: Ylang-ylang

Combine All Your Energies

On this day in 1825, the Erie Canal opened, connecting the Hudson River to Lake Erie. In a busy life, it's difficult for us to remain connected body, mind, and spirit. To reestablish a connection to our spiritual comfort, bring together a blanket, a pillow, and sandalwood incense. Light the incense and lie down, covering yourself with the blanket. As the grounding power of the scent fills you, go into a deep relaxed state. In your mind's eye, see your body surrounded with beautiful colors. From your head, see clear light shine out and combine with the colors surrounding you. From your heart, see a wonderful green color come out and combine with these colors. Feel all those energies combine in an ecstatic dance and feel the energy of your combined self. As you relax, feel that energy merge in your body. Rest with that connection until it is time to return to the here and now.

Gail Wood

Notes:

October 27
Wednesday

3rd ♊
☽ → ♋ 3:14 pm

Color of the day: Topaz
Incense of the day: Honeysuckle

Ritual for Clairvoyant Tools

This is a good workout ritual for those who are in training to be clairvoyants because it can be performed as many times as you wish—even after starting out in clairvoyance. This ritual also allows you to realign with spiritual objects that are used as tools in your work. Such items are crystal balls, crystal pyramids, tarot cards, I Ching, and all other types of card decks. On a day when you are undisturbed, place all your tools on the altar. Meditate until you are able to hold an unwavering meditative state of mind. Pick up each object one at a time and get to know it; observe its lines, designs, and qualities. Know that you are getting better acquainted with it. Send loving energies to each item. Personify each by letting them assimilate with your natural electromagnetic energy levels. Visualize the tool and you working smoothly and accurately together.

S. Y. Zenith

Notes:

October 28
Thursday

 3rd ♋

Color of the day: Green
Incense of the day: Clove

Release to Retool

Autumn is a time of change. The lazy pace of summer quickens into harvest. The still air begins to stir with brisk winds that bring the autumn rains. The colors brighten from placid greens to fiery reds and yellows, then fade to brown. As the seasons change, so do our lives. The pace quickens or slows. Old things that no longer serve us must be released so that we can take up new tools and challenges in the future. Think of four things you want to release—bad habits, bothersome memories, broken relationships, anything that holds you back. Write each one on an autumn leaf and toss them into the wind to be carried away. Walk among the fallen leaves, without looking back, and chant:

> Gold and brown
> Gold and brown
> Wind blows up and
> Leaves fall down

Let go of hindrances as the trees let go of dead leaves.

Elizabeth Barrette

Notes:

October 29
Friday

3rd ♋
☽ → ♌ 8:39 pm

Color of the day: Coral
Incense of the day: Yarrow

Exile Negative Emotions

Take a red piece of construction paper and write a list of things you wish to banish from your life. Astrologically, the Moon is currently waning and the Sun is in Scorpio. One of Scorpio's rulerships is emotion—namely the hidden, deeper aspects of one's emotional body. Therefore, think not only about general hindrances in your life, but about those connected to your emotions. How do you hold back your happiness and peace? When you have spent some time constructing this list, read over it a number of times. Next, place a mixture of banishing herbs (such as nettles, black pepper, and valerian root) onto the paper and crumple it. Tape, glue, or staple shut the makeshift pouch. On the smooth side of the paper, draw a big black X. Say something like:

> These hindrances I do not
> want, and I ask the Universe
> to guide me out of them.
> I banish these things and
> employ the Divine for assis-
> tance in seeing that these flee
> from my life. So mote it be.

Leave offerings to the spirits, burn some incense, and throw the spell in the trash.

Raven Digitalis

Notes:

H oliday lore: Many villages in the English countryside share the tradition of "lost-in-the-dark bells." Legend tells of a person lost in the dark or fog, heading for disaster, who at the last moment was guided to safety by the sound of church bells. The lucky and grateful survivor always leaves money in his or her will for the preservation of the bells. This day commemorates one particular such case, a man named Pecket in the village of Kidderminster, in Worcestershire, who was saved from plummeting over a ravine by the bells of the local church of St. Mary's. In honor of this event, the bells still ring every October 29.

October 30
Saturday

3rd ♌
4th Quarter 8:46 am

Color of the day: Gray
Incense of the day: Sandalwood

Dancing in the Dark Spell

T raditionally known as Merry Mischief Night, I think of this night as a time to work my personal magic, before the public festivity of Hallowe'en, or the circle ritual of Samhain. It's a time to take care of myself before attending to the needs of my children, family, circle, and community. While everyone is safely tucked into bed, I quietly slip into dark clothes and go outside. Standing with my bare feet on the cold earth, I dance slowly, feeling secretive and mischievous. What giddy joy. My family sleeps. In the waning light of the fourth quarter Moon, let yourself dance in the dark, celebrating the private magic that lies within you. Free from the demands of family, friends, or community, dance mischievously in the dark, summoning your deepest desires. As they are revealed to you, know the blessing of the Dark Goddess is upon you.

Dallas Jennifer Cobb

Notes:

October 31
Sunday
halloween – Samhain

4th ♌
☽ → ♍ 11:51 pm

Color of the day: Orange
Incense of the day: Heliotrope

A Remembrance Ritual

In a simple ritual, we remember those who have passed over this year. At Samhain we remember those who have left us for a time. We are saddened, and we may even shed a tear remembering them. It is all a part of the grieving process that we need to complete. Raise a glass to those who have moved on between the veils, salute them on the completion of a memorable life, thank them for allowing us to lean on them when we needed to, and remember them for their kindness and for their laughter. Give thanks that you had gotten to know them. Tell them that you look forward to meeting them in the next cycle of life. Drink to their life, and then drink to the life we all have left to enjoy. Let go of your grief. The wheel of the year turns again, and we all move on to the next cycle.

Boudica

Notes:

November is the eleventh month of the year. Its name is derived from the Latin word *novem*, meaning "nine," as it was the ninth month of the Roman calendar. Its astrological sign is Scorpio, the Scorpion (October 23–November 23), a fixed-water sign ruled by Pluto. The harvest season is complete and the land is now at rest, for a moment. The bare beauty of nature can still be seen—in the true shape of trees, their naked branches in silhouette against the sky, the ground covered with a soft mantle of brown leaves. Frost glitters upon the grass; see your breath in the gray morning. There may be a hint of wood smoke in the air, and you might glimpse a deer nibbling on bark. Thanksgiving is the major holiday this month, a time for families and friends to come together and celebrate life—to express gratitude and enjoy a feast. November is a month for remembering, beginning with All Souls' Day on November 2. As families tend to gather this month, and people spend more time indoors, remember loved ones and tell stories. Honor memories. November's Full Moon is called the Frost Moon—spend some time this night reflecting on your ancestry or practice scrying by lighting some incense and watching the tendrils of smoke by candlelight.

November 1
Monday

Day of the Dead – All Saints' Day

 4th ♏

Color of the day: Gray
Incense of the day: Clary sage

Create an Ancestral Altar

Traditionally celebrated November 1 and 2, Dia de Los Muertos, or Day of the Dead, is a celebration of the Beloved Dead in Mexico. Families gather at the graves of their dearly departed to share a meal and give food and gifts. Large and elaborate altars are created with pictures of their beloved friends, foods they liked, special possessions, and plenty of orange marigolds. Many of them also display religious icons such as the Virgin Mary and Jesus. Though many of the original practices have been Christianized or lost to antiquity, scholars trace the origins of this holiday back thousands of years to the indigenous Aztec tribes. The festivities would be dedicated to Mictecacihuatl, goddess of the dead. As Christianity became more prominent, the practices blended with All Saints' Day. Create your own Dia de los Muertos altar by gathering pictures of your beloved dead, trinkets, flowers, and candles. Leave the altar up for the day or make it a permanent part of your home.

Abel R. Gomez

Notes:

Holiday lore: The time between sundown on Samhain to sundown today, the Day of the Dead, was considered a transition time, or "thin place," in Celtic lore. It was a time between the worlds when deep insights could pass more easily to those open to them. Through the portals could also pass beings of wisdom, of play, and of fun. And while in time these beings took on a feeling of otherness and evil, as our modern relationship between the realms has been muddled, today can be a day to tap into the magic and wonder of other worlds.

November 2
Tuesday
Election Day

 4th ♏

Color of the day: Red
Incense of the day: Basil

A Child's Blessing

While not all of us are parents, grandparents, or guardians, children are part of our lives and our communities. Children are the manifestation of our love and our future. Children are precious. Too often, children are the victims of violence, abuse, and bullying. While we cannot be with them always, nor fight all their battles for them, we can bless the children and invoke a spell of protection over them. Let us all bless the children:

> Sweet babe asleep in mother's
>   arms,
> Goddess keep you safe and
>   warm,
> Toddler bounding on eager
>   feet,
> Goddess bless you and keep
>   you sweet,
> Child at play running long,
> Goddess make you healthy
>   and strong,
> Teenager creating a separate
>   identity,
> May the Grace of the
>   Goddess be with thee,

> In her embrace you children
>   are safe,
> Goddess be with you
>   throughout your days.

Dallas Jennifer Cobb

Notes:

November 3
Wednesday

4th ♏
☽ → ♎ 1:19 am

Color of the day: Yellow
Incense of the day: Honeysuckle

The Lullaby of the Earth

When the life of the fields begins to slumber and Old Man Winter pulls his coat on, we gently put our yards and gardens to rest. As you bed down your scrap of Earth or window box for the winter, stroke the soil gently and tuck it in with leaves or other winter mulch to encourage fresh life in the spring. This is a great way to snuggle in bulbs for springtime blooms and it can encourage us to let go of the cycles of the past and embrace the future. Singing to the Earth is a sonic offering of love and gratitude, which reminds us of the larger cosmic vibrations that we are a part of. As the wheel spins ever 'round and change greets us anew, singing the Earth to sleep can inspire us to give thanks for what we have harvested. This opens us to experience the fullness of each season in turn.

Estha McNevin

Notes:

need to be dramatic, just something new for you to spice up your life and inspire you. Or, go all-out and have a mischief night theme party. Light a purple candle or wear something purple. Before your activity, recite the following:

> Discovering new sides of me,
> the freest person I can be—
> take a break, have some fun,
> mischief night has begun!

Ember

Notes:

November 4
Thursday

 4ᵗ ♏ ♎

Color of the day: Turquoise
Incense of the day: Carnation

Mischief Night

This is Guy Fawkes Eve in Britain, a traditional night for making mischief and celebrating with firecrackers and bonfires. In your own way, to honor the need to enjoy some good-natured rule-breaking, do something surprising or unusual for yourself—safely and legally, of course! Go out dancing or dance at home, call an old friend, try new food or listen to different music—take a break from your routine. It doesn't

November 5
Friday

4ᵗ ♎
☽ → ♏ 2:16 am

Color of the day: Coral
Incense of the day: Rose

Two of Swords Meditation

Find a quiet, comfortable place to sit. Tie a blindfold gently around your eyes. Folding your arms across your chest, visualize holding the gilt of two crossed swords pointing upward. Focus on your heart chakra. See if you can hear or feel the pulse of your blood. Become very still, softening to the sound of your internal rhythm. Engage your center. Now raise your awareness to your third eye chakra, Ajna, which houses your psychic sense. Allow initial random thoughts to float through your mind like a carousel. When you feel the moment is right, stop the circling mental motion and focus sharply on whatever becomes totally present. Hold on to that thought. Freeze this frame. Now find yourself guided by asking questions of whatever picture you have "taken," whether it is a person, place, or thing. If it is simply a sensation, ask it to show you a sign. If it is a color, ask it to express an emotion. If it is a person, ask them to give you a message. Pass through the portal that is the Two of Swords, seeking inner vision and hold the knowledge close to your heart.

Igraine

Notes:

November 6
Saturday

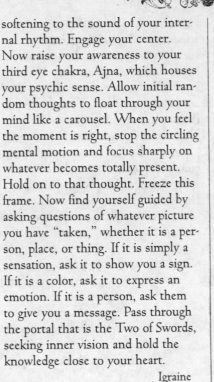

4th ♏
New Moon 12:52 am

Color of the day: Blue
Incense of the day: Rue

A Time to Look Within

Tonight is the New Moon. The Earth's shadow casts a dark cloak across the shining Moon, hiding her from our eyes. This is the turning point, when the energy reaches its inmost focus, for tomorrow the Moon begins her return. For now she lies in balance. The world below pauses in the indrawn breath of the Moon. Now is a time for introspection and scrying. If you have relevant tools to dedicate—such as a crystal ball, tarot deck, or black mirror—this is an auspicious time. Past-life regression is another good choice. The three-faced goddess Hecate oversees this phase of the Moon for she can see the past, the present, and the future all at once. To aid your scrying, gather a black altar cloth, a black candle, white sandalwood incense, and your favorite scrying tool. Light the candle and say:

> Here is the light of the
> hidden Moon.

Light the incense and say:

> Here is the smoke of the
> Earth's shadow.

Hold your scrying tool and say:

> By light and shadow, may
> Hecate show me the way.

Then do your reading. Remember to thank Hecate for her insights after you finish.

Elizabeth Barrette

Notes:

burned up in a ritual fire—in an attempt to achieve a larger vision, such as victory, social change, or a better future. Sometimes you don't know if or how sacrifice will pay off, but believing in the reciprocity gives the act meaning. So do something today for the greater good, the bigger picture, and infuse your action with your belief that it will make a difference. Consign your overtime, extra change, or one less trip out for coffee to the powers that be, and see what happens.

Castiel

Notes:

November 7
Sunday

Daylight Saving Time ends 2 am

 1st ♏
)) → ♐ 3:28 am

Color of the day: Amber
Incense of the day: Eucalyptus

Sacrifice for Change

Try something today that is often greatly misunderstood by others—make a sacrifice. Though this may conjure images of blood-stained altars, think about how often we talk about the sacrifices made by great athletes, politicians, or anyone who works hard to achieve something. Sacrifice is giving something you are not going to get back—time, money, energy, gone as sure as something

November 8
Monday

1st ♐

Color of the day: Silver
Incense of the day: Neroli

Protection Spell for a Child

I think we all know about the "Star Light" spell that we all come to realize is probably the first spell we learned as a child. Here is special spell to teach a young child for protection and to instill a feeling of

warmth and security. It is a great way to introduce another spellworking that your child will benefit from and never misunderstand. You may substitute your deity's name for *Goddess*, and *Father* for *Mother*.

> As I work and as I play,
> Goddess watch me night
> and day.
> Keep me safe in all I do,
> Mother Goddess,
> I thank you.
>
> Boudica

Notes:

patchouli incense, a pen, fallen leaves (dry), and a fireproof bowl. At your altar, honor the directions and call in the guides and deities that sustain you. Light the black candle in honor of your grief and light the silver candle in honor of love and hope. Light the incense and let its grounding power envelop you. Write messages and blessings on the leaves in honor of your grief. Present the leaves to the directions and the deities and the lit candles; and then burn them one at a time. Watch the smoke waft upward as prayers for blessings and comfort.

> Gail Wood

Notes:

November 9
Tuesday

1st ♐
☽ → ♑ 8:37 am

Color of the day: Maroon
Incense of the day: Bayberry

A Grieving Ritual

None of us are exempt from sorrow and grief; and mourning takes its own time and its own path. For a spell to honor our sorrowful heart, gather a black candle and a silver candle, special items to commemorate who or what you are grieving,

November 10
Wednesday

1st ♑

Color of the day: Topaz
Incense of the day: Marjoram

Protective Clothing

Part of being a Witch is seeing all life as sacred. Our experience of existence is the most holy ritual we will ever perform. Because of this, magicians and Witches should always be conscious of how they are living in metaphysical consciousness from day to day. First and foremost, we must be centered in our bodies and minds; we must holistically be at peace with ourselves—and protected. There are countless ways to weave magic into our lives. The most mundane tasks can easily become sacred mini-rituals or acts of magic. I recommend the book *Instant Magic* by Christopher Penczak for gaining such ideas, and recommend performing the following spell to influence your daily cycles. When in public, all sorts of energies surround us and can influence us on many levels. To help secure daily energetic protection, simply go into your room with a smoldering wand of sage. Quickly smudge every article of clothing you own—everything from the elegant wear to the underwear. Say:

> *Flee, all foreign vibrations!*
> *This clothing is mine, and*
> *shall protect me for all of my*
> *days. May they continually*
> *serve as strong barriers of*
> *protection. So shall it be!*

Raven Digitalis

Notes:

November 11
Thursday
Veterans Day

1st ♑
☽ → ♒ 5:32 pm

Color of the day: Green
Incense of the day: Jasmine

Healing, Peace, and Hope

On Veterans Day, the U.S. government asks that we honor all the men and women who have served in our nation's military. Some may not agree with the military actions the United States has engaged in during their lifetimes, and others, who may not know any soldiers, struggle to connect to the meaning of this holiday. But whatever one's political beliefs or personal experiences, today is a good day to work for healing. Whether you want to direct energy toward ending a world conflict, increasing tolerance in your own community, or a soldier you know who has been wounded or psychologically injured in combat, take time today to create an altar. On the altar, place three candles—for hope, healing, and peace. Visualize a world in which the soldier's job is no longer necessary, and acknowledge the value of fighting for freedom and human rights. Close your ritual with a salute.

Castiel

Notes:

November 12
Friday

1st ♒

Color of the day: Purple
Incense of the day: Thyme

Keep a Secret Spell

When a friend tells you a deep dark secret and swears you to secrecy, sometimes it's hard to keep your mouth shut. Now that the Sun is in Scorpio, this is a favorable time to work a spell that will help you guard a secret. For this spell you'll need black paper, a black ink pen, black ribbon, and an old key you don't need. Write this verse on the black paper with black ink (the idea is that you can't see it):

> My lips are locked, my lips
> are sealed,
> Your secret will never be
> revealed.

Place the key over the verse and fold the paper around the key. Tie the bundle with the ribbon. Hide this bundle. When and if the time comes that you no longer need to keep the secret, burn the paper in a ritual fire. Then take the key to a muddy body of water and throw it away.

James Kambos

Notes:

Historical lore: Veterans Day commemorates the armistice that ended the Great War in 1918. Oddly, this war ended on this day, November 11, at 11 am (the 11th hour of the 11th day of the 11th month). Though Congress changed Veterans Day to another date in October at one point during this century, in 1968 they returned the holiday to November 11, where it stands today. The number 11 is significant. In numerology, it is one of the master numbers that cannot be reduced. The number 11 life path has the connotation of illumination and is associated with spiritual awareness and idealism—particularly regarding humanity. It makes sense then that this collection of 11s commemorates the end of an event that was hoped to be the War to End All Wars. Unfortunately, it wasn't the last such great war, but we can at least set aside this day to ruminate on notions of peace to humankind.

November 13
Saturday

1st ≈≈
2nd Quarter 11:39 am

Color of the day: Gray
Incense of the day: Ivy

Prepare for Winter

The runic period of Nyd, also known as Nauthiz, begins today. As the rune of necessity, Nauthiz urges us to make ready for winter. What tasks do you give yourself this time of year to prepare for winter? Whether it's packing up your summer clothes and bringing out the quilts, cleaning the chimney, mulching the garden, or all of the above, these activities bring us in line with the rhythms of our world and, if done mindfully, can be a spiritual practice. As a deepening of this practice, consider what needs mending in your emotional life. This is a time to pay back old debts and heal old grudges. If you view the upcoming winter with dread, try to identify what makes this season hard for you and brainstorm how you might remedy the situation.

Lily Gardner

Notes:

November 14
Sunday

2nd ≈≈
☽ → ♓ 5:24 am

Color of the day: Yellow
Incense of the day: Hyacinth

A Coffee Spell

As the cold returns, we often choose a hot beverage in the morning for comfort and cheer. Let coffee infuse you with delightful good dark magic. Whether you grind your own beans or use preground coffee, take a moment to smell the stimulating aroma. As your coffee brews, know that light transforms into darkness, just as the water transforms to coffee. As you gaze at the coffee in the pot, look also to the dark, rich places inside you. What parts of you need stimulating and enlivening? What energy do you need to awaken? What aspects of the darkness will you most enjoy in this time? Pour yourself a cup of coffee and fix it to your taste. Sip the magical brew, incanting:

> Into the darkness I safely
>   slide,
> Knowing my magic dwells
>   inside.
> Strength and safety, dreams
>   and insight,
> Darkness befriends me just
>   like the light.

Dallas Jennifer Cobb

Notes:

your offering, walk away whispering
your hopes and dreams for peace
and unity. Continue repeating these
prayers as you travel home and give
energy to them often.

Estha McNevin

Notes:

November 15
Monday

2nd ♓

Color of the day: Lavender
Incense of the day: Lily

healing Tribal Blood Lines

Collect your fingernail clippings
and excess hair from combs
or brushes. Place them in a loose
muslin bag and bury them in an
undeveloped area or woodland park
close to you. When finished, place
your hands over the fresh soil and
chant the following mantra slowly
and clearly ninety-nine times, to
invoke the number of change and
progression.

> *Oh, spiral life;*
> *all tribes are one.*

When you have finished, give your
own personal prayer to the ancestors of all people on the Earth. Try
to evoke a feeling of global unity
and humanitarian love. Let this
flow freely from you into the Earth;
keep nothing for yourself. When
you feel that the Earth has accepted

November 16
Tuesday

2nd ♓
☽ → ♈ 5:59 pm

Color of the day: Black
Incense of the day: Ginger

Long-Distance friendship Spell

When things get rough, it
helps to remember that we
have people in our lives who care
for us. Even when we're far away,
traveling or away at college, they still
bless our lives. Sometimes we need a
reminder that we aren't alone, especially when we're feeling down. Get
a beeswax candle, preferably one that
will burn for a long time. Next, ask
permission from those closest to you
to carve their names into the candle;
if they're of the magical persuasion,
you might even ask them to put a

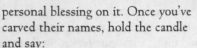

personal blessing on it. Once you've carved their names, hold the candle and say:

> I am blessed by every friend
>
> Who helps me get back on
> the mend.

Whenever you're having a bad day or feeling like you're all alone, burn the candle for a little while and meditate on those whose names are on it and their relationships with you.

Lupa

Notes:

and recite the following as you tie each knot:

> Learning, living, loving—life
>
> Contains both happiness and strife.
>
> Help me see, and learn, and know—
>
> So that I may always grow.

Carry the ribbon with you in a purse or wallet for as long as you like.

Ember

Notes:

November 17
Wednesday

2nd ♈

Color of the day: White

Incense of the day: Lilac

Wisdom

Most people say wisdom comes with age, but it also comes with experience. Use this spell to help you gain the most wisdom you can from your daily experiences. Find a long piece of yellow ribbon. You will tie three knots into this ribbon

November 18
Thursday

2nd ♈

Color of the day: Purple

Incense of the day: Nutmeg

Offering to Cernunnos

Today is sacred to Cernunnos, the Celtic god. Cernunnos is associated with shamanism magic and rebirth. In his darker aspects, he is connected to the mysteries of death and sexuality. He is the wild and untamable force in nature. Make an offering to Cernunnos today. What part of you is wild? What part of you is completely free and untamable? Think about this today. Even in the age of computers and technology, there lives a deep, primal power within each of us. How does it look for you? Journal in your Book of Shadows if you like. Go to your ritual space and meditate on the meaning of freedom and untamability in your life. Breathe deeply and allow your true self to come forth. Listen. What do you vow to do to foster your wild nature? Offer this to Cernunnos today. May your day be blessed.

Abel R. Gomez

Notes:

the air, screaming, "I'm not going to take it anymore," anger—as long as you don't dwell on that kind of rage. To magically express those emotions so that eventually your cooler head will prevail, go to a private place outdoors near some trees. Take a dozen eggs in a biodegradable carton. After you are sure you are alone, scream, rage, and express your anger. Name names and be as cussed as you wish. When the anger peaks, take an egg and throw it at a tree. When it breaks, see the anger release and the energy transform. Repeat as necessary. When you are finished, break up the carton, thank Mother Earth for her transformative powers, and put the carton in compost or recycling.

Gail Wood

Notes:

November 19
Friday

 2nd ♈
☽ → ♉ 5:04 am

Color of the day: Rose
Incense of the day: Yarrow

Today is "have a Bad Day" Day
There is nothing wrong with being mad—the kind of stomping, raging, yelling with your fists to

November 20
Saturday

2nd ♉

Color of the day: Brown
Incense of the day: Pine

Sophia the Internet Goddess

There are those who say the goddess of the computer is the motherboard. While I do not disagree, I also believe that Sophia is an important goddess invoked by the computer. We find Sophia (wisdom; derived from the Greek *sophos* meaning "wise") buried in among the many Wikipedia listings that are unattributed, in the online encyclopedias and dictionaries, the university information pages, and the millions of blogs and newspapers. What we need to understand is that not everything we read on the Internet is true, and we need to ask Sophia to help us see past the opinions, hearsay, and gossip to find the truths. Ask Sophia to guide you as you rummage through the Google entries when you are researching a paper or looking for information on the Web. Listen, because she will point out the well-documented information by showing you the footnotes and bibliographies you should be looking for.

Boudica

Notes:

November 21
Sunday

2nd ♉
Full Moon 12:27 pm
☽ → ♊ 1:46 pm

Color of the day: Gold
Incense of the day: Juniper

Invoking Hecate

Tonight is a perfect time to work with the goddess Hecate for protection and wisdom. This Triple Goddess has many forms and faces. She can appear as the Maiden in a shining headdress. As a mature woman, the Mother, or a wise silver-haired grandmother, the Crone. Hecate is a powerhouse and is fiercely protective of magic users. Light three candles: one white, one red, and one black. If you own a dog, call it to your side for this invocation, as dogs are sacred to her.

> *The Mourning Moon of November rises softly this night,*
>
> *Illuminating the night skies with a magical light.*
>
> *Hecate hear my call and send me your blessings,*
>
> *How you may appear, will keep me guessing.*
>
> *With the dramatic howl of dogs, your presence is known,*

I will honor your magic no matter where I roam.

Grant me the gifts of your protection and wisdom,

For I will hold these dear, within my Craft lessons.

By Hecate's power of earth, sky, and sea,

I accept your wise teachings, So mote it be.

Allow the candles to burn out in a safe place. Pay attention and see what messages Hecate sends to you in the next month.

Ellen Dugan

Notes:

go into rut; bucks will then battle it out for the right to mate with does. Both sexes possess sharp hooves and a powerful kick any time of year, and deer have been known to attack people, especially this time of year. Likewise, you may be underestimated by others because they may not understand you as much as they think they do. Today, take a page out of Deer's book and show others what you're really capable of! Of course, you don't have to resort to violence. Instead, shatter people's illusions about you in positive, constructive ways. Above all else, be true to yourself. Deer doesn't stop being aggressive just because people think Bambi is the real deal. In the same way, don't compromise yourself just to please others.

Lupa

Notes:

November 22
Monday

 3rd ♊

☉ → ♐ 5:15 am

Color of the day: White
Incense of the day: Clary sage

Buck Misconceptions about You
Most people think of deer as a gentle totem. However, this time of year many species of deer

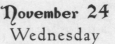

November 23
Tuesday

 3rd ♊

☽ → ♋ 8:14 pm

Color of the day: Gray
Incense of the day: Ylang-ylang

Fireside Nights

Deep in November, when the night settles quickly over the hills and the wind moans through the pines, I'm drawn to the fireside. Nights such as this are times to perform fire magic. You may begin by divining the future. Start by burning a piece of bark; as it burns look intently at the shape of the bark as it curls. What do you see? After building the fire more, watch the flames. If there are no flames in the center of the logs, you'll have a break in a problem you've been facing. If the flames build higher in the center, news is coming. To send a message to someone, write it on a piece of paper and feed it into the fire; you'll receive an answer. As you let the fire die, look deep into the embers, and you'll see the dawn of civilization.

James Kambos

Notes:

November 24
Wednesday

 3rd ♋

Color of the day: Brown
Incense of the day: Bay laurel

Saraswati Knowledge Ritual

The Hindu goddess Saraswati is the patron of the arts and sciences. She can be invoked using her mantra for help in studies, exams, memory retention, intellectual pursuits, insight, wisdom, writing, singing, dancing, choreography, and composing as well as in scientific studies and research. Wash or clean a statue, idol, or framed picture of Saraswati. When it is dry, adorn it with flowers and perfume. Light some incense and candles or a ghee lamp where possible. A ghee lamp is nontoxic and does not have black fumes. Offer fruits, sweets, honey, milk, sweet cakes, yogurt, and unsalted nuts. Sit in a comfortable position before commencing mantra chanting. The mantra for Saraswati is "Om Aim Saraswatiye Namaha." The mantra should be recited at least 9 times each day, but if you are able to chant up to 108 times per day in one sitting for thirty days, this is even better.

S. Y. Zenith

Notes:

November 25
Thursday

Thanksgiving Day

3rd ♋

Color of the day: Crimson
Incense of the day: Myrrh

A Thanksgiving Blessing

Family gatherings can be a challenge, but since Jupiter, the planet that rules Thursday, inspires us to share our thoughts, beliefs, and prosperity, it is the perfect day for a Thanksgiving spell. You don't need to convert your family to the Pagan practice, but offer to say a blessing when your family gathers for the traditional Thanksgiving meal. Sometimes the simple, nondenominational blessing is the most powerful, speaking metaphorically to everyone gathered.

We give thanks for all that we are blessed with democracy, peace, prosperity, and abundance.

Let us give thanks for the food that fuels us, the abundant earth that has produced it, and our family that gathers in harmony to enjoy it.

Let each of us quietly reflect on the great riches that are ours, collectively and individually.

As we gather here, let us be grateful for all we enjoy and share our bounty together.

Dallas Jennifer Cobb

Notes:

November 26
Friday

3rd ♋
☽ → ♌ 1:01 am

Color of the day: Pink
Incense of the day: Mint

Spell for Detachment

During a period of Christian persecution back in the fourth century, St. Peter of Alexandria instructed his followers to conquer their fear of pain and death by detaching from the idea of self. What neuroscientists have concluded in this century is there is no part of the brain wherein the self resides. What gives us the illusion of self is our brain giving us an ongoing narrative of the "Me." Whether you buy into this idea fully or not, practicing detachment is an excellent tool when you're experiencing difficulties. Find yourself a quiet place where you can

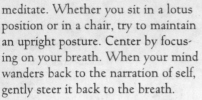

meditate. Whether you sit in a lotus position or in a chair, try to maintain an upright posture. Center by focusing on your breath. When your mind wanders back to the narration of self, gently steer it back to the breath.

Lily Gardner

Notes:

November 27
Saturday

3rd ♌

Color of the day: Gray
Incense of the day: Patchouli

Prescription for Life

I am a crone. You are a warrior refining your skills. She is a maiden or perhaps a mother with babe swollen in her belly. Our day begins, each one of us with different needs, different expectations; each of us requiring our own personal medicine. What is your prescription for life today? We might ask this question and simply draw a tarot card, rune, or ogam. But it is interesting to discover what nature whispers softly to us. Go out into the day. Sharpen your senses. Listen, look, smell, and feel. Allow yourself to experience this heightened expectation of magic brewing. Go for a walk and remain very alert and aware of what's around you. Begin to collect objects that come into your sphere. An acorn, a playing card, a perfect branch of birch, a goose feather that falls from the tree right into the palm of your hand, an electric-blue shard of glass, someone's discarded newspaper. It can be anything that catches your attention or simply happens before you. Make it like a scavenger hunt, discovering hidden treasure. When you return home, spread out all of your findings. Think about what they may represent in your life that you need right now. Create your own medicine by divining the secrets of your found objects and then writing a personal prescription for your life.

Igraine

Notes:

November 28
Sunday

3rd ♌
☽ → ♏ 4:34 am
4th Quarter 3:36 pm

Color of the day: Amber
Incense of the day: Almond

Remove Workplace Negativity

Before the workweek starts back up, let's remove any negativity and envy others may be directing toward you at your job. This crystal spell taps into the energies of the Sun and the waning Moon and uses the crystal carnelian. A beautiful, orange-red, and inexpensive tumbled stone, carnelian encourages protection, passion, and healing (and is rumored to remove jealousy and hatred). Hold the tumbled stone in your hand and repeat the spell verse three times. Afterward, slip the enchanted stone in your pocket—keep it close to you until the New Moon.

> The carnelian is linked with
> the element of fire,
>
> Surround me with your
> healing strength and grant
> my desire.
>
> Ward me against anger,
> envy, and spite,
>
> Let this week at work turn
> out just right.

> By the powers of the Earth
> and Sun,
>
> As I will it, so shall it be
> done.

Ellen Dugan

Notes:

November 29
Monday

 4th ♏

Color of the day: Ivory
Incense of the day: Narcissus

Andrzejki Fortunetellings

A traditional Polish method for fortunetelling involves young unmarried women who, starting at the back of a room, would line their shoes up in a straight line one after another. After all the shoes are in place, the person at the end of the line takes their shoe to put it at the front of the line until someone's shoe reaches the door. It is said the owner of the first shoe to cross the threshold will be the first to marry within twelve months. Another fortunetelling method is the "Fruit Rite," in which several fruits are placed in a

line on a table. Participants are blind-folded and told to pick a fruit. A ripe, red apple signifies a healthy relation-ship. A lemon represents a wrong choice of partner. A pear or banana means fertility. A prune means that the person will live a lonely life. A strawberry signifies a lifetime partner-ship.

S. Y. Zenith

Notes:

November 30
Tuesday

 4th ♏
) → ♎ 7:15 am

Color of the day: Black
Incense of the day: Cedar

Sleep Tight!

With night comes sleep, and with sleep come dreams. Ordinary dreams give the mind a way to process the day's experiences and turn them into memories. True dreams may bring messages from the subconscious or from the higher self. Nightmares can make for restless sleep and lethargic days, so here's a spell for sweet dreams. For this spell,

you need a clear glass jar with a tight lid, some white sugar, clean sand that is dark enough to contrast with the sugar, and a wire. Pour a ½-inch layer of sand in the bottom of the jar, then a layer of sugar, then another layer of sand. Poke the wire down through the layers at the sides of the jar to make V-shaped patterns. Visualize the sweetness of the sugar blend-ing with the sand, which represents sleep and dreams. Continue adding layers, and making designs with the wire until the jar is full. Seal the lid and keep the jar near your bed. Sweet dreams!

Elizabeth Barrette

Notes:

December is the twelfth month of the year, its name derived from the Latin *decem* meaning "ten," as it was the tenth month of the Roman calendar. Its astrological sign is Sagittarius, the Archer (November 23–December 22), a mutable-fire sign ruled by Jupiter. Winter settles in, with this month being cold, yet filled with mirth. Although the Winter Solstice is the official start of the season, it also marks the return of the Sun and, even though we won't notice it for a few months, the days are growing longer. In many cultures, this has traditionally been a time for celebrating with friends and family, enjoying music and giving gifts. The Romans celebrated Saturnalia during this month, one of the origins of Christmas. Other winter holidays such as Hanukkah and Kwanzaa are celebrated with feasts, candles, and other bright decorations that remind us of the continuing cycle of life—the great wheel of the year keeps turning. Yuletide evergreens, such as pine trees, and garlands and wreaths of holly, symbolize that despite the bleak appearance outside, the land is only sleeping and will return with vigor in spring. Stars are used to symbolize the divine spirit and also to represent the Sun—whose glowing gift of light gives us life. As one year ends, so another begins, amid a sparkling and icy winter landscape. December's Full Moon is called the Snow Moon.

December 1
Wednesday

4th ♎

Color of the day: Yellow
Incense of the day: Lilac

Early Activity Planning

December may seem like a strange time to celebrate fertility; however, Barbes Diena, a traditional Latvian celebration today, focuses on the fertility of sheep. While generally lambing season occurs in the spring, winter births are not unheard of. Winter is generally seen as a gestation period, and while spring may seem far away, the solstice approaches and the equinox will arrive before you know it! Thus, December is a good month to start planning projects for the upcoming new year. It's also a favorable time for drawing together resources in general, taking stock of what you have and what you need. Spend some time today daydreaming about things you'd like to accomplish in the next year and see what ideas you come up with. Then start making plans to bring these desires into reality. While you may not be able to do much now, early preparation can pay off down the line.

Lupa

Notes:

December 2
Thursday

hanukkah begins

4th ♎
☽ → ♏ 9:44 am

Color of the day: Green
Incense of the day: Clove

Spend Wisely

As holiday shopping season is in full swing, it may be useful to exercise some caution with spending. Often people become so caught up with buying gifts that they exceed their budget. If you tend to do this, use this charm to help you spend wisely during the holidays. Wrap a dollar bill with one green ribbon and one black ribbon. As you wrap the ribbon, and tie each in three knots, say these words:

> Wisdom guide me in my quest
>
> To find my loved ones what is best;
>
> To find all that I need and yet
>
> Keep from ending up in debt.

Tuck this away in your pocket or purse while you shop.

Ember

Notes:

December 3
Friday

 4th ♏

Color of the day: White
Incense of the day: Rose

Focus on Abilities

Today is recognized as the International Day of People with a Disability. For this spell, altruism is the key. If you have been diagnosed with a disability of any type, consider this spell as one that will partially affect you. Otherwise, focus your energy solely on assisting and helping other individuals—this is one of the most important parts of living the Craft. Take a white candle and inscribe the word *ability* on it. Anoint it with a "solar" oil for courage, such as orange, cinnamon, or marigold/calendula. To add an extra boost to the candle spell, place a mixture of the aforementioned herbs (or other herbs associated with the Sun) at the base of the candle. Next, speak the following:

> I ignite this flame to recognize and honor all those individuals who struggle with a disability. As this candle burns, I send forth the energy of strength to those who feel disadvantaged in their minds or bodies. I project the energies of life and love, and ask the spirits of healing and balance to bless the disabled with the awareness of their abilities. Ability of the mind. Ability of the body. Ability of the spirit. So mote it be.

Raven Digitalis

Notes:

December 4
Saturday

 4th ♏
☽ → ♐ 12:59 pm

Color of the day: Gray
Incense of the day: Magnolia

The Dark of the Moon

The dark of the Moon is a powerful time to banish obstacles, troublesome situations, and difficult people out of your life. Saturdays are sacred to the god Saturn, a god of harvest and karma. Today, all the astrological energies are correct for a banishing and a cleansing. Light a black candle at sunset and begin the spell. Visualize the problem and see it removed from your life in a positive way.

Tonight I banish and cleanse all negativity,

With the dark of the Moon phase, and the power of three.

Now I push all discordant energy away,

Forever gone, broken and banished it must stay.

As this black candle burns your power will fade,

My magic grows stronger as the charm is made.

By all the power of three times three,

As I will it, so shall it be.

Allow the candle to burn out in a safe place.

Ellen Dugan

Notes:

December 5
Sunday

4th ♐
New Moon 12:36 pm

Color of the day: Yellow
Incense of the day: Hyacinth

Rowan Protection Sachet Spell

A protection sachet is one of the easiest to make of protective charms. Cut a piece of white cloth into a seven-inch square. Put some rowan in a bowl. Place the white cloth on the altar. Put rowan in its middle and tie up the cloth in four corners with a thin red or yellow ribbon. Make several knots to your satisfaction. When ready, light altar candles and some incense. Hold the sachet with both hands and say:

> I command thy protective spell, To serve me well!

Other herbs such as angelica, basil, bay laurel, dill, fennel, mugwort, rosemary, rue, tarragon, and vervain can be mixed with rowan for use in the sachet. The ancient Babylonian method of binding stems of rowan and other protective herbs together with red thread for hanging is still used in many Pagan and non-Pagan households today. In Italy several centuries ago, people tied many dozen yards of red thread or yarn around a twig of rowan for placing at a window where it was visible outdoors for

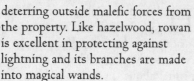

deterring outside malefic forces from the property. Like hazelwood, rowan is excellent in protecting against lightning and its branches are made into magical wands.

S. Y. Zenith

Notes:

children and the less fortunate. Old St. Nick's wisdom and generosity is worth emulating. Donate a bag of oranges, to symbolize the famous bag of gold, to a soup kitchen today. Think twice before you rush to judgment. And procure a special little treat for a child. Surround yourself today with the magic of giving.

Castiel

Notes:

December 6
Monday

 1st ♐
☽ → ♑ 6:16 pm

Color of the day: White
Incense of the day: Clary sage

The Magic of Giving

St. Nicholas, who would become the mythic Santa Claus, is a guy who's easy to connect with. A bishop who lived in the third century, he became famous for using his inheritance from his wealthy parents to give gifts to the poor (in one case dropping a bag of gold down a chimney, where it fell into a stocking hung up to dry there), and for defending the falsely accused (he knew whether you were naughty or nice.) In many parts of Europe, it is on this day that people give gifts to

December 7
Tuesday
Islamic New Year

 1st ♑

Color of the day: Gray
Incense of the day: Ylang-ylang

A Gaea Spell

Gaea, the Greek name for Mother Earth, is known as the Deep-breasted One. She is called the oldest of divinities. She is the beginning of all life, all wisdom, all mystery, and our eternal Mother. While the light dwindles, and the darkness stretches across the land, we often retreat indoors to the warmth of home and hearth, and lose touch with our Mother Earth. Renewing our connection to Gaea, even while we dwell indoors, keeps us green-minded and ecological, balanced and well grounded. Stand with your feet apart. Psychically reach down through your socks and the floor-boards to pull the balancing energy of the Earth up into your body, saying:

> By the earth that is her body,
> I ground mine.

Now, send your negative thoughts and fears back down into the Earth, quite literally grounding yourself. Through the winter use this spell to invoke Gaea and stay grounded.

Dallas Jennifer Cobb

Notes:

Holiday lore: Cultures around the world have shared a penchant for the ritual burning of scapegoats, enemies, and devils. There's something primal about the roar of a large bonfire and its ability to bring purging light to a community. Today is such a day in the highland towns of Guatemala. Men dress in devil costumes during the season leading up to Christmas, and children chase the men through the streets. On December 7, people light bonfires in front of their homes, and into the fires they toss garbage and other debris to purify their lives. At night, fireworks fill the air.

December 8
Wednesday

 1st ♑

Color of the day: Brown
Incense of the day: Lavender

Awaken through Sacred Sounds
This is a very holy day in both the Christian and Buddhist faiths. It is celebrated as the Immaculate Conception of the Virgin Mary as well as the enlightenment of Buddha. What a day to consider life's

potential and all that we are capable of becoming! In every faith from the beginning of time, the practice of chant or sacred sound has encouraged our awakening, stimulating dormant powers in our minds through music and mantra. Repetitive intonations encourage our capacity to open our hearts to what is Divine in us. Chanting "Om," the universal sound of peace, is the seed syllable to begin with. It is the basic sound of the Absolute and allows us to know what is unknowable. Vibrating this single tone attunes us to an eternal state of being. Then try to extend this out to *Om Namah Shivaya*, intoning on a single note or creating your own sacred melody. This core mantra loosely translates to "Salutations to all that I am capable of becoming!"

Igraine

Notes:

December 9
Thursday
hanukkah ends

 1st ♑
) → ♒ 2:30 am

Color of the day: Crimson
Incense of the day: Apricot

Personal Passion Day

For a spell to energize our personal passions, bring together a red candle for passion and energy, and a white candle for sincerity and purity, peppermint essential oil for mental clarity, a sage and lavender smudge stick, and the symbols of your personal passion. Dress your candles with the peppermint oil, asking for clarity and purpose. At your altar, call in the directions and deities. Smudge yourself and the candles with the smudge stick. Holding the symbols of your personal power, smudge yourself again and feel the wisdom, purity, and centeredness of the herbs filling your being and creating clear pathways for your personal passion's full expression. In your pure, passionate state, light the white candle and ask for blessings. With another breath, light the red candle to energize. Meditate there until you feel the fullness of your passion. Extinguish the candles and thank the deities. Whenever you need inspiration, burn the candles.

Gail Wood

Notes:

Keep the ornament in a window, or hang it on a holiday tree if you wish.

Elizabeth Barrette

Notes:

December 10
Friday

 1st ♐ ♒
Color of the day: White
Incense of the day: Cypress

Mirror Magic

In the dark of winter, we see the harsher side of the world. The shadows lie sharp on the snow; the light flares on the ice. Challenges come upon us. It helps to have protection—but you don't want to let the dark side of your emotions rule you. So put up a shield to deflect negative energies. For this spell, you'll need a holiday ornament covered in mirrored tiles (easily found at this time of year) and four silver or white candles. Light the candles and hang the ornament between them. Visualize yourself surrounded by flashing, dizzying mirrors on all sides and say:

> Hall of mirrors in the mind:
> No malicious force shall find
> Any path to my ill cost
> But shall be waylaid and lost.

December 11
Saturday

1st ♐ ♒
☽ → ♓ 1:41 pm

Color of the day: Indigo
Incense of the day: Sage

The Light Within the Darkness

Light a single white candle within a dark room and sit watching it for ten to fifteen minutes. As you look at the flame, imagine the innovation that fire has been for humanity. Picture all of its uses and powers. Acknowledge the flame as a living, moving force of creation. In your mind, dissect its many layers as it consumes the wax as fuel. Then focus your mind on the knowledge of the flame, which can only be created by the act and transition of combustion. When you have fully drawn in the energy of light, snuff the flame and sit quietly in the dark room. Feel the cool air engulf you and commune now with the absence of light. Let the walls of the room dissolve until you find yourself in utter cosmic darkness. Then relight the candle and experience the light anew!

Estha McNevin

Notes:

To enhance the spell, include mistletoe with other holiday greenery as you decorate your home for the season. These could include pine, holly, rosemary, and boxwood. And for some old-fashioned love magic, hang a branch of mistletoe over a doorway, and exchange a holiday kiss with those who enter.

James Kambos

Notes:

December 12
Sunday

 1st ♓

Color of the day: Orange
Incense of the day: Marigold

A Mistletoe Love Spell

Mistletoe was the most sacred of herbs to the Druids and is one of the oldest holiday decorations—even older than the Yule tree. It's excellent as a love-attracting herb, and this is the perfect time of year to perform this spell. In a dish, combine mistletoe leaves with its berries, some pine needles, and pink glitter. Cast your magic circle and carry the dish to each of the directions. Return the dish to your altar and say:

> Mistletoe, herb of love, bring
> me the perfect romance.

December 13
Monday

 1st ♓
2nd Quarter 8:59 am

Color of the day: Gray
Incense of the day: Hyssop

The Last-Minute Shopper

Time once again to work with Sadie, the goddess and queen of the bargain shoppers, for last-minute decoration ideas, and inspired meals for the holiday season. Decorating your home will require a careful eye as you wander through the dollar stores and bargain outlets this year. Follow Sadie through the store and see where she stops. You know what

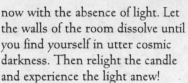

she looks like—you can only see her from behind and both her hands are filled with overstuffed shopping bags with brand names on them. She will show you the bins with the just the right holiday decorations and the closeout and deeply discounted holiday trimmings. If you are really lucky, she can lead you to the one-day-only supermarket specials that will help you create a holiday meal your family and invited friends will praise you for all year long. Watch for Sadie and follow her to the best deals in town.

Boudica

Notes:

winter. Earth is the realm of silence, death, sleep, and darkness. Its powers include those of healing, prosperity, and manifestation. Build an earth altar in a quiet corner of your house as a place to rest your spirit. Use cloths of brown, black, and green and place on your altar a vase of bare branches and a pentacle, the tool associated with the earth. A representation of your totem animal and your favorite crystals are excellent additions. Go to this special altar whenever you need a moment of peace. Allow your eyes to soft-focus on the symbols you've assembled. Breathe slow, even breaths. There. Don't you feel better?

Lily Gardner

Notes:

December 14
Tuesday

2nd ♓
☽ → ♈ 2:15 am

Color of the day: Black
Incense of the day: Geranium

Earth Altar

Are you exhausted from the holiday craziness? If you need a break from all the manic energy, consider building a special earth altar. Earth is the ruling element in

December 15
Wednesday

2nd ♈

Color of the day: Topaz
Incense of the day: Honeysuckle

The Consualia Festival (Roman)

The Consualia was a yearly festival for Consus, the Roman god who protected the grain. Mars, and the Lares (household gods) were often also celebrated on this day. Today we often take food for granted; even in the dead of winter one can go to a supermarket and get fresh produce. There are plenty of people in the twenty-first century who never have enough to eat, and the Consualia is a reminder to not assume food will always be available. When you prepare supper tonight, set aside a plate for the deities and spirits who protect the harvest. Say the following prayer before you eat:

> Thank you to all of those
> who have given of themselves
> to feed me (us),
>
> Both directly and indirectly.
>
> May I (we) learn to be as
> generous as you.

This is also a good prayer to say before every meal, if you like.

Lupa

Notes:

December 16
Thursday

2nd ♈

☽ → ♉ 1:49 pm

Color of the day: Purple
Incense of the day: Jasmine

A Spell for Strength and Courage

On this day in 1773, the Boston Tea Party occurred. Tea is a symbol of courage and strength. To build up your courage, make a strong cup of Earl Grey tea. As you prepare the tea, make each action a mindful task. The bergamot in Earl Grey is an essential oil that draws money and strength. Open the package and sniff the tea, letting the aroma fill you. Fill a pot with cold water and bring it to a boil. Take your cup, add some hot water, swirl it around, then discard. Pour water over the tea, letting it steep for three minutes while meditating on your courage. Discard the bag. Hold the cup, letting the warmth fill you as you breathe in the aroma. Say:

> Devas of tea, devas of tea
> bring your wisdom into me.
> As I drink this Earl Grey,
> bring your courage here to
> stay.

Gail Wood

Notes:

December 17
Friday

 2nd ♉

Color of the day: Pink
Incense of the day: Alder

Psychic Vision Spell

Use the powers of the upcoming Full Moon and the attractive powers of Friday to boost your psychic vision. Gather a purple candle, some mugwort, three pieces of amethyst crystal, and the High Priestess tarot card. Cleanse the candle with your breath and imbue it with your intention. Place the candle in a firesafe (noncombustible) area on your altar and place the crystals and herb around the candle to boost its energy. Hold the tarot card to your heart and visualize yourself becoming the high priestess, keeper of the deepest source of magical vision. Say something like:

> Powers of crystal, herb, and candle,
>
> Open my sight to what I can handle.
>
> Grant me the gift of true and deep knowing,
>
> I surrender to my own inner power growing.

Allow the candle to burn out, and carry the crystals to boost your psychic sight. Sprinkle the mugwort in your ritual space to produce visions.

Abel R. Gomez

Notes:

Holiday lore: Saturnalia was the Roman midwinter celebration of the solstice, and the greatest of the Roman festivals. It was traditional to decorate halls with laurels, green trees, lamps, and candles. These symbols of life and light were intended to dispel the darkness of the season of cold. The festival began with the cry of "Io Saturnalia!" Young pigs were sacrificed at the temple of Saturn and then were served the next day. Masters gave slaves the day off and waited on them for dinner. Merrymaking followed as wine flowed and horseplay commenced. Dice were used to select one diner as the honorary "Saturnalian King." Merrymakers obeyed absurd commands to dance, sing, and perform ridiculous feats. It was also a tradition to carry gifts of clay dolls and symbolic candles on one's person to give to friends met on the streets.

December 18
Saturday

 2nd ♉

☽ → ♊ 10:37 pm

Color of the day: Blue
Incense of the day: Patchouli

Welcome the Winter Faeries

As you "deck the halls with boughs of holly," remember to hang up some fresh greenery in your home for the winter faeries. According to legend, the faeries enjoy coming into a magical home for a little vacation from the cold and to enjoy the lights, decorations, and excitement of the holiday season. Arrange your fresh greenery on the mantle or hang it above your doorways and repeat this charm. Here's wishing you an enchanting holiday season!

> These fresh holly, ivy, and evergreen boughs,
>
> Provide a shelter for the faeries right now.
>
> Welcome to our home, and enjoy your stay,
>
> No tricks or pranks during these holidays.
>
> When the Yuletide is over, you must then depart,
>
> Know that you will always have a place in my heart.

> By all the powers of the green holly,
>
> As I will it, then so must it be!

Ellen Dugan

Notes:

December 19
Sunday

 2nd ♊

Color of the day: Gold
Incense of the day: Frankincense

A Solitude Spell

We're surrounded by people at work, at home, and in the community. We play so many different roles and fulfill their demands. We work magic in many areas, extending ourselves to others—volunteering, collaborating with neighbors, contributing to our kids' schools, even raising money. We need a solitude spell. Take five minutes alone. Close your eyes and envision peeling away the roles that demand your time, energy, wisdom, and money. Now just be. Breathe, and pull energy from up through your feet. Draw it through your body, and cascade it out the top of your head, spilling down and over you. Feel tingling at the back of your neck, a sign of the shifting energy. Know that the Great Mother is there to help you, her energy flowing to you, through you, and around you. She is the source to return to in solitude, to refill, regenerate, and renew. She is the source of all being.

Dallas Jennifer Cobb

Notes:

ribbon, and light a white candle. Suspend the crystal and swing it clockwise around the candle flame. Chant the following:

> The time is old,
> the time is new
> In all seasons may I prosper
> As I await the time renewed
> New hopes and joys I foster.

Give your crystal a clockwise spin whenever you need the momentum of anticipation.

Castiel

Notes:

December 20
Monday

2nd ♊

Color of the day: Lavender
Incense of the day: Narcissus

The Energy of Anticipation

It is a time now of great anticipation. The Moon is almost full, the Sun is almost reborn, Christmas is coming, and then the New Year is nigh. Everyone is poised, and the excitement is palpable. The time to start preparing for the adventures and trials of next year is at hand. Try this spell to tap into this powerful tide of energy and slingshot yourself into a prosperous, joyous new turn of the wheel—or just survive the holidays! Tie a crystal to a white or silver

December 21
Tuesday

Yule – Winter Solstice

2nd ♊
Full Moon 3:13 am
☽ → ♋ 4:22 am
☉ → ♑ 6:38 pm

Color of the day: White
Incense of the day: Cedar

Rite for Gathering Moon Water

Witches and Pagans use water charged under the Full Moon for purification rituals and miscellaneous cleansing work, such as washing religious statues, crystals, pentagrams, magical mirrors, and other tools. Moon water can also be added to baths and for cleaning wounds. Moon water is one of the greatest liquids for anointing the body's energy points before starting ritual work. Different paths anoint the body in different ways. Purification points for the Celts were the forehead, lower stomach, and feet. This is also called the "Threefold Blessing." Gather your own Moon water during the night of a Full Moon for storage until ready for usage. Use only a silver container such as a mug, chalice, or bowl. On a Full Moon night, fill up the silver container with spring water and place it outside or on an open windowsill. Let it sit undisturbed for several hours to absorb lunar rays. For more Moon-charged water, use several more silver vessels with spring water. When you feel the water is well charged, pour it into a glass jar with cap for storage. When you need to use the water, write some short verses relevant to your magical intent before opening the jar.

S. Y. Zenith

Notes:

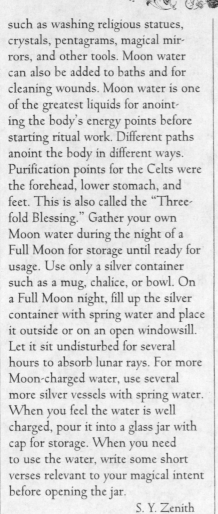

December 22
Wednesday

3rd ♋

Color of the day: Brown
Incense of the day: Bay laurel

Charged-Up Housekeeping

Devote the day to cleansing and clearing your home. This should work on both an energetic and physical level, and should be performed in the daytime (when the Sun is shining at its brightest). Start by getting some paper towels and a cup of lemon juice and vinegar—an all-natural, nonchemical cleaning solution. Cup your hands over the mixture and visualize cleansing, radiant yellow energy surrounding the bowl or bucket. Say something like:

> By the power of the sun, I do charge and enchant this cleansing mixture. As the mixture touches stagnant energy, it sends the vibrations into oblivion. By the power of water and fire, this mixture is enchanted. So mote it be.

Walk all around the house, moving widdershins (counterclockwise) in each room. Wipe down all the counters, the tops of doors, cabinets, and shelves, visualizing all the stagnant energy (lying dormant in the dust and grime) being exorcised by the cleansing solution—only to be gathered in the paper towels and thrown in the trash. When finished, sprinkle a handful of salt in the trash. This will help ground the energy and successfully banish stagnation. Smudge the house when finished.

Raven Digitalis

Notes:

Holiday lore: The Yule season is a festival of lights and a solar festival, and it is celebrated by fire in the form of the Yule log—a log decorated with fir needles, yew needles, birch branches, holly sprigs, and trailing vines of ivy. Back porches are stacked with firewood for burning, and the air is scented with pine and wood smoke. When the Yule log has burned out, save a piece for use as a powerful amulet of protection through the new year. Now is a good time to light your oven for baking bread and confections to serve around a decorated table; sweets have an ancient history. They are made and eaten to ensure that one would have "sweetness" in the coming year. Along these lines, mistletoe hangs over doorways to ensure a year of love. Kissing under the mistletoe is a tradition that comes down from the Druids, who considered the plant sacred. They gathered mistletoe from the high branches of sacred oak with golden sickles. It is no coincidence that Christians chose this month to celebrate the birth of their savior Jesus. Now is the time when the waxing Sun overcomes the waning Sun, and days finally begin to grow longer again. In some Pagan traditions, this struggle is symbolized by the Oak King overcoming the Holly King—that is, rebirth once again triumphing over death. And so the holly tree has come to be seen as a symbol of the season. It is used in many Yuletide decorations. For instance, wreaths are made of holly, the circle of which symbolized the wheel of the year—and the completed cycle. (*Yule* means "wheel" in old Anglo-Saxon.)

December 23
Thursday

3rd ♋
☽ → ♌ 7:51 am

Color of the day: Turquoise
Incense of the day: Balsam

Larentalia (Roman)

Larentia (one of her possible names) was the Roman guardian of "good ghosts"—a protector of

families. She was called the Mother of Ghosts. Offerings were made to her to protect the beloved dead and spirits of slaves. Create an altar with pictures or objects to represent those you wish to ask Larentia to protect—it could be a departed family member or friend, or someone you don't know—a historical figure or personal hero. Light white candles on the altar and use this chant, or write these words on a piece of paper and place it on the altar:

> *Departed ones be safe and rest,*
>
> *Your spirit be forever blessed.*

> Ember

Notes:

December 24
Friday
Christmas Eve

3rd ♌

Color of the day: Rose
Incense of the day: Orchid

Avert holiday Tension

Christmas Eve is a time to gather with family and close friends who are family-of-choice. Although this holiday does not belong to a Pagan religion, it is closely related to Midwinter and other Pagan holidays. Plenty of Pagans still celebrate Christmas with their non-Pagan relatives. So here is a spell to help the holiday go smoothly for everyone. Think about who you're going spend Christmas with and cut a two-foot length of ribbon or yarn for each person. Use green for your relatives and red for your friends. Tie the ribbons together at one end, divide them into three hanks, and braid them together. Concentrate on creating unity out of diverse parts, and visualize a peaceful holiday season. Finally, knot the ends together to form a wreath, and hang it on the Christmas tree. If tension arises, look at the braid and remind yourself of its peaceful intent.

> Elizabeth Barrette

Notes:

December 25
Saturday
Christmas Day

3rd ♌
☽ → ♍ 10:14 am

Color of the day: Black
Incense of the day: Sandalwood

Braggadocio Ritual

Whatever your religious persuasion, Christmas is a holiday of merrymaking. Families and friends gather in festive spirit. Houses are festooned with tiny lights and garlands of fresh pine and there is a general up swelling of a celebratory heart. One of the cheeriest ways to commune on this day is to participate in the ancient rite of sumbling. This is a sharing of toasts and boasts that gets everyone laughing and sharing in spirit and good cheer. You will need a huge chalice full of brew, wine, nog, or mead. Gather friends 'round in a circle. The host shall be the first to begin the sumble. Raise the chalice and proclaim something that you want to brag about, some accomplishment of yours this year. You can make this very dramatic and overly full of yourself. Then take a sip of brew and pass the chalice to the next celebrant. He then raises the chalice and boasts of his achievement this year or something he is very proud of. Make it loud and boisterous. The second round is about gloating over

how fabulous you are. Each participant in turn will raise the chalice and say something about themselves that they think is their best quality. Be imaginative and in good humor. The third and final round is an oath, kind of like a New Year's resolution in which you swear to something important to you. Don't forget to save a last sip to pour into the fire as an offering to the attending gods and goddesses. Merry meet!

Igraine

Notes:

December 26
Sunday
Kwanzaa begins

3rd ♍
Color of the day: Orange
Incense of the day: Heliotrope

Take Care of Your Health

During the holidays nobody really thinks about their health. But here's a little hint that will help you take care of all those medical tests that you should have had done this year and didn't. This time of year, the doctor's offices, health centers, and medical testing centers are empty because everyone is more focused on family and holidays than doctor's appointments. For women, this means you could probably call your doctor's office or health center tomorrow and probably get in to see the doctor for your annual Pap smear and mammogram by the end of the week (even with the New Year's holiday). For men, this is a good time to schedule that physical that you keep putting off. Take advantage of the empty waiting rooms and short waiting times and have that preventive testing done for your own sake, and the sake of your family.

Boudica

Notes:

December 27
Monday

3rd ♏
☽ → ♎ 12:38 pm
4th Quarter 11:18 pm

Color of the day: Silver
Incense of the day: Lily

Cleansing Spell

As the Moon begins to wane and the year draws to a close, take time today to cleanse all that no longer serves you in the coming year. Get a pad of paper and a pen and reminisce on all of the difficult moments of the year. How did these experiences serve you? What gifts did they grant you? What are you ready to release? In your ritual space, meditate on the lessons these experiences have taught you. Speak them. Cry if you need to. There is no wrong way to release. When ready, burn the paper in a fireproof dish and say:

> *I release the cords that bind*
>
> *What does not serve is far behind*
>
> *I cleanse my body, mind, and soul*
>
> *Through the fire, I am whole.*

Collect the ashes and release in the wind or bury in the earth.

Abel R. Gomez

Notes:

Light the candle each evening through New Year's to complete this purification ritual.

James Kambos

Notes:

December 28
Tuesday

4th ♎

Color of the day: Scarlet
Incense of the day: Bayberry

A Bayberry Purification Ritual

As one year ends and another begins, it's a good time to purify our homes to receive the New Year. One of the favorite purifying scents to use is bayberry. For this ritual you'll need one bayberry-scented pillar candle. Raise your power hand and walk clockwise around your home as you visualize a stream of light coming from your fingertips. Seal your home with this psychic energy. Light your candle and place it on your altar or coffee table. Allow it to burn for about an hour. Snuff out the candle, and think about anything in your life you want to change. List these on paper. Also include the names of anyone you want to bless. Lay your list in front of the candle.

December 29
Wednesday

4th ♎
☽ → ♏ 3:49 pm

Color of the day: Yellow
Incense of the day: Marjoram

A Familiar Blessing

Here is a spell to bless a pet and familiar. Hold your pet in your arms or sit down and allow your pet to climb into your lap. Now say your pet's name and then look up at the Moon and repeat the spell saying your pet's name in the final line.

May the Moon goddess
Diana look down upon you,

To keep you healthy and
happy in all that you do.

There is a magical bond
between man and beast,

I surround you with magic
beginning in the east.

Now south, west, and north
the power does spin,

(Dog or cat's name), you have
my love without end.

Ellen Dugan

Notes:

"I will remember my dream upon awakening and I will record it." The last tip is to date the journal before you fall asleep. This signals your brain that you expect a dream that night. As a separate practice, journal your thoughts during daylight hours as to what your dreams might signify. Remember to trust yourself to know what your dreams symbolize. Sweet dreams!

Lily Gardner

Notes:

December 30
Thursday

 4th ♏

Color of the day: White
Incense of the day: Apricot

Dream Journal

Winter is a time of rest and reflection. In keeping with these quiet rhythms, begin the practice of recording your dreams in a dream journal. If you've never had luck remembering your dreams, don't despair, these tips will improve your dream memory. It's important upon awakening to immediately record the dream and the emotion you felt upon awakening. Designate a notebook for this practice. It also helps to say a prayer or an affirmation, such as,

December 31
Friday
New Year's Eve

 4th ♏
☽ → ♐ 8:21 pm

Color of the day: Purple
Incense of the day: Vanilla

Rebirth

As we all know, the end of the year is an excellent time for new beginnings. Cleansing yourself with complementary alchemical agents can enhance this opportunity for rebirth by drawing on the basic elements of life. In a large pot, bring the following

ingredients to a boil, then strain,
cover, and let cool until warm to the
touch.

1 bottle of red wine
1 apple, diced
1 book of matches (for the sulphur)
1 T. anise seed
3 T. sea salt
1 cup of apple juice
2 cups of pure spring water
    or fresh river water

When ready, stand naked in a full,
warm bathtub. Lift the pot over your
head and drench your body in the
brew of rebirth. (Do not drink the
body wash). Feel the water embrace
you as you return to the womb of
the Great Mother. Allow your pains
and sorrows to leave you, let her
take them from you. When you
have finished, drain the tub. Feel this
"water break" as the inevitable force
of change and when the water is all
gone, slide or crawl from the tub and
learn to stand once again.

Estha McNevin

Notes:

A Guide to Witches' Spell–A–Day Icons

 New Moon Spells

 Full Moon Spells

 New Year's Eve, Day

 Mabon

 Imbolc

 Samhain, Halloween

 Valentine's Day

 Thanksgiving

 Ostara, Easter

 Yule, Christmas

 April Fool's Day

 Health Spells

 Earth Day, Earth Spells

 Home and Garden Spells

 Beltane

 Protection Spells

 Mother's Day

 Travel and Communication Spells

 Father's Day

 Money and Success Spells

 Litha

 Love and Relationship Spells

 Lammas

 Grab Bag of Spells

Daily Magical Influences

Each day is ruled by a planet that possesses specific magical influences:

Monday (Moon): peace, healing, caring, psychic awareness, and purification.

Tuesday (Mars): passion, sex, courage, aggression, and protection.

Wednesday (Mercury): conscious mind, study, travel, divination, and wisdom.

Thursday (Jupiter): expansion, money, prosperity, and generosity.

Friday (Venus): love, friendship, reconciliation, and beauty.

Saturday (Saturn): longevity, exorcism, endings, homes, and houses.

Sunday (Sun): healing, spirituality, success, strength, and protection.

Lunar Phases

The lunar phase is important in determining best times for magic.

The waxing Moon (from the New Moon to the Full Moon) is the ideal time for magic to draw things toward you.

The Full Moon is the time of greatest power.

The waning Moon (from the Full Moon to the New Moon) is a time for study, meditation, and little magical work (except magic designed to banish harmful energies).

Astrological Symbols

The Sun	☉	Aries	♈
The Moon	☽	Taurus	♉
Mercury	☿	Gemini	♊
Venus	♀	Cancer	♋
Mars	♂	Leo	♌
Jupiter	♃	Virgo	♍
Saturn	♄	Libra	♎
Uranus	♅	Scorpio	♏
Neptune	♆	Sagittarius	♐
Pluto	♇	Capricorn	♑
		Aquarius	♒
		Pisces	♓

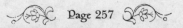

The Moon's Sign

The Moon's sign is a traditional consideration for astrologers. The Moon continuously moves through each sign in the zodiac, from Aries to Pisces. The Moon influences the sign it inhabits, creating different energies that affect our daily lives.

Aries: Good for starting things, but lacks staying power. Things occur rapidly, but quickly pass. People tend to be argumentative and assertive.

Taurus: Things begun now do last, tend to increase in value, and become hard to alter. Brings out an appreciation for beauty and sensory experience.

Gemini: Things begun now are easily changed by outside influence. Time for shortcuts, communications, games, and fun.

Cancer: Stimulates emotional rapport between people. Pinpoints need, supports growth and nurturance. Tend to domestic concerns.

Leo: Draws emphasis to the self, to central ideas or institutions, away from connections with others and emotional needs. People tend to be melodramatic.

Virgo: Favors accomplishment of details and commands from higher up. Focus on health, hygiene, and daily schedules.

Libra: Favors cooperation, compromise, social activities, beautification of surroundings, balance, and partnership.

Scorpio: Increases awareness of psychic power. Precipitates psychic crises and ends connections thoroughly. People tend to brood and become secretive under this Moon sign.

Sagittarius: Encourages flights of imagination and confidence. This Moon sign is adventurous, philosophical, and athletic. Favors expansion and growth.

Capricorn: Develops strong structure. Focus on traditions, responsibilities, and obligations. A good time to set boundaries and rules.

Aquarius: Rebellious energy. Time to break habits and make abrupt change. Personal freedom and individuality is the focus.

Pisces: The focus is on dreaming, nostalgia, intuition, and psychic impressions. A good time for spiritual or philanthropic activities.

Glossary of Magical Terms

Altar: a low table that holds magical tools as a focus for spell workings.

Athame: a ritual knife used to direct personal power during workings or to symbolically draw diagrams in a spell. It is rarely, if ever, used for actual physical cutting.

Aura: an invisible energy field surrounding a person. The aura can change color depending upon the state of the individual.

Balefire: a fire lit for magical purposes, usually outdoors.

Casting a circle: the process of drawing a circle around oneself to seal out unfriendly influences and raise magical power. It is the first step in a spell.

Censer: an incense burner. Traditionally, a censer is a metal container, filled with incense, that is swung on the end of a chain.

Censing: the process of burning incense to spiritually cleanse an object.

Centering yourself: to prepare for a magical rite by calming and centering all of your personal energy.

Chakra: one of the seven centers of spiritual energy in the human body, according to the philosophy of yoga.

Charging: to infuse an object with magical power.

Circle of protection: a circle cast to protect oneself from unfriendly influences.

Crystals: quartz or other stones that store cleansing or protective energies.

Deosil: clockwise movement, symbolic of life and positive energies.

Deva: a divine being according to Hindu beliefs; a devil or evil spirit according to Zoroastrianism.

Direct/Retrograde: refers to the motions of the planets when seen from the Earth. A planet is "direct" when it appears to be moving forward from the point of view of a person on the Earth. It is "retrograde" when it appears to be moving backward.

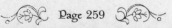

Dowsing: to use a divining rod to search for a thing, usually water or minerals.

Dowsing pendulum: a long cord with a coin or gem at one end. The pattern of its swing is used to predict the future.

Dryad: a tree spirit or forest guardian.

Fey: an archaic term for a magical spirit or a fairylike being.

Gris-gris: a small bag containing charms, herbs, stones, and other items to draw energy, luck, love, or prosperity to the wearer.

Mantra: a sacred chant used in Hindu tradition to embody the divinity invoked; it is said to possess deep magical power.

Needfire: a ceremonial fire kindled at dawn on major Wiccan holidays. It was traditionally used to light all other household fires.

Pentagram: a symbolically protective five-pointed star with one point upward.

Power hand: the dominant hand, the hand used most often.

Scry: to predict the future by gazing at or into an object such as a crystal ball or pool of water.

Second sight: the psychic power or ability to foresee the future.

Sigil: a personal seal or symbol.

Smudge/Smudge stick: to spiritually cleanse an object by waving incense over and around it. A smudge stick is a bundle of several incense sticks.

Wand: a stick or rod used for casting circles and as a focus for magical power.

Widdershins: counterclockwise movement, symbolic of negative magical purposes, sometimes used to disperse negative energies.

Spell Notes: